"In *Tainted Destiny*, Clarke deftly picks up where *Intimate Chaos* left off. This thrilling, suspenseful tale is a rollercoaster ride of love, lust, disappointment and fear."

—Kristin Silvani, *Out IN Jersey* Magazine

"*Tainted Destiny* travels through the many pathways and blockages associated with obsessive love and culminates in an action-packed, growth-filled conclusion. Anyone who has had any contact with a love obsession will gain real hope from following this exciting adventure into the soul and the self."

— Dr. Paul Hannig, Ph.D., author of "Obsessive Love Disorder: A Profile."

"Once again Cheril N. Clarke entertains with a sexy and insightful lesbian drama. On her way to healing lost love, Sadira encounters stalkers and plenty of lusty situations. For anyone who has ever fallen in love and lost a part of herself, *Tainted Destiny* will ring with truth."

—Kathy Belge, Lesbian Life Columnist, About.com

"Cheril N. Clarke brilliantly pulls the reader into the twists and turns of lust, fantasy, lunacy – and what happens when you don't cherish real love when it walks into your life."

—Lynne Womble, *Sable* Magazine

"Cheril's method of storytelling makes you feel like you are right there in every scene watching the story unfold. I would read this book again and recommend it to anyone who has ever felt that there destiny was tainted no matter how hard they tried to make it right."

——-Pmyner Ltd., a Services and Entertainment Company for LGBT artists

"Cheril N Clarke's storytelling skills are natural. Don't miss out on her latest release *Tainted Destiny*."

——-Shelia M. Goss, National Best-selling author of *My Invisible Husband*

TAINTED DESTINY

Rose,
Thank-you!

6/3/07

TAINTED DESTINY

CHERIL N. CLARKE

DODI PRESS – NEW YORK, NY

Copyright ©2006 Cheril N. Clarke
Cover Design by: N'Digo Design

This book was published by Dodi Press, and printed in the United States of America in 2006. All rights reserved.

ISBN: 0-9767273-1-5

ISBN13-978-0-9767273-1-6

Chapter 1

A passenger of the wind, she floated in and out of my life as she pleased without regard to how it affected me. But foolishly I exercised a level of patience and persistence that I never knew possible to chase something I thought was fate, love...destiny. I loved her hard, and with everything I had. Now that I look back I think I may have even been obsessed with her. Something about this woman was magnetic, pulling me toward her even when her actions should have pushed me away. With golden skin, blue-gray eyes, neat locs, a beautiful body, and a smile to die for; without embellishment, that was Jessie—a symbol of perfection. My attraction to her was swift, definite, and of an intensity I'd never experienced. There were times with her that felt as though our souls mingled with each other though our bodies didn't. I knew her...or so I thought, but I was wrong. I didn't know anything. I was being led by my misguided heart down a lonely road of misfortune.

I remember the day Jessie and I met on the subway just as clearly as if it had happened the day before. An incredible nervousness swept over me as I struggled to muster the courage to approach her. She was wearing tight fitting black leather pants, high-heels and a tan corset top, but it was a rainbow pendent on her necklace that made me take a chance on assuming she was lesbian or at least bisexual. After a few glances back and forth I walked over to her, holding a flyer for a gay pride event, hoping to use it as a conversation starter. It worked. She fell for my corny pick-up line and gave me her contact information. I was elated.

Though she was elusive, Jessie and I did eventually settle down, initially in New York and then to Miami where we relocated after she had accepted a promotion and raise from the firm for which she was working.

Going to Miami was a big deal for me because I had painful memories from my childhood there. My parents died when my sister, Khedara and I were young, and shortly after, we were split up and bounced around from foster home to foster home as seemingly unwanted twin girls. I didn't want to go back there, but not as badly as I wanted to be with Jessie, so I went and never once dug up anything from my past. I didn't even visit my parents' gravesite, which I now kind of regret. I just tried to forge a life with Jessie and focus on the present and future.

We experienced a short period of domestic calm before drama entered our relationship. Surprise, temptation, fear, ecstasy, a near death encounter, insecurity, jealousy, infidelity, turmoil and pain—you name it, we experienced it until the point of my becoming emotionally bankrupt. Our dysfunctional relationship didn't work. We sold our condo. She moved out and I relocated to the familiarity of New York, ready to move on.

I sat staring out a taxicab window and tried to relax as it sped through the wet streets. The hurried people on sidewalks and the unparalleled hustling and bustling to get to one's destination was a comforting scene. It's funny how a noisy, filthy, and crowded place like Manhattan could be so welcoming. There was only one thing from my life with Jessie that would resume and that was my taking a position at WSOL, a radio station at which I used to work. As my cab driver maneuvered through the busy streets, my mind wandered back in time. A sigh escaped me as I remembered what I'd been through over the last couple of years, but I shook my head to free myself from my own thoughts. It worked. I rode the rest of the way with a clear mind.

After the cabbie dropped me off, I stopped for a bagel with cream cheese and glanced at the *Daily News* but decided against buying it. *The news is always depressing,* I thought. I took my breakfast and quickly

2

headed into the radio station. My co-worker and old friend, Devonte' Parks was on the air in the middle of his morning show. I waved at him when passing his booth and he gave me a broad smile.

I said hello and talked with a few other people before filling out forms and doing a urine test, the same way I'd done the first time I was hired. My prior employment there didn't exempt me from their background checks. Since I didn't actually have to do any work, it was basically a free day for me. The engineer working with Devonte' hated the morning shift and was grateful to take the afternoon or even midnight shift if I wanted my old time slot. I definitely wanted it back so I could work with Devonte' and be a team the way we used to be.

After he wrapped up his show, we had a late lunch at Wendy's, and I told him the entire story of how things ended with Jessie, starting with my attraction to another woman.

Devonte' took the last bite of his chicken sandwich and drank his soda. "Well I don't want to rehash everything. You're about to start a new life. This time around you'd better listen to me when I tell you to leave a woman alone."

"Yeah, yeah."

"Don't 'yeah yeah' me. Anyway, where are you living now?"

"I'm in Brooklyn—Bed-Stuy. I didn't want to go back to Harlem. Actually I'll probably buy an apartment after I get settled in with work. I signed a six-month lease with a month-to-month option afterward."

"How the hell did you find a lease like that?" Devonte' asked.

"The lady needed the money and was willing to be flexible. I paid four months rent up front."

"Oh."

I drank a little water before speaking again. "Are you still in Crown Heights?"

"Nope, I bought a co-op in New Jersey."

"Jersey?"

"Yeah, but it's just on the other side of the George Washington bridge in Ft. Lee. It's cheaper to buy over there. Plus I wanted a change from Brooklyn."

3

"Apparently so. That's a big change."

"The commute isn't bad. It's cool, you know?"

"Yeah."

A few seconds of silence passed before he looked at his watch. "Man, I'm tired. Listen, it's good to have you back. I missed your ass while you were gone."

"I missed you too, Devonte'."

"All right, enough of that." He stood up. "Let's call it a day. We'll have plenty of time to catch up. Right now I need to go to sleep."

Following his lead, I too got up. "Okay. I'll see you tomorrow."

We went our separate ways, and I continued to soak up the city that I'd so badly missed, but I missed Jessie more.

Things were still fresh in my mind despite my wishing they would go away. They came with force and were frequent and strong, especially at night. I wondered what Jessie was doing, how she was feeling, and who she was with. I knew I shouldn't care, but I did. I never loved anyone the way that I loved Jessie, and I wondered why, since I never totally had all of her. I didn't know it then, but through my soul searching I began to wonder if I ever loved her at all. I started to believe that it was the possibilities of what I *thought* I could have with her that I loved so much it ached. For whatever reason, when I saw her, I saw a representation of heaven, nirvana—paradise on Earth—but it was an illusion. Jessie was a mirage. It wasn't her fault. It was the power of my own mind and the desires of my own soul that made me stay with her and go through what I did. My revelation didn't make me hurt any less though.

In an effort to speed up the process of getting over her, I buried many feelings. All I had to occupy my mind was work and a couple of new friends who lived in my neighborhood, but it was difficult to keep my mind from wandering to her. I could still hear her voice in my head thinking she was in a room with me. I could remember the scent of her and remember the softness of her touch. The first time we made love our souls conceived a link that to this day I feel hasn't been fully broken. In my mind, I lost my lover and my friend. But I'd also lost something else.

4

Tainted Destiny

I lost my idol, my model of perfection. To break my obsession with Jessie I needed to redesign my mind, reprogram my feelings, renege on what my heart told my mind all of those nights before we moved to Miami when I craved her like a stray animal desperately searching for sustenance. I needed to sever the link.

Chapter 2

After a few weeks went by I slowly fell into a comfortable routine. Going to work, coming home to spend hours on the Internet, going to bed, and doing the same thing the next day. It was June. The days were hot, and all the skin women loved to show during the summer proved to be a good distraction for me. I did, however, spend many of my breaks at work with Devonte'. One day we were hanging around talking after our shift was over.

"I'm telling you, Sadira. Some women don't want men, or in your case women, who treat them right. It's a damn shame, but the worse you treat them, the more they hang on to you. And the better you treat them, the more they play games and act stupid. Not all women are this way, but some of y'all are really unstable creatures." He shook his head and sighed.

"I'm not even going to argue with you on that considering how long I stayed with Jessie. I won't be like that for anyone ever again. I've learned my lesson."

"Good. And don't date anyone exclusively for a while either. Just try to relax, take your time, and see what's out there before you go committing to someone just to have an attachment."

"I'm not ready to date anyone at all right now."

"Well when you jump back into dating, make sure you're among the few women who still have common sense. Don't put up with bullshit just to fill a void. To hell with that."

"I know. I know. Anyway, what are you doing this weekend?"

"I'm helping Tricia move into another apartment. I don't have any other plans outside of that though."

Tricia, I thought. She was Devonte's cousin and I purposely hadn't seen or asked him about her since I'd returned to New York. I did think about her though. I thought about the few nights we'd spent together when she came to visit a few years ago, before Jessie and I officially considered ourselves a couple. What I shared with Tricia was more sexual than emotional, though I'm sure we could have built on it if we'd wanted to. There were no strings attached, and both of us were content with moving on after our fling. I thought about her even after I moved to Miami with Jessie. I wondered how she'd adjusted to living in New York coming from Alabama. Did she like her new job and was she was seeing anyone? I didn't let the questions linger for too long though. What was important to me at that time was focusing on my relationship with Jessie.

"Why did you get so quiet, girl?" Devonte' asked, pulling me out of my thoughts.

"No reason."

He gave me a look that told me he knew I was lying, but he didn't say anything.

I sighed. "Does Tricia know that I'm here?"

"No. I didn't know if you wanted me to say anything or not, so I didn't. Do you want her to know?"

I thought before answering. "I don't know. Is she involved with anyone right now?" Seeing her in love with someone else would make me feel uncomfortable.

"Nothing serious that I know of. She has quite a social life though. That girl is never at home."

"Oh."

A few seconds passed before he spoke again. "Hey, I have to get out of here. Do you want me to tell her or not?"

"Um, yeah. Give her my number."

"All right. Are you working overtime today or are you leaving soon?"

7

"No, I'm leaving now."

He got up. "C'mon, let me walk you to the subway then."

Despite the heat, it was a beautiful day. Devonte' walked me to 34th Street station and then decided to ride downtown with me. He got off in lower Manhattan, and I stayed on the train all the way into Brooklyn where I got off and then walked the rest of the way home. I missed my car, but not enough to keep it. I hated driving in New York, plus it was too expensive, so I sold my car before leaving Atlanta. Before relocating to New York, I lived in Atlanta with my sister for a short period of time.

Luckily, it was easy for me to melt back into my old routine at WSOL and with Devonte'. I still wasn't used to being alone at night and on the weekends though. Laying in a state of lonely aggravation, I would toss and turn before I finally fell asleep. I knew I needed to get out and meet more people, but I didn't want to go out alone. In the meantime I decided to start an online journal about how I felt. Sometimes I wrote stories and other times I wrote poetry. I bought a software program that allowed me to create background music for my poetry and I uploaded audio versions of my readings. It was the best thing to help me work through my feelings. A couple of people e-mailed me compliments, which was somewhat soothing. They said they could feel my pain and encouraged me to be strong. I kept telling myself to go out to an open mic poetry event to get back in the swing of things but was reluctant to actually do it. I didn't have the motivation and the lust I once had for reading in front of people. It used to give me a rush, but I was starting to feel as though I'd outgrown the whole scene.

A few days later I was in downtown Brooklyn trying to do some shopping, but after looking around for an hour I got frustrated and left empty-handed. With no destination in particular, I got on a southbound A train. When the train went above ground, my cell phone beeped alerting me of a new voicemail message, but I didn't check it until I got off at the end of the line at Rockaway Beach.

As soon as I walked out of the subway station, I could smell the ocean. The sun was shining, and I could hear music playing. There was an eclectic group of people in the area. Destitute individuals, teenagers and elderly were all enjoying the beautiful weather. I reached in my pocket for my cell phone as I walked toward the beach. The air was refreshing, and I was glad I decided go *somewhere*. My eyes locked with those of a homeless man as I dialed into my voicemail. Something about him struck me. I could see the pain, the despair, and the desire for help. I felt as though I were a human sponge, absorbing his emotions. His blue shirt was torn, his pants were filthy, and the soles of his shoes were held in place by dull gray duct tape. I closed my flip phone and walked over to him so I could put money in his cup, which surprised me because I'd long noticed that New York had desensitized me to homeless people. There were so many of them begging, sleeping, drinking liquor, or talking to themselves that I didn't want to give, fearing I was supporting a bad habit.

This man was different though. I put two dollars in his cup and he looked me straight in the eyes. "God bless you," he said.

I nodded.

"I'm a vet, you know. Army, but you know how the government…" He paused and looked down, perhaps ashamed, but I wasn't sure. "Anyway, I appreciate your help."

I could have built a conversation with him around the military, but decided against it. I had served four years in the Air Force as an audio engineer, but his living on the street told me that whatever he had gone through was a lot worse than what I'd seen in my career. "You're welcome," I said and walked off.

"Always expect the unexpected!" he yelled.

I looked back to see him laughing hysterically.

Still laughing, he shouted again. "Magical beginnings have tragic endings. Expect it!"

Okaaay? I thought and proceeded to make my way toward the beach. A slight wind was blowing but the sky was absolutely clear. Once I got closer, I sat down on a bench facing the water, reached in my pocket for my cell phone, and dialed into my voicemail again. I smiled when I heard the voice. It was Tricia. She'd left a brief message with her phone number, asking me to call her back.

9

Not wasting a second, I pressed a two-button code that would automatically dial back the number from which she had called. It rang three times before going to voicemail. I sighed and left her a message. In a way, I was a bit thankful. I realized after I hung up that I wasn't even sure how to pick up where we'd left off. *At least I called.*

As the sound of the water hitting the sand relaxed me, my mood changed from drab to good. I stretched my legs and leaned back to soak up the serenity. Birds chirped above me, and music came from a radio somewhere nearby. I exhaled peacefully, then reached into my bag for a pen and pad to write, but found myself blocked. I couldn't come up with anything to put down on paper. After struggling for a while I decided to take a stroll on the boardwalk and take pictures instead, hoping it would inspire me. I shot the water, the sky, the restaurants, and even the dirty corners. From afar, I used the zoom function of my digital camera to photograph the man to whom I'd given money. I was busily taking the pictures when my phone rang.

"Hello?"

"Sadira, hi, it's Tricia."

I smiled. "Hi."

"How are you? I hear you live in New York again."

"Yes, I'm back." I walked over to a bench and sat down. "It's good to hear from you."

"So," she said and paused.

"So…"

There was an uncomfortable silence before she spoke again. "How has life been treating you?"

"Fair I suppose. I've gone through a lot in the last couple of years but don't have the time or energy to explain it all. I'm rebuilding myself right now, I'll tell you that much. I'm learning from past mistakes."

"I see. Well, I don't have much time to talk now, but I'd like to see you if that's okay."

"Yeah, that's fine." I felt good. "When do you want to meet up? I mean, I heard you're super busy now, so you tell me when a good time will be."

10

She laughed. "I am quite busy, but I'll make time for you. Unfortunately this week won't work because tomorrow I'm going to Tampa for business."

"Look, why don't you just call me when you get back?"

"Ew. You don't have to say it like that."

"Like what?"

"Like, 'whatever bitch, just call me whenever you get time, damn.'"

I couldn't help but laugh. "That's not how I meant it, geez. I'm just saying that you should call me when I can have your undivided attention because I won't settle for less."

"Yeah, okay. Listen, I have to go now, but we'll speak again soon."

"All right," I said. "I'll be around. My phone is always on, but I don't answer it all the time so leave a message if you don't get me."

"I will."

"Cool, I'll talk to you later."

"Bye."

I hung up the phone feeling refreshed and in an even better mood. Seeing Tricia again would be great. I hung around the beach a bit longer before going home. On the train ride, I scrolled through all the photos I'd taken and my creativity kicked in. I started writing a long poem about my feelings, but the subway car was so hot I couldn't finish. It was too uncomfortable to concentrate, so I just rode listening to music. When I got home, I saw a familiar face.

"What's up, Sadira?"

"Hey, Rick. What are you up to today?" I smiled at him. He wasn't the most attractive guy but he had the kind of confidence that could override a not so pleasant face. He was a sharp dresser and a smooth talker. When I first moved to the neighborhood, I saw him every day on my way home from the subway. He always said hi, and then I noticed him visiting Melissa.

"Not much. I'm waiting for Melissa to get home." Melissa was a quiet young girl who lived in the brownstone next to mine.

11

"What's up with you two?"

"See now, why are you being nosey?" He sat down on the stoop and smiled. "We're just friends."

"Mm hm. Anyway, I'm going inside. I'm tired."

"I'll see you later then."

"Bye." The sun was setting as I walked up to my place.

I took a shower, watched some TV and finished up the poem I had started on the train. When I was done I spent two hours working on music to go with it and then went to lie down.

Arguing coming from next door interrupted my catnap. It was Melissa and her roommate, Jasmine. I didn't know either of them very well, but Jasmine came off a bit odd to me. They fought all the time. And though they said they were roommates, it sounded like bitter lovers' quarrels to me. I tried my best to mind my business as far as those two were concerned. Eventually, I went back to sleep.

Chapter 3

Some time during the following day I made up my mind to go to an open mic lounge that evening. Even if I didn't perform, it was time I made some new friends. Wanting a fresh start, I decided against going to the club that I used to frequent. I'd looked into a few venues and decided to check out a place in Brooklyn called Piper's that was supposed to be gay friendly.

It was humid and a slight drizzle had started sprinkling the city when I left work. I debated not going out, but refused to let the weather stop me. When I got home I turned on my computer to finish the musical track that I was making to go behind my poem. After tinkering with it for a while, I got it to sound just the way I wanted it. I logged onto the Internet to check my e-mail and post my latest creation on the message board I'd started frequenting.

Two private messages from people I didn't know popped up. One of them was a generic message from the board moderators with a reminder of the forum rules, and the other one said: *I love what you post and I think you're cute. Send me a note sometime. I live in Brooklyn too.* Without thinking about it, I clicked the link to look at the person's profile.

"Damn," I said out loud when I saw the photo. The picture was nice. She had a very bright smile accented by dimples and piercing brown eyes. I couldn't tell what her hair was like because she was wearing a head wrap, but she had beautiful skin. I skimmed over her hobbies, *swimming, drawing, singing, and reading.* I wondered if it were someone bullshitting me by putting a different person's photo in her profile. *There's only one way to know.* I replied to her message to find out that she was online, so I responded immediately. We chatted for a while. Her name was Brianna, and that really was her picture. She turned on her webcam to prove it to me. She was younger than I was, and I was impressed by her ambitiousness when she told me that she was finishing a five-year program to get a Bachelor of Arts in political science and a master's degree in public administration. The more I looked at her bright smile, the more intrigued I became. She was wearing a fitted white sleeveless t-shirt that slightly revealed the impression of her breasts. Looking beyond her and into her background of the room, I noticed that it was very neat.

We didn't get into a deep conversation but breezed over light things like the last movie we both saw, what our dream vacations were, and the type of music we liked. I did flirt a little and asked if she wore bikini cut panties or thongs. She laughed but answered *thongs*. I was amused and interested, but I didn't want it to show too much so I cut our conversation short to shower and get ready to go to Piper's. Brianna was pleasant and promised to send me an instant message when she saw me online again.

I logged offline and started getting ready. After getting dressed, I printed out a few of my poems just in case I felt like going on stage, but as it was, I was only going that night to get a feel for the place and the people there.

The first thing I noticed when I got there was the artwork. There were a lot of paintings hanging on the walls, the lights were dim, and candles were on the tables. A small band was playing and people were scattered at tables and the bar. A waiter smiled and said hello to me as he walked by. I looked around for an empty table and spotted one in a corner. As I was walking over, two women sat down before I could get there. *Damn, they took my spot.* One of them made eye contact with me. I smiled at her, then turned to look for another empty table, but there weren't any so I went to the bar.

"What can I get for you?" the bartender asked.   He had a deep voice and was sporting a spiky red and black Mohawk.

"Just a bottle of water for now, thanks."

"Coming right up."

When he came back I gave him four dollars for the water and left a dollar tip on the bar. The band finished up a song and an androgynous woman sporting a chaotic hairdo walked on to the stage. She was upbeat, welcoming everyone to Piper's. It was a new establishment, only open for a month with one night reserved for poetry and the open mic crowd. The room revealed an even mix of men and women, gay and straight. I saw some men holding hands as well as men and women sitting closely together. It was definitely comfortable.

The MC's name was Alison, but she told everyone to call her Al. She wore black boots, ripped jeans with a chain hanging from them, and a white tank top that read BITCH on it in bold. She was attractive in an alternative way. After going over the house rules and announcing the bar specials, she called the first person up to the microphone. From poems about Big Macs to the public school system and even interracial dating between men, there was a fusion of thoughts, emotions and opinions that filled the room. Everyone didn't sound good, but those who went up tried their best and the crowd was appreciative and applauded their efforts.

There was one guy who was especially impressive at the end of the first set. He was different, fresh, and a relief from some of the people who were all starting to sound alike in rhythm and pattern. His piece was about how the commercialism of the black culture's spoken word was ruining it. I totally agreed and had a piece on that subject myself, but mine stated that the movie "Love Jones" was partly responsible for the downfall of originality in spoken word. I loved the movie, but after it came out everyone who could put rhyming words together thought she was the next Sonia Sanchez or Nikki Giovanni. I'd written my poem after getting fed up with what I was hearing from a lot of new people on the poetry scene. In my opinion they lacked unique rhythm, tone of voice, and animation that would make them stand out from others. But whatever, I could just be an arrogant prick and annoyed that there were new artists coming out. *Nah, they lacked originality.*

"Can I get another drink for you?" the bartender asked, interrupting my thoughts.

"Um, yeah. Give me an apple martini." I noticed one of the women from the table at which I was originally going to sit trying to making eye contact with me again. I smiled back.

"Coming right up," the bartender said.

When I turned around I saw that the woman at the table was now approaching. She was dressed casually in black Capri pants and a peach v-neck shirt. She looked a little nervous, so I smiled at her.

"Hi." I decided to break the ice as soon as she sat down.

"Hello," she said, seemingly relieved that I had spoken first. "How are you?"

The bartender brought my drink over without interrupting. I put money out to cover my drink and continued talking to her. "I'm fine, and you?"

"A little unsure. I can't believe I came over here to you."

I laughed. "What made you do it?"

"Well, I thought you were attractive. And…"

"And?" I raised my eyebrow wanting her to finish her sentence.

"And I wanted to say hello. There, I said it."

"Good. Courage is good. You are attractive too. My name is Sadira." I extended my hand. "It's nice to meet you."

"Olivia," she said with a smile while shaking my hand.

Before we could speak more, the music faded out and Al was back on the stage to announce the next poet. I wanted to ask Olivia where she was from because I heard an accent when she spoke. She sounded like she was from one of the Caribbean islands—Jamaica maybe. To avoid being rude to the artist on the stage, I held my question until he finished. Olivia followed my lead.

When the guy on the mic was finished I spoke again while people were clapping. "Olivia, do you want to move to the back of the room so we can talk?" I thought about offering to buy her a drink before we left

16

the bar, but decided against it. Hell, *she* came up to *me*.

She looked over to the table where she was sitting to see the other girl was now talking with a guy. "Sure, we can go in the back."

"Come on." I grabbed my drink and made my way to a small unoccupied couch in the corner. Olivia followed. "Is this comfortable for you?"

"Yes, it's fine."

"So," I said after we sat down. "Where are you from?"

"St. Thomas, but I've been in the States for twelve years."

"I see." I moved in closer to her and put my glass on a table in front of us.

We talked for a while about where we were from and what we liked. I was feeling a nice buzz from the alcohol and was a bit surer of myself than usual. By the end of the conversation I had her phone number, a kiss on the neck, and a tentative date the following weekend. I remained on the couch after she excused herself to go back to her friend who was now sitting alone.

Shortly afterwards, I left Piper's thankful that I made myself go out. When I got home there was a message from Tricia on my voicemail. *Hey, Sadira. I'm just calling to say hi. Don't call me back because I'm getting ready to go to sleep. I have a long day tomorrow but just wanted to let you know I was thinking of you.* I smiled and listened to it again before disconnecting.

After undressing and changing into my pajamas I crawled into bed.

Chapter 4

The next morning I woke up with just enough time to get dressed for work and get out of the house. On my way into the radio station, I bought a raisin bagel with cream cheese and an orange juice from a woman running a sidewalk café. It was a quarter to six in the morning and Devonte's show was supposed to be about pet peeves. In my workspace, I put on my headphones, checked the sound levels, and got ready to start my shift.

My mind drifted to Olivia and Brianna, the two women I had just met and I grinned to myself. Finally, I was easing out of the rut I let Jessie put me in. I also couldn't wait until Tricia got back in town.

Off air Devonte' yelled over to me. "What's up, girl? Have you talked to my cousin?"

"Yes, I did. I'm going to see her when she gets back."

"Gets back? Where is she?"

"She told me she had to go to Tampa for business."

"Damn, I can't keep up with her. Anyway, I'll catch up with you after the show."

"Okay."

Devonte' and I really didn't get to talk for long after the show. He was in a hurry. "Hey, I have to get out of here," he said. "I'm going to Alabama tomorrow and haven't packed yet."

"Why?"

"I haven't been home in a long time and my mama has made it

18

clear she doesn't like it."

"Oh. All right, man. I'll see you when you get back."

"Later."

After work I went to the movies by myself to see "The Day After Tomorrow" and thoroughly enjoyed it. I got so wrapped up in the movie's special effects, I didn't think too much about the suggestion that global warming might bring a new ice age. It was good entertainment. I felt funny going alone, but I didn't want to go out with Olivia earlier than we'd planned, and I wasn't ready to meet Brianna in person yet.

Afterwards I took the bus home and ordered Chinese food for dinner. I looked on my nightstand at the piece of paper with Olivia's number, debating if I should call. *I'll wait,* I thought, and got on the Internet. Brianna was there. I decided to linger and let her speak to me first, and she did. We talked about our day and shared more about ourselves. My eyes started to get tired after a while and I told her I was logging off. She gave me her phone number and asked me to call when I had time. I didn't share mine, but I promised to call her. Not long after I logged off, my food was delivered.

"Here you go," I said. "Keep the change."

The deliveryman nodded, smiled, and rode off. As I was going back up to my apartment, I heard arguing coming from next door. Jasmine and Melissa were at it again.

Melissa's voice was enraged. "You are fucking crazy! I'm leaving."

"Where are you going to go? You don't have any money. Don't think Rick is going to come to your rescue," Jasmine shouted.

I heard what sounded like running downstairs. Then their voices faded. Snooping, I looked outside to see if Melissa had left. She did, and Jasmine was following her closely. *Damn,* was all I could think and went back up to mind my own business. Drama.

After eating, I turned my television on the smooth jazz channel and stretched out on my bed. I was glad the arguments next door had stopped, but a part of me worried about Melissa. She couldn't have been older than twenty. I knew Jasmine was about twenty-eight and strange. I

19

only spoke to her in passing and it was never more than a hello. I did speak to her grandmother, Etta, who always sat outside on nice days. There was something about Jasmine that annoyed the crap out of me though. I avoided her.

Glancing over at the clock I decided to give Brianna a call before it got too late.

"Hello?" She answered after three rings.

"Hi, may I speak with Brianna, please?"

"This is she."

"Do you know who this?"

"I sure do. You're the only person I've given my number to in months." She sounded as though she were grinning. "Hi, Sadira. I'm glad you called."

"I promised I would."

"Well, it's good to know you don't break promises."

I smiled. "Yeah."

"So what's up?"

"You tell me."

"Well..."

There was a brief silence before I spoke. "Well, what are you feeling right now?" I asked, trying to help move the conversation along.

"I'm feeling a little nervous but excited at the same time."

"Mm hm. Well let's just talk. You don't have to be nervous. I'm not crazy."

"You better not be."

"No, not anymore. They let me out of the mental hospital last week," I said playfully.

She giggled. "Shut up."

"Made you smile. So, anyway, you said you haven't given your number out in some time. What made you give it to me?"

"That's a good question. I've been asking myself and haven't come up with an answer yet. I guess there's something special about you."

"I suppose that is a good thing."

"We'll see."

We ended up talking for hours into the night. I knew I would feel tired the next day but didn't care. I hadn't spent that much time on the phone with someone since I was in high school. She told me about her life and dreams of going into politics and working at the Capitol. When I asked her how she got interested in politics in the first place, she told me it was because of a militant history teacher that she had in junior high school.

"He would always bad mouth white people and go off on political tangents saying how the Republicans were going to be the death of society because they didn't care about poor people. 'Blacks shouldn't vote Republican. Remember that when you get old enough to vote!' That is what he said at the end of the year."

"Damn that's blunt."

"It was. Half of the students let it go in one ear and out the other, but I wanted to find out more."

"Mm hm."

"Through all of my reading over time I really started liking politics and analyzing policies. The next year school year I joined the debate team and kept it up through high school. I also started paying attention not only to what the local politicians were saying when they came out to our neighborhood, but comparing it to the results. All promises and no positive outcomes, that's how I felt and still sort of feel about Democrats today."

Not sharing much about my past, I continued to listen to her. I was more interested in getting to know her, and I only sprinkled bits and pieces of my childhood and being in the military. When the conversation did shift to me, I told her about just breaking up and adjusting to being single. By the time our talk wound down, it was 2 a.m.

I yawned. "Hey, Brianna, I'm starting to get tired."

"Me too."

"Mmm. I can tell. You sound kind of sexy."

"I do, do I?" I could tell she was smiling again. I imagined she was lying on her back, in the dark, with her eyes closed, talking to me.

"Yes. I better get off this phone with you. We had a great conversation and I don't want to ruin a potential friendship by flirting too much or moving too fast."

"I agree," she paused before speaking again. "Hey, it was nice talking to you. Thanks for calling."

"My pleasure."

"Good night."

"Night. I'll call you again."

"Okay."

I closed my cell phone, got up to adjust the air conditioner, and went in the bathroom.   I brushed my teeth and then eased into a late night slumber.

The two days before my date with Olivia went by quickly. She and I met for lunch at a Mexican restaurant in the Greenwich Village and walked over to the pier afterwards. We talked about our pasts and where we were at the current moment in our lives. Olivia was trying to find her way. She wasn't sure which career path she wanted to take and was working through a temp agency. She loved to cook and design homes but wasn't sure if she wanted to invest the time and money to go to school to get the proper credentials. Her conversation didn't impress me, but she was beautiful. I could tell from our dialogue that she was the type of person I could sleep with and with whom I could have a good time, but not much more. There wasn't enough chemistry for us to make it beyond three dates.

We stopped and stood facing the water. I took her hand and turned to look at her. "So, what are you looking for?" I hoped she'd say that she just wanted something casual.

"What do you mean?"

"What are you looking for, something serious or laid-back with dating?"

"Nothing too serious. I mean I'm not looking for a wife right now if that's what you're getting at. I'm okay with casual dating. If things got to be more than that with you, then I'll have to make some decisions."

22

"Okay."

She looked at me and smiled.

"Come here," I said and leaned in to kiss her. She didn't stop me so I kept going deeper into a sexually charged kiss.

She put her hand on the back of my neck and moved closer to me. With closed eyes I leaned against the guardrail and put my arms around her waist as we continued to kiss. I wanted to move my hands farther down her body but kept in mind that we were in public, and thought that though it felt good, we should stop. I slowly eased out of the kiss, opened my eyes, and stared into hers. I was aroused, but knew I wouldn't sleep with her—at least not that day.

Olivia and I stayed on the pier a while longer before bringing our date to a close.

"I'll call you," she said before turning to leave.

"Okay, see you later." We parted, and I walked to the nearest subway to head home. When I got in I went straight to the bathroom for a warm shower. After turning on the water, I stripped out of my clothes and stepped inside to let the warm beads of water massage my body. I tried to clear my mind of all things and just enjoy the peace that came with cleansing but was unsuccessful. Thoughts of Jessie crept into my mind against my will. Memories of us living in Miami and the times we made love in the shower, in the kitchen, and even on the beach flooded my mind. I wondered what she was doing and how she felt at the moment. Did she miss me? I closed my eyes and sighed. To combat my thoughts, I turned on the cold water hoping the temperature would shock me out of the relapse into which I was falling. *You have a new life now.* I got out of the shower, dried off, and put on my black terrycloth bathrobe.

"Damn, I need to go grocery shopping," I said aloud as I looked in my barren refrigerator. There was nothing in there but cheese, Sprite, leftover Chinese food, and eggs. With no real options, I reheated the leftovers and plopped down on the couch to watch TV. From "Oprah" to "Wife Swap" to a PBS special on the gold rush, I flipped back and forth among programs not watching any one in its entirety. *I should call Brianna.* Before the thought could fully exit my mind, I dialed her

23

number, but to my disappointment the call went straight to her voicemail. I left a message and went to my desk to log on the Internet.

Khedara was online so I turned on my mic and we used a messenger to do a voice chat.

"So how have you been, sis?" I asked.

"Not bad, I've been on a couple of more dates with Lance, and I really like him. Finally, I think I found someone I click with."

"That's great. So tell me a little bit more about him."

"Well, he's an electrician. He's a little on the chubby side, but he has the most beautiful smile I've ever seen. You should see his cute dimples and cocoa brown skin. He makes *me* smile! His eyes are dark brown, and his voice is so deep. I feel safe around him." She was rambling!

Definitely in love, I thought. I laughed. "I've never heard you talk about anyone like this. Good luck with him."

"Thanks. I just have to make sure I don't get too excited. I don't want a big letdown if things don't work out."

"It's too late for that. I bet you've already thought about what your kids would look like."

"No I haven't. Well..."

"You're sprung. I can't wait to meet this guy."

"Well, bring your butt out here to Bermuda and you can." A while back she'd gotten an opportunity to work in Bermuda for a year. She liked it so much she was debating on staying there permanently instead of returning to her home in Atlanta.

"I will soon. I promise. I miss you."

We conversed a little bit longer before saying goodbye and signing off the Internet. I took the mic off my head and went to lay down and watch television. After flipping through all of my channels, I put the remote down and ignored the TV, annoyed that with over 800 stations, I couldn't find a program that interested me. I felt lonely. Lying on my side staring at the wall, I tried to think of something to occupy my mind, but I couldn't. When boredom finally got the best of me I decided to call Olivia. She sounded surprised to hear from me.

24

"Hey!" she said. "What's going on with you?"

"I can't sleep. What are you doing?" I glanced at the clock on my cable box. It was 10:30 pm.

"I'm just watching TV. I didn't want to go out tonight."

There was silence on the phone line for a few seconds as I thought about what to say next. I wanted to invite her over to my place, but it would be moving too fast. *How slow should I go with someone I know I don't want to get serious with?* Before I could speak again, my phone beeped. Someone was on the other line. "Hold on a sec, Olivia," I said, and then took the other call. It was Brianna. *Yes.*

"Hello?"

"Hi," said Brianna.

"Hey, what's up?"

"I hope it's okay that I called. You never actually gave me your number but it was still on my caller ID. I'm sorry, I know it's late."

"Of course it's okay. Hold on a moment, let me clear my other line." I clicked back over and told Olivia I had to go, but I'd call her back if it didn't get too late. She didn't sound happy that I was cutting her off for someone else but I didn't care. "Okay, Brianna, I'm back."

Again, Brianna and I talked for hours. Even after we hung up the phone I met her online and she turned on her webcam so I could see her. I e-mailed her a couple of pictures of me so she could see what I looked like too. We clicked. I was intrigued by her interest in politics and how easy it was to talk to her. Her laugh was contagious, and I caught myself smiling a lot during our conversation. I suggested that we meet in person soon and she agreed. We chatted a bit more and I sent her some spoken word audio files that I'd been working on. I really liked her.

After speaking to Brianna I didn't feel like calling Olivia back so I ordered a movie on demand and relaxed by myself.

The next day went by slowly. It was Thursday and I had a date with Brianna on Saturday. Meanwhile, Tricia called me from the airport in Tampa to let me know she was thinking of me and that she'd be back in New York by nightfall. Single life was turning out nicely for me. My mind drifted to thoughts of the three women I was talking to, but I was pulled out of the moment when I noticed a lady sitting across from me on the bus. She looked like a die-hard butch and she was smiling at me. *Oh hell, not today!* I wanted to roll my eyes, but I didn't. Whenever I wore fitted clothes and was having an overall more feminine day, I had a tendency to attract more men and butches. I didn't want either one of them.

I eased my demeanor into one that I hoped would read, *don't bother me,* but it didn't work. She was still smiling in my face. I was dressed in a gray v-neck t-shirt and dark blue fitted jeans. I was also wearing a rainbow bracelet that obviously identified me as gay to people who knew what it meant. When the two people who were also sitting up front got off the bus, the woman moved closer to me. *Here we go.*

She spoke first. "Hi."

"Hey."

She smelled like cigarettes and incense. "My name is Jovi."

I shook my head and acknowledged her name but didn't give her mine.

"You're not going to tell me yours?"

"Actually I'm getting off at this stop," I lied.

"At least tell me your name."

"Sadira, but I only date femmes," I said and walked off. *Punk,* I thought and laughed at myself. I took the easy way out, but I didn't care. I just wanted her out of my face.

I decided to walk the rest of the way home. Rick was getting up and leaving Melissa's stoop. He said hello to me before walking off and leaving her sitting by herself.

I smiled. "Hey, Melissa."

"Hi."

Before I could say anything else my cell phone started ringing. I waved at her and took the call as I walked inside. It was Tricia.

"Hey, Tricia."

"Hi. I lucked out and caught an earlier flight. I'm already in New York."

"Really? That's great. So when I can I see you," I said as I walked to the kitchen to pour myself something to drink.

"I'm kind of tired, but you can see me later on tonight if you really want to."

"I do want to see you. Where do you live, and what time should I come?"

"You can come over around 9:00. I want to relax a bit by myself first. I live in Greenpoint now."

"Okay."

My doorbell rang just as I was about to turn my television on. "Hold on a second, Tricia."

"Actually, let me call you back when I'm ready for you to come over," she said.

"All right, that's fine. Don't go changing your mind."

"I won't."

"Okay, bye."

We hung up and I looked through the window before going downstairs to answer the door. It was Melissa.

I was surprised to see her. We spoke often in passing but never anything more than that. When I opened the door, she looked disheveled and her eyes were red.

"Come on up. What's wrong?" I had a feeling it had something to do with Jasmine but waited for her to tell me. I wasn't sure what I could or would say, but I had to do something to help her feel better. She looked awful.

"I hate her." She spoke slowly and with pure disdain after sitting down. "I hate the fact that she breathes." Tears flowed from her eyes before I could say anything. "And I hate that I got myself into this situation and am struggling to find a way out."

I sighed.

She tried to say something else but all that came out was a sob. Melissa lowered her head and cried.

Unsure of what to say or do, I moved closer to her and put my arm on her shoulder. "It'll be okay."

27

She exhaled and her tears subsided a bit. "I'm sorry to come over like this. You don't even know me that well, but I just needed someone to talk to."

"It's all right. What's going on over there?"

"I have to get away from her." She spoke fast, running one sentence into the next. "I have to get out. She's crazy and she doesn't even know it."

"What's stopping you from leaving?"

"I don't have any money."

"What about your family? Don't you have family here?"

"No, my father is in Kentucky, and I don't want to ask him for help. If he knew what was going on, he would have a fit." She shook one of her legs nervously as she talked.

"Well what are you going to do?"

"I'm looking for a job now. I'll do whatever it takes to get away from her. She's nuts, I mean nuts! One minute she seems normal, then the next minute she is obsessive and controlling."

I remained quiet.

"As soon as I went inside after Rick left, she started asking me all these questions about why I'm talking to him so much. Then she started talking about her birthday and gave me a wish list. Next she tried to kiss me, and when I didn't respond she started crying. I left her crying and went to the bathroom. Before I could sit on the toilet she was banging on the door demanding that I come out."

"Jesus."

"Yeah, the bitch is insane." Melissa ran her hands over her head, which was clad in a blue bandana. She was wearing gray windbreaker pants and a gray t-shirt with her school name in blue letters.

I nodded negatively, recognizing that I'd always had a funny feeling about Jasmine, but this was more than I thought.

"I'm sure I'll have better luck getting a job as soon as the semester is over. I just don't know how I'm going to make it through the next month. I can't focus in class."

"You'll be okay. Try your best. I mean, just hang in there for the

28

next couple of months and then get away from her."

"Tell me about it." She sniffled and then wiped her face.

"Let me get you a tissue."

"Thanks."

Melissa was deep in thought when I returned. She didn't even see me walk up to her. I handed her the tissue. She cleaned herself up and then stayed a few minutes longer before getting up to leave.

"Thanks for listening and being there for me."

"You can come over whenever you need to talk, okay?"

"All right."

"Just be strong," I said as I walked her to the door.

She stuck her hands in her pockets and tried to smile. "Bye."

I nodded and smiled before closing the door behind her. After Melissa left I walked to the bodega on the corner to get a sandwich and protein shake.

"Where's Sammy?" I asked the guy behind the counter flirting with me.

"He is gone home to Yemen to visit his wife. When will you go out with me?"

I laughed. I was used to the question from him and answered it the same way I always did, with a smile and a polite brushoff before leaving. About nine men who rotated running the store lived in a brownstone a couple doors down from where I lived. They were very friendly to me and only one made passes at me every now and then. I never felt like explaining that I didn't date men so I avoided it as much as I could. There was always the option to walk to the store on the other end of the block, but I didn't like the family who ran it. And as funny as it may sound, *that* end of my block was too ghetto for me.

The weather was beautiful and I wanted to soak up the sunshine when I got back to my place. Jasmine's grandmother was now sitting outside in her favorite old wicker chair. Everybody on the block called her Grandma. She was so pleasant, always waving at people who walked by. I said hello to her and made small talk while sitting on my stoop.

29

In the middle of our discussion, Jasmine walked outside wearing tight blue jeans, a sleeveless brown shirt, and a brown hat. She looked at me with her large eyes and smiled before speaking.

"Hi!"

"Hello."

Before saying any more, she stretched and the visible hair under her arms immediately turned me off. *Eww.* I know I made an ugly face as I squinted in disgust.

"It's getting too hot out here for me," I lied and got up.

She rolled her eyes. "Bye, then."

Jasmine's grandmother had dozed off in her chair so I didn't feel bad about abruptly leaving.

"I'll see you around, Jasmine," I said and went up to my apartment. Forget about her.

I knew Tricia would be calling soon so I took a quick shower after finishing my food. A bit of anxiousness consumed me as I thought about seeing her again. While drying off I heard my phone ringing, but it stopped before I could get to it. When I checked my voicemail there were two messages. One was from Brianna, and the other was from Tricia. *I'll call Brianna later.* Wrapped in a towel, I sat down and called Tricia.

She answered on the second ring. "Hello?"

"Hey, it's me Sadira."

"I know who it is."

"Well excuse me," I said sarcastically and she laughed. "Are you ready to see me now?"

"Yes, I am."

"Good, because I've been looking forward to seeing you. It's been a long time."

"Yeah, a couple of years. I didn't think I'd ever run into you again."

"Well, I'm back now. And you can see me as soon as you give me your address." I didn't want to talk about what happened in my life during the period Tricia and I hadn't seen each other. I didn't want to think about Jessie.

30

"I live at 158 Broadway. You can either take the train to Lorimer Street or take a cab over. I don't think it would be very expensive in a cab, but it's up to you."

"Well I'm not in the mood to walk to the subway station. Plus I'd have to take two trains. I'll just call for a car."

"All right. I live on the first floor so I'll look out for you."

"Okay, I'll be there soon."

"See you."

"Bye," I said and hung up the phone smiling.

I got dressed then called car service. The operator said a driver would be there in three minutes. After spraying on a little perfume, I went outside to wait. A minute later a beat-up looking white Lincoln town car pulled up in front of me.

"You called for cab?" the driver yelled.

"Yeah." I walked to the jalopy and got in.

Despite speeding, running a few red lights, and making an illegal left turn from a far right lane, he got me there in one piece. I tipped him two dollars before getting out and walking up to Tricia's building. Dressed comfortably in black pants and a fitted burgundy button-down shirt, I reached up to press the buzzer but saw Tricia peek through the window before I could push it. Quickly, I popped a Tic-Tac in my mouth to make sure my breath wasn't offensive.

She smiled as soon as she opened the door. "Hi."

"Hey," I said, returning the smile. I leaned in to hug her. It surprised me how good it felt to be in her familiar arms. She smelled good and made me feel warm inside.

Tricia gave me a soft kiss on the neck and said, "Come in."

Still smiling, I squeezed her for a second longer before easing out of our hug and following her inside her apartment. It had a baby blue, brown, and white color scheme. The small end tables on each side of her sofa had unlit candles on them, and there was a candle and rock arrangement as a centerpiece on her coffee table. The only thing that looked out of place was a paperback book that was on the table. I looked more closely at it to see the title, "Making Gay History." *Interesting,* I

31

thought. Maybe she was reading it before I came over. Her phone rang before I could comment.

She motioned for me to have a seat and I did. I kept glancing around the room. A large decorative vase with artificial flora and peacock feathers was in a corner next to one of two full bookshelves that were on both sides of her entertainment center. I could see fresh flowers in a small glass vase on her dining table, which had complementary baby blue placemats with tassels on both ends. An abstract painting hung on a wall behind the table. Tricia's place was warm, inviting, and relaxing.

Wow. I thought about how different she was from when we had met a few years earlier. Back then she seemed so ... so naïve and filled with an aura of exploration and finding her way. She had since settled down. Dressed in a light pink summer skirt and a white shirt, Tricia wore her hair pulled back in a ponytail, bringing out her neatly arched eyebrows and beautiful brown eyes.

I heard her one-sided phone conversation. "All right, but I have to go now. I have company and don't want to be rude." She stayed on the phone a moment longer before hanging up and turning her attention to me. "Do you want something to drink?"

"Sure. What do you have?"

"Water, soda, juice, wine, I have just about everything." She smiled.

"Juice is good. I'm cutting back on soda, and wine is just disgusting."

"It is not disgusting, but I guess it can be considered an acquired taste."

"Whatever, I'd drink water out of a rusty faucet first. I'd rather swallow lead than drink that French furniture polish. Ugh."

She laughed. "Furniture polish? What the hell are you talking about?"

"Wine tastes the way furniture polish smells."

"Yeah, okay, sure. You've been hanging around Devonte' too long because that sounds like something stupid he would say." She went into the kitchen and came back with two glasses of fruit punch.

32

"Thank you."

"You're welcome," she said with a smile. Everything about her seemed calm and together. The way she looked, smelled, the way she carried herself, and even her apartment said *together*. Her life was in order.

Tricia reached for a remote and turned the television on a smooth jazz music channel before sitting down next to me. We just looked at each other first. I felt a comfort being around her and I wanted to move closer to her, but resisted.

"So..." I didn't know where to begin. I leaned back, stretched my legs, and relaxed a bit more.

She looked me directly in the eyes and put a hand on my knee. "So, how have you been? What are you doing back in New York?"

I sighed. "Well, to make a long story short, I moved to Miami to be with Jessie but it didn't work out, so I decided to come back to New York."

She looked at me without surprise. "How long have you been back?"

"Three months." I felt awkward.

"Tell me how you are really feeling, Sadira."

"I'm okay. I mean, I've been adjusting to being single, you know. I'm not seeing anyone seriously now." I paused. "I'm not ready for that yet, but I am talking to a couple of girls."

"Okay. I understand that."

I adjusted in my chair. "What about you?"

"I'm dating, but I haven't found anyone I want to settle down with yet."

"Wow."

"What?" she asked.

"Settle down. You're actually ready to settle down already?"

"Yes. I'm ready for a wife. I've had enough of the dating and three-month relationship scene. It's just getting old and I want to settle down. I don't *need* a woman for anything outside of partnership and I

33

refuse to settle for just anyone. That's probably why it's taking me a long time to find the right person."

I was silent. New York had molded her. Tricia no longer had the innocent sincerity that I remembered but rather a concrete, no-nonsense attitude. I looked her up and down after she spoke, taking in her beautiful presence.

I was staring at the book on her table when she interrupted my thoughts. "It's a good book. I started reading it on the plane."

"Huh? Oh, the book. Yeah?"

"Yeah. Wait, what were you really thinking about?"

"You," I said.

"What about me?"

"Just stuff."

"Mm hmm." There again was the weird silence in halted conversation. "What are you doing tonight?" she asked to move things along.

"I don't have any plans. Why?"

"I was just wondering. I'm not doing anything and if you wanted to stay the night, you could."

I raised an eyebrow.

"Oh relax. You can also go on home if you please. All I'm saying is that I wouldn't mind spending the night with you."

"What about all that stuff about your wanting a wife and not settling?"

"Well," she exhaled and took a moment to think before continuing, "I have a soft spot for you. No strings attached can apply if you want them to, and that is *only* for you. I'm not sleeping with anyone right now anyway. I'm just dating and none of them have made me think about them as a serious potential partner."

"So you want me to be your Ms. Right Now until Mrs. Right comes along?"

She shook her head and smiled. "I want you to stay with me tonight, that's all. God."

I thought about it, wondering if she could really handle doing no strings attached with me and not getting caught up. I didn't want to hurt or disappoint her. I knew full well that I couldn't be the wife she wanted and didn't want to selfishly block a potential suitor. Well, I did want to block, but I knew it wouldn't be fair to her.

"So?" she said.

"Are you sure you'll be okay with it, Tricia?"

"I'm sure. Besides," she said, locking eyes with me and finishing slowly, "I think it'll do you some good."

"Mm. Hm."

Neither one of us said anything for a while. We just sat there and listened to the melodic sounds of jazz coming from the TV. Tricia moved over close to me, putting her head on my shoulder. I put my arm around her and closed my eyes as I sat with my head back on one of the cushions. Stroking her soft skin, I enjoyed the moment of reconnecting that we were experiencing. I kissed her on the forehead and she hugged me.

Just stay the night, yeah right. I pulled her closer to me and kissed her on the lips. She climbed on top of me. I grabbed her by the waist and moved to meet her half way for a kiss. She began unbuttoning my shirt as she eased out of our kiss and looked me directly in the eyes. Without using words to communicate, we shared a stare that had the power of conversing. Looking, gazing, and admiring, I took in all of her, saying everything I needed to say in variations of intense looks and glances.

"I want you," she finally said.

I moved my body upward into hers and pulled her close to me. "Come here." I kissed her full and hard.

She ran her hands through my hair as I continued to thrust up into her. She moaned. Her hands then ventured down to my breasts and she managed to finish unbuttoning my shirt. I was wearing a black sleeveless undershirt.

"Let's go in the room," I whispered, then picked her up. Her legs were wrapped around my waist and before we got to the bedroom I had her up against the wall. She held on to me tightly, as I kissed her. Slowly, I let her down to stand on her own but then moved her left leg aside and began to grind on her as we stood against the wall. She pulled my shirt all the way off and tugged on my undershirt so that it was no longer tucked in my pants. I slowly moved back a step and ran my hands up between her legs.

"Mmm," she moaned as my hands passed over her center.

She pulled her shirt over her head to reveal a sparkling white bra and well-defined abdomen. *Goddamn!* I slid my hands down her stomach while I gently kissed her cleavage. *Lucky me.*

"Come on." Tricia grabbed me by the belt and led me to her bedroom. We could still hear the music from the television.

Inside her room she took her skirt off. I couldn't think of anything but being intimate with her when I saw her firm ass in a matching white thong. On her hands and knees with her face down, Tricia climbed in bed giving me a lovely view of what I was about to have. Quickly, I kicked my shoes off and slid out of my pants all while watching her. *Relax,* I told myself.

I got in bed with her and told her to lay all the way down. Then I licked her from the base of her spine to her neck where I stopped to kiss and massage. I could feel her moving her behind toward me as I kissed her on her neck. She moaned. I focused my attention on her shoulders, then down her arms. Kissing and licking, I grazed her sides and went back to her spine, licking it up and down as well as in a circular motion from top to bottom. She grabbed the sheets as I moved down and kissed past her back, softly biting her cheeks before venturing lower to her legs and behind her knees. I kissed all the way down her legs, one at a time and back up again.

"Turn around," I said and she did.

I was on my knees looking at her in awe as she turned around and opened her legs. The white bra and panty set against her smooth brown skin and her toned body was beautiful. I looked at her from head to toe before lying on her. She hugged me, and I kissed her on the cheek. She turned and kissed me on the lips. Our tongues caressed each other as I ran my right hand down her side. I shifted my weight more toward the bed, then pulled her on top of me. It reminded me of the first night we'd had sex and how she had straddled me in my Harlem apartment.

36

"Why don't you let your hair down?" I asked.

"If that's what you want, okay." She took her hair out of a ponytail and let it fall silkily against her shoulders.

With her eyes closed, Tricia slowly moved her neck around in a circular motion as if to stretch it out. As I moved upward into her, she arched her back and then exhaled. Music from the other room wafted through the air as she slid her hands beneath my undershirt and pulled at it. I leaned forward, took it and my bra off, and guided her head to my breasts. One by one she took them in her mouth, sucking and licking. I could feel her hair brushing against my skin as she kissed down my stomach. Tricia pulled my boxers off and then kissed my inner thighs. She looked up at me, smiled, and then gave me a long slow lick up my center.

I gazed down at her as her head moved up and down as she sucked on my womanhood. I had the strongest case of penis envy, so much so that I actually felt as though her sucking was causing me to rise like a small hard mound in her mouth. She looked up, locking her eyes on mine, and with a snake-like swiftness, flicked her tongue against me so I could see her every move. Her bedroom eyes pierced mine. I began to shake. I inched back, but she moved forward.

"Hold on, slow down. Wait, wait, wait, I don't want to finish yet," I whispered.

She eased into slower kissing, then licked down to my opening and slid her tongue inside. In and out, she massaged me with her tongue. Again, I looked down to watch. Her face was buried in me and her behind was in the air. I felt myself getting closer to a climax, and though I didn't want to finish too soon, I didn't want her to stop either. *Shit*. I wrapped my legs around her neck to lock in more of the pleasure she was giving me and let myself go, moaning and becoming lost in the moment. Within seconds my own hands were on my breasts as she continued to please me. I took it for as long as I could and was feeling myself reach a peak before trying to stop her again.

"Come here."

37

She didn't stop. *Don't climax yet, Sadira,* I thought to myself. I opened my eyes as if it would help slow things down. It did. *Focus, and hold out.*

"Tricia, baby, please come here." I reached down to pull her up, but she still didn't come up immediately. I moved back, trying to pull away, but she continued. "Pleeeeaase." I had to get her up or I was going to release in her mouth, plain and simple. Not that I didn't want to do that, but it would be over too fast. I wanted to enjoy her for longer than a few minutes. Finally, she came up for air and lay down on top of me.

"I want to stretch this moment out with you." I kissed her on the forehead.

She smiled, then used her index finger to trace the contours of my body.

No strings attached, I thought and for a second wondered if *I* could handle the arrangement. Already I knew I didn't want anyone else to have her. After a few minutes I turned over and was on top of her. I unfastened her bra and ran both my hands down the sides of her body. I pulled her panties off, looked at her, and smiled. Nakedly lying against the golden detailed sheets, she looked gorgeous. Moving down to the foot of the bed, I started to please her. As I moved my mouth to kiss up her calves, I put her leg on my shoulder. Down into the crevice of her inner thighs, I kissed and lightly grazed my tongue over her center.

She squirmed, grabbed the sheets, and moaned. After slowly moving my tongue back to her center, I gave her the same pleasure she gave me. With the meticulousness of a perfectionist, I sped up, slowed down, and changed my style from smooth to wild, tasting and reaching my tongue as far inside of her as I could. Inhaling with my mouth open to catch my breath, I gave her the sensation of a quick cool breeze, pleasurably alternating from the wet warmness her body was exuding.

"Oh, Sadira," she moaned.

Slowing down, I moved up and kissed her perfectly chiseled stomach, then ventured to her breasts. Cupping one while sucking the other, I felt her hands rubbing my back. Then I lay directly on her and held her hands down above her head before rhythmically moving my body

38

on top of hers. I could feel her wetness against mine as our centers grazed each other. She began to moan louder as I sped up.

Again I wanted to control the length of our passionate session so I slowed down and kissed her some more. She held on to me tightly and kissed me back. "How does it feel?" I whispered in her ear, and she moaned in a positive response. I tasted her neck with my tongue and gradually sped my body movement back up to the point of inducing beads of sweat between us. I moved faster and harder on top of her and could hear the contact of our bodies. A few minutes later she screamed when reaching her climax and I reached my peak shortly after.

She looked at me with her pretty brown eyes.

"Give me a kiss," I said and she did.

We lay still for a while, before I rolled off her. She got up and got something to drink. I couldn't move.

Chapter 5

When the alarm on my cell phone went off at 5 a.m., I was jolted out of my sleep. I blinked a few times, and then looked around as if to remind myself where I was. Tricia stirred next to me but didn't wake up. *Damn, I have to go to work.* I yawned and slowly got out of the bed to go to the bathroom to relieve myself and wash my face. I looked at myself in the mirror after drying my face and smiled while remembering the previous evening. I had to be careful with Tricia. She gave the kind of sex that would have me spending my last dime on her.

Just as I was walking back in her bedroom, I heard her say my name softly. "Sadira."

"Yeah?"

"Where are you going?"

"I have to go to work."

"This early?"

"Yes, I work the first shift, remember?" I walked over and sat on the edge of the bed next to her.

"Oh," she said and paused. "Okay. Whatever."

She was curled up in fetal a position and the deep blue and gold sheets were covering her from the shoulders down. Her hair lay softly against the pillow as I leaned in to kiss her on the cheek. She smiled without opening her eyes. I kissed her on the forehead and then on her lips. She moaned softly at my pecks of affection.

"I'll call you," I whispered and got up to pick up my clothes that were lying all around the bedroom.

"Hold on." Tricia sleepily got up and walked me to the door. We exchanged a short but sweet kiss before I left.

By the time I walked to the subway and waited for what seemed like forever, I knew I wouldn't have time to go home and change. *Oh well,* I thought. Though I did stop to buy a mini toothbrush and toothpaste, I went to work in the previous day's clothes. I slipped into the bathroom to freshen up before bumping into Devonte'. I was glad to see him when I walked down the hall into the station.

"Welcome back, D."

"Hey, girl. What's up? You look good. I mean you look happy."

I smiled. "Thanks. You look tired as hell."

"Yeah, man I am. A lot has changed since the last time I went home. I had no idea I would get stuck with my Uncle James for most of the time."

"I bet you have a bunch of stories."

"Hell yeah. I love my family, but they're country as hell."

"And you're not?"

"You ain't seen country until you go to Alabama. I took my uncle to the racetrack one day and every chance he got he would keep talking about how he was drinking cappuccinos. I tried to tell his old ass that they ain't serving real cappuccinos at no damn *racetrack*. That ain't nothin' but watered down coffee with some evaporated milk in it. Please."

I laughed. "Your whole goddamned family is crazy except for Tricia, huh?"

"Shut up. Anyway, have you heard from her?"

I hesitated before answering him. "Um yeah."

"What does that mean?" He looked at me inquisitively.

"Nothing. I saw her last night."

"Oh, okay."

There was a brief silence before I spoke. "It was good to be around her again."

"All right, all right. Say no more."

41

"Yeah." I felt uncomfortable and was glad he brushed the conversation off.

"Hey, let's get ready to start the show."

"Okay, later."

Whew. I don't know why I felt the way I did. It wasn't like Devonte' didn't know about his cousin and me being together before I moved away from New York. I still felt a little uneasy talking to him. Maybe it was because I wasn't sure what I wanted to do next. At least Tricia and I talked beforehand and she knew that I wasn't ready to date anyone seriously. I'd just have to see what happened as it happened.

After work I took a bus up to Central Park and enjoyed the afternoon by myself. It was a comfortable summer day and I wished I had my camera on me. Trees, people, the sky, I took mental pictures of a little bit of everything before I stopped at a hot dog stand to grab a bite to eat. After paying, I walked a few feet to a section of grass where I ate and then laid down on my back and closed my eyes. The sun didn't bother me one bit.

I relaxed for a while until being disturbed by some children who ran by. I sat up, brought my knees closer to my chest, and rested my folded arms on them. There was a woman not too far away blowing bubbles and playing with her kids. Two pre-teens to my far left were spraying each other with water guns. I smiled. *Good weather in New York brings out the best in people.* I decided to hang out in the park a bit longer before getting up and heading home. A bright pink flyer taped to a light pole caught my attention as I walked to public transportation. It was advertising piano lessons. I stared at it for a few seconds, intrigued, before tearing off one of the small pieces at the bottom with the person's contact information. I hadn't played a musical instrument since high school, and that was the trumpet, but as I traveled home I thought about the piano lessons. *It would be fun.*

The first thing I did after settling in at home was call Brianna. She and I had a date the next day.

"Hello?"

"Hey. What's up, Brianna?"

"Not much. I was studying."

"Do you want me to call you back?"

She didn't answer immediately. "Yeah, why don't I call you back when I'm done. I have a test tomorrow morning and I'm getting some last minute cramming in."

"You have a test on a Saturday?" I asked incredulously.

"Yes," she responded. "In my dual-degree program we have classes on Saturday mornings. It's a drag, but it's worth it to get the two degrees in a shorter period of time."

"Okay, I'll be around."

"All right. I'll call you soon," she said.

"Bye."

Seconds after I hung up I could hear wailing sirens and fire trucks blasting through the street as I assumed the FDNY was off to put out a fire. Not a day went by that I didn't hear loud sirens. As much as I liked my little section in Brooklyn, the noise was starting to get annoying.

To kill time while waiting for Brianna to call me back I pulled out an old deck of cards and played Solitaire over and over until I won.

When she finally phoned, I glanced at the clock and noticed it was 8:30.

"Hello?"

"Hi, Sadira."

"Hey, bookworm. Are you sure you studied enough?"

"Yes, I don't think my brain can hold any more information even if I tried."

I smiled. "Well good luck on your test."

"Thank you. I can't wait to get it over with."

"I can imagine."

"Did you go to school?"

"Yes, but in the Air Force's community college. I don't know what university life as a civilian is like."

"What did you study?"

"Audiovisual production services and music. I must not have told you about my job. I work at WSOL with Devonte' Parks."

43

"Really? He is nuts!" she said then laughed. "I listen to the show some mornings."

"Yeah, he's a trip. You'll never hear me though because I work behind the scenes."

"Sounds like a lot of fun."

"I like it," I said. "What do you want to do after you graduate?"

"Well, before I even finish school there's an internship this fall to work for a state senator and I really want it. I could learn so much. If I get it, I'd work in Washington full-time for a semester. It's unpaid but the experience is priceless in my eyes."

"That does sound like a great opportunity."

"Yeah. I submitted my application, resume', and everything. I'm just waiting to hear good news."

"Good luck."

"Thanks." There was a brief pause in our conversation before she spoke again. "So are we still on for tomorrow night?"

"Yes. Actually, I was wondering if we could make it a lunch date instead of dinner. I'd like to walk around and enjoy the day with you if that's okay."

"That's fine. I don't have plans after my test. The earlier the better. I can't wait to meet you in person."

"Same here." I smiled.

We chatted for at least another hour or so about music, books, and politics before she got a call on her other line. After clicking over and then coming back to me, she said it was her mother, and that she'd have to call me back.

"Okay," I said and let her go.

She called me back shortly after and told me her mother's dog was sick. Her mother wanted Brianna to go with her to the vet for an emergency visit.

"I better go meet her now. She loves that dog like a second child."

"All right. I hope everything goes all right."

After we hung up I logged online to tinker with my music program and my poetry. I spent a bit of time on a website that had free samples of

44

artists on independent labels. I wanted to hear what others were doing. Although I had no desire to pursue music full-time, I entertained the thought of making it a bigger hobby.

When my eyes began to get tired from staring at the computer screen, I logged off and shut the machine down. I stood up and stretched before going in the bathroom to take a shower. While I was emptying my pockets I found the pink piece of paper, with the contact information for piano lessons, that I'd taken earlier that day.

"Damn," I said aloud. I'd forgotten about it but decided to follow up and see about possibly signing up for lessons.

I turned on my radio while I was in the bathroom and took a long steamy shower. When I was finally finished and dressed for bed, I turned my television on. Usher's "Burn" music video was just beginning to play. A bit of sadness came over me as I listened to the words. I started thinking about Jessie, wondering how she was and what she was doing. I closed my eyes and remembered her smile. The song couldn't have been much longer than four minutes, but thoughts of Jessie lingered in my mind long after. I don't know why I didn't just change the channel. Even after a new video was showing I thought about her. A single tear rolled down my cheek as my mind traveled back in time. Lost in somber memories, I think I eventually drifted off to sleep somewhere between 3:00 and 3:30 a.m.

My ringing phone woke me up the next day. I peered over to my clock radio trying to see what time it was, but all I saw were blurry red numbers.

"Hello?" I answered.

"Hey. Are, you still asleep?"

"Brianna?"

"Yeah, it's me."

Oh no, tell me I didn't sleep through our date! I rubbed my eyes to help me wake up faster. "What time is it?"

"About 12:30. I just got out of class."

"Oh." *Whew.*

"I'm sorry I didn't call you back last night. My mother was frantic, but her dog will be fine."

45

"That's good to hear."

"Yeah, well I'm about to leave Manhattan now. What time did you want to meet and where?"

"Why don't we go to Ft. Greene Park? I can be there in less than an hour."

"Okay."

"Um. What are you wearing?" I asked. I had a good idea of what she looked like from the photos we exchanged online but wanted to be sure I could spot her.

"A canary yellow shirt, dark blue jeans, and sandals. I'm wearing my hair in a ponytail today. What about you?"

"Um, I'm not sure yet, but I'll call you when I'm on my way."

"All right."

"Okay, I'm going to get up and get dressed. I don't want to keep you waiting."

"You better not. As a matter of fact, tardiness is one of my pet peeves."

"Gotcha. Well where in Manhattan are you now?"

"Downtown, right by my school, Pace."

"It doesn't take me long to get ready, and I'll be taking a cab over to the park so you won't have to wait. We should get there at the same time if not within minutes of each other. Stand by a bus stop so it'll be easier for me to spot you, and then we can walk into the park together."

"All right."

"I'll see you in a few."

"Bye."

Quickly, I got out of bed and went in the bathroom to wash my face and brush my teeth before getting dressed. Multitasking, I called for a car while putting my shoes on, then sprayed a hint of CK1's summer scent on. Finally ready, I grabbed my bag with my camera and portable CD player in it and went outside to wait for my ride. It didn't take long for a cab to pull up in front of my place. I got in, told the driver where to go, and then turned my headphones on. When the he pulled up a few feet away from a bus stop, I saw Brianna on the opposite side of the street reading a book. *I hope she hasn't been waiting long.*

I paid the fare and got out of the car. Keeping my eye on her as I crossed the street, I reached in my pocket for my cell phone and called her as I was approaching. While dialing, I saw her look left and right, then put her head back down and continue to read. A second or two later she heard her phone ring and pulled it out of her bag.

I decided to walk up to her from behind. "Hey, Brianna. I'm here."

"What are you wearing?"

"A white shirt and jeans." I was few feet behind her. "Turn around."

She smiled when she saw me. "Hi." We both hung up our phones at the same time.

"Hey, have you been waiting long?"

"No. I haven't been here longer than ten minutes, so you're off the hook."

I laughed, slightly relieved that my first in-person impression wasn't a bad one. She was cuter in person. I gave her a quick hug and motioned for her to walk with me. "What book are you reading?"

"Oh, it's called 'Capitalism and Freedom'."

"Interesting. Have you learned anything from it yet?"

"Well I just started reading it yesterday. So far it's pretty good."

"I see."

"Uh huh." She looked at my CD player. "What were you listening to?"

"Mostly instrumentals that I made, but some of them have me reading poetry on them. I'm listening so I can see where I need improvement."

"What do I have to do to get a copy?"

"Hmm, let me think about it."

She put her hands on her hips in protest.

I smiled. "You don't have to do anything. I guess I can burn you copy of some of my stuff and bring it to you the next time we see each other."

47

"How do you know there will be a next time?"

"Because I have something you want."

Defeated, she blushed and tried to change the subject. "So…"

"So?"

"What did you want to do today?"

"To be honest I didn't make any specific plans. I just wanted to see you. Are you hungry?"

"A little. I didn't eat breakfast this morning."

"Okay, why don't we have brunch or something?"

"Sure."

Brianna and I walked to a little private restaurant close by and had a good time getting to know each other better. The environment was relaxed and I believe that we were both comfortable enough to just be ourselves and go with the flow. She was really focused on school, telling me more about her goals and how badly she wanted the internship. After we finished eating we walked back to the park, sat down on the grass, and talked more.

"You know there is only one thing that I will have to be careful with from now on though," said Brianna.

"And what's that?"

"Being openly gay."

"Ah, yes of course. You are going into politics. Can I assume by the book you're reading that you're a Republican?"

"I am. What are you?"

"I'm unsure right now. I voted Democrat in the last election though."

"Why?"

"Because that's what I always vote."

She shook her head.

"I know. That's not a good reason to vote a particular way. That's why I said I'm not sure right now. I have to do some reading on both parties and then decide."

"I hope you make the right choice."

"Me too."

There was a moment of silence as we looked at each other. I smiled first; then she returned one of her own.

"Come over here," I said.

She moved closer to me.

"I don't bite you know."

"How can I be sure?"

I smiled. "Because I just told you so."

She rolled her eyes. "Yeah, yeah."

Eventually our talking slowed to intervals mixed with silence, which I broke when I got an idea. "Hey, remember I told you one of my hobbies was photography?"

"Yeah."

"Well, I have my camera on me. Do you mind if I take some photos of you?"

"No, I don't mind," she said.

I pulled my camera out of my bag and took a variety of pictures of her. I even let her use it to get some shots of me. A guy walking by asked if we wanted one of us together and volunteered to take it. I told him *sure* and gave him my camera.

"Thanks," I said when he was finished.

"No problem." He smiled at us and then walked off.

I shot a few more photos of her and then sat down to look at them all on the camera screen.

"Brianna, you're beautiful."

She smiled bashfully displaying her dimples. My cell phone rang, interrupting the moment. When I looked at the caller ID and saw that it was Olivia, the girl I met at Piper's open mic, I sent the call to voicemail. After Brianna and I looked through the pictures, I asked her if she wanted to go to the movies, and she agreed. We left the park shortly after and went to a theater in downtown Brooklyn.

When the film was over we both went to use the ladies room. It was while I was in the stall that I realized I'd spent almost all day with her and was enjoying every minute of it. We left the theatre and walked in the direction of the Brooklyn Promenade to take in the serenity of being around water and stroll with the backdrop of the Manhattan skyline. I stopped at a Baskin Robbins to buy ice cream cones for us to eat as we walked down to the water. This was one of the best dates I'd ever had, and it was totally unplanned. Brianna and I spent an hour or so at the Promenade before deciding that we should call it an evening.

"What train do you need to get home?" I asked, and then suddenly wondered if I should have hailed a cab for her. *Darn it!*

She answered immediately and seemed unbothered by my suggestion of her taking the subway home. "I need the C train. I live in East New York."

"You do?" East New York was an awful neighborhood. I don't know why I was surprised she lived there; it wasn't like I hadn't met plenty of good people from bad neighborhoods. As cliché as it may sound, I guess there is always a diamond in the rough.

"Yes, I do." Her voice brought me back to reality.

"Okay, we can either walk or take a bus back over to Jay Street to catch our trains."

"Let's walk." She spoke with ease.

"All right."

On the way home I told her how much I enjoyed spending the day with her, and she said she felt the same. We rode the rest of the way in silence.

"My stop is coming up," I said as we approached Utica Avenue. I gave her a quick hug and got up. "Call me when you get home, okay?"

"I will." She smiled at me before I exited the car.

On my walk home I heard music playing and smelled food on a grill. *There's a block party nearby.* My mind traveled back to when I when I was a kid and how I always heard about New York summers, the parties, the people, the food, the kids playing in the fire hydrants, oh, and the crime. I had an image of the city being magical, despite the negative comments. As I traveled down Lewis Avenue I heard rap music blasting through the speakers. Though it was only one block having a party, everyone was outside. The sun was a half an hour away from setting and the burnt orange sky was initiating the simple yet elegant fading of day

50

into evening. I noticed some older men playing with dice on the sidewalk, women sitting on stoops talking, and kids running around in the street. Some of the young women were very scantily clothed, and dare I say 'ghetto-fabulous.'

Getting closer to where I lived, I saw Rick a few feet ahead of me. I knew he was going to see Melissa.

"Hey, Rick," I said when I got to my house. He was standing outside of Melissa's place.

"What's up, Sadira? I haven't seen you in a while. Where you been?"

"I've been around, man."

"Uh huh." He rang the doorbell. "You know I might be leaving New York, right?"

"No, I didn't. Where are you going?"

"Down south for a little while to take care of some things, but I'll be back."

Jasmine answered the door. "Melissa isn't here, Rick."

"Where is she at then?"

"I don't know."

"Liar. Where is she?"

"Negro, move from in front of my house. She's not here." Jasmine closed the door.

I could see his jaw clenched. "Bitch," he mumbled then turned to leave. "I'll see you around, Sadira."

"All right, man. Later."

There was a small box outside from Amazon.com. *My book;* I remembered that I decided to buy the book I saw at Tricia's house. It also made me realize that I hadn't checked my mailbox all week so I cleared it out. Once inside my apartment I changed out of my clothes and checked my voicemail. There were two messages and they were from Olivia. I decided against calling her back right away. I really wanted to talk to Brianna or Tricia. While I waited for either one of them to call, I picked up the book that I'd just received and started reading it. Not long after, however, my phone rang. It was Brianna.

51

"Hey, Sadira. I just got home."

"Hi. I'm glad you called." I smiled, assuming that she was doing the same or blushing on the other end of the phone.

"Oh hold on a second," she said. When she clicked back over she told me that her mother was on her other line. "Let me call you back later."

"All right. Bye." I hung up and turned on my television to search for something to watch instead of reading. Finally, I ordered a movie. I was feeling intellectually lazy and didn't really feel like jumping back into the book. My phone rang a couple of times, but I didn't answer. I don't like being interrupted in the middle of a good movie. I'd return calls when it was over.

Two hours later I reached for my cell phone to see who was trying to reach me. Tricia, Olivia, and Brianna had called. I felt like some sort of player, but brushed it off. *Who should I call first?* I was losing interest in Olivia; Tricia and I had the best sex, plus I genuinely cared for her; and Brianna's personality intrigued me.

I decided to call Olivia first because I remembered that she'd called me earlier.

"Hello, stranger," she answered.

"Hi."

"You are a very busy woman."

"I guess you could say that. What's up?"

"I was wondering if you have plans for tonight."

"No, actually I don't. I had a pretty full day."

"Too full to spend a little time with me?"

I thought before answering. "What do you want to do?" *I'm not hungry, I've already been to the movies, and I did a lot of walking today.*

"I don't know. Maybe we could go to a lounge or something. It's still early, so if you wanted to relax for a while first you could."

I wasn't sure I wanted to go back out but remembered just the night before how loneliness and thoughts of Jessie kept me up half the night. "Sure, we can meet somewhere in the city. Where do you live again?"

"The Bronx."

"God damn, that's far."

"*Brooklyn* is far."

"Let's meet in the middle. Why don't you choose a place somewhere in midtown and call me back?"

"Okay, I'll do that."

"All right, I'll wait for your call."

I hung up and tried Tricia's number, but got her voicemail. I left a message, and then went to the kitchen for something to drink. While I was washing a glass my phone rang again. *Well damn.* This time it was Olivia calling me back.

"Hello?"

"Hey, it's me."

"Who is me?"

"Olivia!"

"I know, I was just joking."

"You better know."

"Mm hmm. Anyway. Where do you want to meet?"

"A friend of mine just told me about a new place called Opaque. It's in the Chelsea area, so it's actually closer to you than me, but I'll make the trip if you do."

"I will. Are you ready to leave now, or do you need to get dressed and all that stuff?"

"I'll be ready to leave in a half an hour, so let's say meet there at midnight."

"Okay, I'll be there," I said.

"Good. I can't wait to see you."

"All right."

When I hung up with Olivia and called Brianna back, she was asleep. I was kind of relieved because I didn't want to start a conversation and cut it short to go out with Olivia. On the other hand I didn't want to lie and tell her I was going to bed or that I was going out with someone else, not after the day she and I had just had together, no way.

I got to Opaque a few minutes before midnight and decided to wait outside for Olivia. She finally showed up about fifteen minutes later.

"I'm sorry I'm late."

Femmes. "It's okay." I lied. "C'mon, let's go inside."

The club was crowded on the first level, but we were able to find a comfortable room upstairs. There was a racial mix of black, white, and Latino women in the building. Not long after being there I realized that I really didn't miss the club scene at all. I felt like I was getting too old to enjoy the environment. Either that or everyone there was too young to be in clubs, plus it reminded me of Jessie. She was the reason I even built up a tolerance for clubs in the first place. When we first started dating it was one of the sole places to which I could count on her showing up.

By 3 a.m. I was ready to go. House music was being pumped through the speakers, and Olivia wanted to stay a little bit longer so I pushed myself to 4:00 and then we finally left. I was surer than ever that I did not want to hang out in clubs anymore.

I hailed a yellow taxi for Olivia, gave her a hug and a kiss, and sent her on her way. It was too late for either of us to be on the subway alone, so I flagged down the next cab for myself. It was almost 5 in the morning when I got home. I thought about Brianna while I was undressing and getting ready for bed. I really liked her and wondered how things would play out. Not long after lying down, I realized that I was too hungry to go straight to sleep. I got up and made an egg and cheese sandwich to make my stomach stop growling and then collapsed in bed just an hour before the sun rose.

Chapter 6

I spent the next day alone taking care of things I'd been putting off, like doing laundry, going grocery shopping, signing up for a 24/7 fitness gym, and flipping through the Sunday paper to look at the real estate ads. Commotion coming from next-door was actually what reminded me to give more thought to moving out of the neighborhood. When I first moved back to New York I wanted to get into a place quickly so I settled for renting again, but I knew I needed to buy something in a quieter neighborhood. Between the summer heat and the noise coming from Melissa and Jasmine, I wasn't in a good mood at all.

I talked to Tricia briefly later that evening.

"I want to see you," she told me, "But things are so hectic at my job I don't see myself getting out of here at a decent hour any day this week."

Tricia worked as a marketing analyst for a mutual fund group at a large investment bank. She wanted badly to move up from being an analyst to getting involved in the real day-to-day activities of investment management, but she had her work cut out for her since she only had two years of work experience in the industry.

"I'd like to see you too, but it's okay. I understand. I'll be around whenever you're ready to get together." I was disappointed but tried not to let it be obvious.

"Okay, I have to run now, but I'll call you tomorrow. Maybe we can squeeze in an hour or two one of these evenings."

"Cool." That made me smile. But a sigh escaped me when I hung up with her. I wished I were ready for Tricia. It annoyed me that I was letting a good woman slip away, but what could I do? I was trying not to be selfish.

The following morning at work was the usual routine, but I went shopping for a keyboard when I got off. After going to three stores, I settled on one that cost me about $300 and arranged for it to be delivered. The rest of the evening faded into late night, watching television. At some point my mind drifted to Jessie. I bit my bottom lip in defiance and suppression. *Screw Jessie.* My thoughts were only projections of how I wanted to feel, but I hoped that one day I really wouldn't give a damn about Jessie. I sighed and decided to turn in early. Sleep wasn't pleasant for me though. I tossed and turned in aggravation all night.

The next morning I felt sluggish but my emotions weren't running rampant the way they were the night before. I took my time getting dressed for work and stopped to buy a breakfast sandwich on my way in.

"Smile, baby. Whatever's bothering you will go away," a man said as he walked by me.

I didn't even realize I was frowning, but apparently I was. His passing comment did get me to smile. It's funny how strangers can impact you with only a sentence or few seconds of their time. I put a little pep in my step and got in to work. After our shift, Devonte' and I went out to lunch and chatted about random topics before he picked up the check. He had to go home and clean up for some woman who was visiting him that night.

"Who did you trick into visiting you at home?"

"I didn't trick anybody, fool. I've been talking to her for about a month now. There's something special about her."

"Really now?" We walked toward the exit.

"Yeah. We'll see where it goes. I'm tired of the dating game, man. It's time for me to settle down."

"You sound like Tricia."

"She said that?"

"Yes, that's what she told me."

56

We stood outside of the diner for a little while to finish talking.

"So does that mean you two are going to try again?"

"No. I'm not ready, and I don't want to hurt her or block her from meeting someone else." It saddened me to say it out loud.

He didn't respond immediately, perhaps absorbing my words before finally speaking. "Well I guess I'm glad you have her best interest at heart."

"I do."

"All right."

"Hey, I'm going to get going," I said, changing the subject. "Thanks for lunch, D."

"You're welcome. I'll see you tomorrow. Take it easy."

"I will."

We separated and I walked to the nearest subway to travel home. It had started drizzling and the food I'd eaten made me want to lazily sit around my apartment. As soon as I got inside I tossed my bag aside and went to take a shower. That's when I noticed the pink piece of paper for piano lessons still sitting on my desk, so I decided to call for more information. I reached for my phone to make the call and spoke to a woman who told me that she taught classical and jazz piano. Her name was Jenny, and she was straight to the point.

"If you're interested, my first lesson would be free. And if you want to continue, it would be $60 a session thereafter. The sessions are an hour long," she told me.

Jenny taught out of a studio in Ft. Greene, Brooklyn, which was one of the neighborhoods to which I was considering moving. She was soft spoken, but as she ran off names of pianists and other musicians, Herbie Hancock, Dave Brubeck, Tchaikovsky, Johannes Brahms, she drew me in. Almost everyone she mentioned sounded familiar to me. All of those years I spent in band in high school and around bands in the military made me pretty well-versed in music. She asked me what my goals were and how serious I was about learning because she had a tight schedule and only two openings that she wanted to fill quickly. I didn't want to make a career out of playing the piano, but I did want to learn well enough to

57

entertain people. Interested, I scheduled an appointment for that Wednesday at 3:00 p.m.

Later that night Brianna called, and as usual we stayed on the phone for hours. I couldn't remember a time that I spent so much time on the phone with someone. We ended up talking about how the debate over legalizing gay marriage was getting bigger.

"How do you feel about it, Sadira?"

"I think we should be able to get married. Why not be able to get the benefits of heterosexuals?"

"So you wouldn't be satisfied with a civil union?"

I thought about it for a second. "It depends." I had to pause again to get my response together in my head. "Civil unions would only be okay if it gave same gender loving people the same rights as heterosexuals. We should get tax breaks. We should be able to be with our partners and handle their estates if they should die. We shouldn't be denied a pension if our partner were entitled to one and she died. I mean there are so many things that are granted to heterosexuals that we are denied. It's not fair."

"Well—"

"And get the federal government out of the issue. It's up to individual states, not the president. Sorry, to cut you off. Go ahead. How do you feel about the subject, Ms. Republican?" I was surprised at how engaged I got answering her question.

"It's okay. As far as my feelings, I think there are various legal ways of protecting your partner."

"Yeah, but everyone can't afford to file the legal paperwork that's necessary."

"There are Legal Aid programs for people like that."

"What if the lawyers are anti-gay?"

"Then sue the lawyer."

"With what representation...Legal Aid?"

She paused. "You have a point...hmph."

"What?" I laughed. "All I'm saying is that it's unfair and everything going on with this presidency makes me sick. I realize that there are existing legal loopholes, but like I said, everyone can't afford an attorney and some just don't want to have to go through that. Why can't we be treated equally? Civil unions are just pacifiers to make it look like we're separate but equal, but we all know how that attitude worked out for black people." I paused. "Why shouldn't we get married?"

Brianna spoke again. "For me, all I care about is that my legal rights are available to me. And most people who are really against it feel that way because they believe the institution of marriage is set on a religious foundation. They feel under attack because The Bible says nothing about same sex people having that type of union."

"Don't tell me you feel that way. The Bible is a collection of stories written by men. Supposedly inspired by God, but written by men, no less. If it's the *word* marriage that these big babies don't want to share, then call it what you want just make the recognition *identical*."

"No, I don't feel that way. I'm not even ultra-religious."

"Then why the hell are you a Republican, Bri?"

"Because, Sadira. I *am* for a strong defense and military. I'm pro-family, in favor of a small government, and a strong dollar. Outside of this one issue, I don't think I'm very liberal." She sounded frustrated. "Too many people think Republican means ultra-religious."

"I wonder whose fault that is," I said sarcastically but not aiming it directly at her. "Hey, I can understand all of your reasons and even agree somewhat. But look at what's going on now. The R in Republican is seamlessly starting to mean Religious. I can't support that because it's forcing a single interpretation that should be left up to individuals."

"You have a point."

"If you ask me, the only thing that'll help in regards to equal rights for gays is people coming out of the closet in droves," I said. "That's the only way for others to see how many of us there really are and how many are already doctors, parents, schoolteachers, accountants, and even politicians. If people stopped being afraid that we're all freaks and perverts, maybe they'd look at us in a positive way rather than being scared we're attacking them and their structure. Please, gay people can't tear up the institution of marriage any more than straight people already

59

have. But everyone is scared! One side is afraid to be themselves, and the other side is afraid of reality. They're scared of a frigging commitment. We have people flying jets into buildings, suicide bombers in the name of God, and this is what people choose to put on the same level to fear?" I rolled my eyes and exhaled loudly. I wasn't mad at her, but she got me thinking about the whole situation and it irritated me.

"I know. I know. It sounds stupid. But you can forget about people coming out like that. Maybe in the next generation people won't be as hesitant to come out, but I don't see it happening now. *I'm* even about to tiptoe back in the closet for the sake of my career."

"Is that so?"

"Well, if I don't, it will get in my way, and as much as I love women, I love my career more."

"That's interesting."

She paused before speaking. "You know I feel a little hypocritical saying that, but it's how I feel. I'm not saying I'll never be out or that I will marry a man for the sake of image. If things go the way I want them to, I will come out later in my career. But I most likely won't have the opportunity to grow if I just walk up wearing a pride outfit demanding things."

"Unfortunately, I do understand."

"I actually think I'll have more of an impact to change things from within the party than outside of it." She sighed. "It's a tough position to be in."

"Yeah." I didn't think anyone could change it from within, but anything was possible. At least that's what I told myself.

"Hey, if you're not busy on Thursday, maybe you could swing by my school. I'm participating in a debate on this topic."

"What time?"

"One o'clock," she said.

"Shoot, I don't get off until 1:00. I'd be late."

"Oh, I understand. Maybe next time."

"I'm sorry. Let me know about other things you're doing and I'll go if I can."

"All right."

Brianna and I talked a while longer before she said she had to go. It was still raining outside, and the evening was hot. I looked around my apartment searching for something to do. When I noticed my camera bag on the floor in the corner, I remembered that I never edited the photos that I took of Brianna that day at the park. I smiled. I took the memory stick that held the pictures out of the camera and hooked it up to my computer to spend some time touching up the images. *Maybe I'll print out the best one and give it to her.*

As I edited the photos, a bit of melancholy fell over me. They were happy pictures. Someone just looking at them would think we were a loving couple rather than two people who had just started getting to know each other. Things didn't happen as easily when I was dating Jessie. The fact that she still crossed my mind really bothered me. It seemed to be a constant battle to deflect her from entering my thoughts when I should have been thinking of someone else...someone better, like Brianna or Tricia.

Despite my efforts to progress into a new life, I still missed Jessie. I went to bed with her on my mind, carrying her into my dreams. I remembered how she took care of me after I had that terrible car accident. Sharp images and staccato pieces of our conversations and dealings filtered through my sleep. I dreamed in brilliant color that night. Jessie's eyes were as blue-gray and beautiful as the day I met her. The soft tint of gold from her warm skin manifested itself and I experienced her in my sleep...I felt her softer-than-a-feather touch caressing me in my vivid subconscious perceptions. She always had a hold on me that presented itself as pure physical attraction to people on the outside looking in, but it was really a soul-intermingling link. *No one would ever understand.* It was what pulled me into her world from the very day we met. Maybe I couldn't let go because she hadn't. I didn't know. Trapped in a cyclone of emotions and ideas of what may have been true about us or what may have been my twisted fantasies of reality, I felt lost. Some of the thoughts I had made me feel as though I were a character in a science fiction novel. Maybe I needed a therapist.

With all the intricate details and colorful scenes, my dream seemed to go on for days, but when I finally slid off the edge of sleep, I saw it had only been a few hours. The early morning sun made its way into my bedroom and I woke up feeling…well, without feeling. *Jessie.* I only hoped that throughout the day I wouldn't find myself caught up in more reveries of her. The weather was better, which would probably help since the day wouldn't look so gray. Devonte' and I didn't hang out after work, and I didn't feel like going straight home so I decided to grab a bite to eat. I ran into Olivia while I was coming out of the subway.

"Hi, Sadira."

"Olivia, what's up?"

"Oh, I'm just out shopping. It's a nice surprise to see you."

"Likewise."

"What are you up to?"

"Just enjoying the day, that's all."

She looked down at the shopping bags she was carrying. "I'm actually finished out here and heading home. Why don't you come over to my place?"

I was startled by her forwardness, then quickly remembered the night we met at Piper's. Though nervous, *she* approached me. I asked, "Do you live alone?"

"Yes. I have a studio."

I thought about it before answering. "Okay, let's go."

"Come on," she said and smiled.

"All right. Let me help you with some of those bags."

She handed me two bags, one from Bebe and the other from Macy's, and we walked to the nearest uptown subway station. We rode for about thirty minutes before exiting at her stop.

"You changed your hair," I said as we walked toward her place.

"Yeah, I put a new color in it. Do you like it?"

"Yes, it's cute. I bet you didn't think I noticed."

"Well…thank you." She grinned.

"Mm hm."

Finally we came up to her apartment building. It was a small dark red brick and probably had about six units in it. She lived on the second floor. The first thing I noticed when I walked in was the smell of scented candles, vanilla I think, but I didn't say anything. I heard Wendy Williams' voice coming from somewhere. Her radio wasn't on so I assumed it was from a neighbor's place.

"Where do you want me to put these bags?" I asked.

"I'll take them," she said and put them in a corner.

"Hey, can I use your bathroom?"

"Sure, it's right there." While I used the bathroom, I thought about why I was really there. *We can't have sex, because it's that time of the month for me.* I flushed the toilet, washed my hands, and went back out to her. *Well at least my cramps are gone.* I sat down next to her on a futon, and there was silence at first.

"Are you thirsty?" she asked.

"No thank you, I'm okay."

She turned on the television to help ease the mood. We sat for at least ten minutes half watching the TV when she leaned over and kissed me. I leaned back and pulled her on top of me. The pendent from her necklace kept grazing my chin, so I moved it to her back. While kissing her, I unbuttoned her shirt and ran my hands over her upper body. From an open window, I could still hear Wendy Williams chatting away and kids playing outside. It was distracting me.

"What's wrong?"

"Nothing," I lied. I unfastened her bra and took one of her breasts into my mouth.

She moaned and placed her hand on my head. I moved to her other breast and she grabbed my shoulders. I felt like I needed more room.

I slowed to a stop and looked at her. "Can you open this up?"

She laughed. "My legs or the futon?"

"Damn." I laughed hard! *This girl is a trip, man.* "The futon, Olivia. The futon!"

"Yes, I can. Get up and hold on," she said and smiled.

63

The comic relief faded quickly and I realized that I didn't feel right. Actually, I felt lonely. I tried to go through with it anyway. If an orgasm didn't make me feel better then oh well, I couldn't say I didn't try.

There was much more room when she opened up the futon. Before I could say another word, she finished undressing. That's when thoughts started running through my mind. *How long was she out shopping? Did she walk the whole time? Would I offend her if I brought up washing up or safe sex? Goddamn, this is beginning to be too much work!* I unbuttoned my shirt.

"What kind of person are you in bed? Something tells me you're one of those pillow princesses," I said.

"I am not. I like to give and receive. I'm not selfish."

"All right, well, you can't give today because of Mother Nature. It's the last day, but still I'm not into that."

"Oh. Well why didn't you say that earlier?"

"Would you have taken no for an answer when you asked me over?"

She thought about it. "Probably not."

"Okay then."

There was an awkward silence. She put her hand on my belt buckle.

"What are you doing?" I asked.

"I may not be able to eat you, but you can still fuck me."

Oh my. "I don't know, Olivia. I'm thinking maybe I should go."

She looked deflated. "Why? I don't want you to go. Let's just relax a little bit first then."

"All right."

A few minutes later she was unbuckling my belt. *Fuck it.* I kicked off my shoes, but decided to keep my pants on. I was wearing panties that day, rather than boxers, and wasn't sure how she'd react.

Sometimes women could be so hung up on image, labels, and roles that they act stupid over silly things like that. She reached up and flicked off a light switch behind her, and the sound of children I had heard earlier seem to fade away, as if they had all gone inside.

64

Shortly after, we were bumping and grinding. I felt like a kid humping with her clothes on. I actually wanted to laugh out loud but refrained. Olivia was into it and ready to climax soon. As she moaned and held me tighter, I felt myself getting closer to a climax too. It couldn't have been more than ten minutes, but I didn't give a damn. We soon finished, and I got off her. Tiny beads of sweat glistened on her stomach. She looked at me expectantly, as if she wanted more. I looked her up and down, stopping at her center for a second. *Man, I am not eating that. Let me get out of here and stop wasting this girl's time.* I closed my eyes but quickly opened them. I didn't want her to think I was sleepy because I wasn't. I was, however, done with her. She was entirely too easy for me.

I put my arm up and looked at my watch. I could have just looked at a clock that was hanging on a wall in front of me, but I wanted her to see me checking the time.

"Oh, shoot."

"What?"

"I have to go."

"Why?"

"I forgot I had something to do this evening." It was bullshit, but I was ready to go.

"But you haven't even been here long."

"I know, I'm sorry, but I have to go." I got up and started putting my clothes back on.

She sat up and looked at me.

Please don't give me those begging eyes.

She just stared at me.

"I'll call you, Olivia."

She looked hurt.

Damn! I didn't want to sit down and trap myself in her feelings. "Olivia," I looked her in the eyes. "I'll call you."

Her look changed. I wasn't sure if it was hurt or anger. "Okay, fine. Call me then."

65

"I will." I gave her a kiss on the cheek, and she got up to walk me to the door. Grabbing my bag that I'd dropped when I got there I said, "Bye," and kissed her once more.

It took over an hour to get home, and the first thing I did when I got inside was take a shower. After lathering up a few times as if it would wash away what I'd done with Olivia, I got out and slipped into a pair of sweatpants and a t-shirt. I didn't feel bad, but I didn't feel good about myself either. As the evening wore on, I thought about Olivia. I really didn't want to see her again, but I had to at least call and tell her. *I owe her that but not tonight.*

I actually started to think about Jessie again. Not a day went by that I *didn't* think about her. I generally pushed her out of my mind, but it didn't stop her from coming back day after day. Sometimes when my phone rang, a part of me wished it were her calling just to say hi—to stay in touch or to at least let me know that I wasn't the only one who still had longing feelings. But she wouldn't. Jessie was always better at masking her feelings. I sighed. It had only been five months since I had spoken to her, when selling our condo was a done deal. I missed her though.

A good disruption to my thoughts came when my phone rang and Tricia was on the other end of the line.

"Hey, Tricia." I was happy she called.

"Hi. How are you?"

"I'm good, and you?"

"Tired as hell, but I won't complain," she said.

"When are you going to get a break from working these long hours?"

"Tomorrow night. That's actually what I was calling you about."

"What?"

"Well, I got tickets from my job to the Liberty basketball game tomorrow night and was wondering if you wanted to go with me."

"I thought you said you were swamped with work."

"I am, but my boss asked if I wanted them so I said 'Yes.' They're courtside seats at Madison Square Garden."

"Oh yeah, I'll go with you." I said it a little faster than I wanted to.

She laughed. "Don't take me up on my offer just because they're good seats."

"No, no. It'll be great to see you."

"Oh will it?"

"Yes. I'm looking forward to it. I wish I could see you tonight." My mouth was speaking before I could think and choose my words carefully.

She was quiet for a second. "You can."

"Are you serious?"

"Yes. But come now if you're coming because I might not be awake much longer."

"All right, let me get off the phone then. I'll be there in a half an hour."

"See you soon." She hung up.

When I arrived at her apartment, she flashed a beautiful smile and embraced me. I kissed her on the cheek before following her inside. We ended up watching a movie together before retiring for the evening. We weren't intimate as we had been on my previous visit, but it felt good just to hold her all night. The next morning I kissed her softly on her lips before slipping out and going home to get ready for work.

Chapter 7

On Wednesday after leaving WSOL, I had my first appointment with Jenny, the piano teacher. She was a rather rotund woman, not at all the way I pictured her from her soft voice. Her dark red hair was very short and curly. She was slightly taller than I was and wore glasses.

"Hello, Sadira." She welcomed me as soon as I walked in.

"Hi." I scanned the room quickly. There were small photos of pianists scattered against the tan walls. Some of them I recognized, and others I'd never seen or heard of. There was a black baby grand piano on a rug in the center of the room, and there were three keyboards. One was next to the piano, and the other two were in opposite corners.

"Would your lessons be for personal enrichment only?" she asked.
"Yes."

She smiled. "Okay. Can you read music now? I remember your saying you had some sort of background."

"I can read music. I'm probably rusty, but I remember the basics. I used to play the trumpet. Oh, and I'm sure once I learn the notes on the piano, I will be able to play by ear too."

"That's fine, but I want to make sure you can read sheet music."

I nodded positively and we talked for a few more minutes as jazz saxophonist Paul Taylor softly played in the background. When we were ready to begin, Jenny walked behind a desk, reached down for something, and the music then faded out.

"Do you notice a pattern among the black keys?" she asked after I sat down.

I stared at them for a while. "The black keys alternate between sets of two and three."

"Correct." She smiled. "Those are sharps and flats of the white keys."

We continued to talk and she taught me a few things from a beginner's workbook. Ultimately, I ended up staying about ten minutes over the hour and decided to sign up for lessons. Before I left, Jenny gave me the workbook that also came with a CD so that I could practice at home.

That afternoon was uncomfortably hot. When I got to my house I had just enough time to change and venture back out to meet Tricia in front of the Garden for the basketball game. *Don't forget your camera,* I reminded myself. I wanted to remember my dates with Tricia.

Dressed in crisp jeans, a baby blue button-down shirt, and a pair of matching Nikes, I got there a few minutes before I saw her emerging from subway entrance nearest me. She wore her hair in a ponytail and was clad in a soft pink v-neck t-shirt, tight fitting jeans, and a pair of cute sandals. We made our way inside and down to the floor to enjoy the game.

Tricia and I had a great time and even spotted ourselves on the big screen above when the cameras were panning the crowd. The mascot Maddie was dancing by us, commanding the arena's attention. Our dinner that night was hot dogs, popcorn, and soda. After the game was over we made our way through the sea of exiting people, stopping only to snap a photograph with Maddie. I asked someone who was cleaning up if he didn't mind using my camera to take a picture of us and he said no. As we stood on either side of the mascot, we had big smiles on our faces as if it were one of the best nights of our lives.

When we exited the arena, we hung around the 34th Street area just a bit longer, walking and talking, but as it got later we decided to head back to Brooklyn. Tricia and I didn't spend the night with each other that evening, as if it were a first date we wanted to keep pure. She called me when she got in to let me know she'd arrived home safely, and we recapped the night through conversation before hanging up with a promise to speak again soon.

I didn't realize how tired I was until I actually sat down at my desk to check my e-mail. After going through my inbox, I logged into the forum where I posted my poetry and added two new pieces, one of which was an audio file. An instant message from Brianna popped up just as I was about to sign off. I was too drowsy to chat with her for long, but promised I'd call her the next day.

The following day at work was the usual routine, including a fleeting thought of Jessie. I even went to the gym to slip a workout into my day. Once home, fresh, clean, and in a new set of clothes I called Brianna. What started out as a phone conversation ended with an invitation to my place, which Brianna accepted. I gave her directions and told her I would meet her at the subway station so she wouldn't have to walk alone. After we hung up, I printed out five of the photos that were taken of us in the park so I could give them to her.

While waiting for Brianna to come over, I got on the phone with Tricia. She was busy at work as usual, but we did agree to go out on another date soon. I wanted to see her again, and the feeling was mutual. I hung up the phone and stretched, redirecting my mind to Brianna. I waited a little while longer before walking to meet her.

We strolled back to my apartment. "So do you like living over here?" Brianna asked.

"To be honest, I don't think I'll be in the neighborhood a lot longer."

"How come?"

"It's too loud, and I want to own, not rent. I'm living below my means right now, and I don't have to. I rushed into this place."

"And why is that?"

"Because I just wanted to start my new life after breaking up with my ex."

She nodded and turned to me for more information but didn't say anything.

"It's a long story," I said.

"Okay," she acknowledged without pressing me for more information.

"Yeah."

When we got to my place, I saw Melissa and Jasmine coming out of theirs. Melissa looked depressed, and Jasmine looked happy. I said hello and introduced Brianna but didn't carry on too long of a conversation with them. Jasmine was wearing SpongeBob pajamas and sneakers, her braids needed to be touched up, and her glasses looked too small for her head. I had never seen her in glasses before. *Goodness.* I stuck my key in the door to quickly get away from them and whatever drama they were having. I gave Brianna a quick tour of my apartment and then tried to pick our conversation back up.

"So what about where you live?"

"What? East New York, Sadira, I hate it. I can't wait to get out of that hellhole. I just can't afford to right now. My mother sublet her apartment to me. It's still in her name, and it's dirt cheap because of rent control."

"Where does she live now?"

"Two floors up in the same building with my grandmother."

"Wow."

"Yeah. I'm just hanging in there until I get out of school."

"I hear you."

I turned the television on, but we didn't even watch it.

"So can you tell me at least a little bit of what happened between you and your ex?"

I smiled nervously. "Yeah, I guess so. I'm not sure where to begin though."

"You can start with the truth."

"Well, we ultimately broke up because of infidelity. She slept with someone else."

"Ah, I sense a 'but' about to come on."

"Yes, I stepped outside of our relationship too. To my defense it was *after* I found out about her being with another woman."

"Do you think that excuses you?"

"No. I was wrong. I know I was wrong too."

She let my words sink in for a second before speaking again. "Have you seen your ex lately, or the woman you slept with?"

"No, I left both of them in Miami. Hell, they may be together for all I know."

She raised her eyebrows. "What?"

I sighed. "You heard me right. We both slept with the same woman. I told you it was a long story."

She looked at me curiously. "Do you still love your ex?"

I looked down.

"I guess I got my answer."

"Look, I can't honestly tell you that I'm over her. I am trying though. It's not like I'm still *in love* with her. There is a difference. Anyway, we don't speak, and I guess that the only thing that will help me is passing time."

"So is that what you're doing right now, just passing time? I'm just a rebound chick?"

Boy, she's hurling the questions at me. "No, I mean... damn it. Maybe that came out wrong. What I mean is that I don't know what else to do to get over her but try to move on with my life one day at a time."

"I understand."

I couldn't read Brianna's feelings. "What about your ex?"

"I haven't really had a long term relationship with a woman before. Everyone I've dated so far only lasted a month or two. And I ended things with the last woman because she pushed me into a wall."

"I'm sorry to hear that."

"Don't be. I fought her back, and she apologized, but I wasn't about to give her a second chance."

"Good."

"Mm hm."

72

We sat for a while half watching the television and gazing at each other.

"Hey, can I use your bathroom?" she asked.

"Sure."

I glanced at the clock on my cable box when she returned. It was 8:30. "Do you want to order a movie or something?" I asked.

"Yeah, sure."

"Oh wait, I have something for you!" I said, remembering the pictures that I'd printed out.

Her face lit up with a bright smile when she saw them. "Thank you!"

She hugged me, and I kissed her on the cheek. "You're welcome."

I continued to hold her for a few seconds before letting go and sitting down. She gave me a soft kiss on the lips and then stared into my eyes.

"What kind of movies do you like?" I asked to refocus our attention to the television.

"Anything but karate movies and movies like 'White Chicks' or 'Pootie Tang'."

"You didn't like 'Pootie Tang'?"

"Tell me you're joking, Sadira."

I laughed. "I am, I am. Trust me, I don't own any of those."

"Thank God. What do you have?"

"I don't have that many DVDs, but we can order a movie on demand."

"All right, let's see what's available."

We ended up watching "Barbershop II." When Brianna noticed that midnight was approaching, she said she'd better be going.

"Let me call car service for you."

She smiled at me before I could pick up my phone to dial.

"What are you smiling at?"

"You. You're so sweet."

73

I blushed. "Thank you." In the instance of our paused conversation I felt my attraction to her building. "Let me call that cab; it's getting late." I reached for the phone and dialed.

"Be outside in ten minutes," the operator instructed.

"Okay."

She moved over so that she was sitting closer to me. I put my arm around her.

"I enjoyed spending time with you today," she stated.

"Me too." I genuinely liked her conversation.

It seemed as though the car came a lot sooner than expected, because before we could get far in dialogue we heard a horn honking outside.

"That's your ride. Let me walk you out."

Brianna put her shoes on quickly and followed me out to the car.

"Call me when you get home," I instructed and kissed her before she got in the car.

"I will."

I shut the door after she was in and watched the car drive off.

Not long after she left, I turned the television off and pulled out my clothes out for work the next day. I found myself getting tired before I heard from Brianna so I decided to lay down. I turned off the lights and tried to relax, but I could hear the faint sounds of moans coming from next door. I squinted my eyes and shook my head fast, as if that would relieve me of the sounds of Melissa and Jasmine having sex. It didn't work, so I turned on my clock radio. *Not this corny ass song again! Jesus I didn't know what was more torture.* I turned the radio off and tuned everything out, everything except for thoughts of Jessie.

To my luck and surprise, however, Tricia called me back very late that night. I got to know more about her and her past. We never really did get into deep conversations about what went on in our lives before we met. She told me a few stories about growing up in Birmingham, Alabama and what a big difference it was when she moved from there to New York to finish up school. She was a country girl, used to things at a slower pace, but didn't have much trouble adjusting to a big city. Her father was an accountant and her mother was a high school biology teacher. I didn't want to talk about my past in depth just yet, but I promised her I would tell it all one day. She didn't push me, which was good.

Chapter 8

A couple of days went by with lengthy phone calls with both Brianna and Tricia. Unfortunately there was still Olivia who needed to be told that she and I had no future, but I was procrastinating. *Just get it over with,* I told myself before picking up the phone to call her. She didn't answer, and I was glad that I could leave her a message rather than speak to her directly.

"Hey, Olivia it's Sadira. I'm sorry I missed you. Listen, I was just calling because," I paused, "I'm calling to tell you that I think we should maybe take a break from each other you know. I just…" I sighed, thinking of a way to soften my message but couldn't come up with any. "Olivia, I don't think we're a good match, and I'm sorry. I'm really sorry," I repeated before hanging up. I felt like crap.

Closing my eyes, I tried to relax, but it was hard. I really felt like a dog. Never in my life had I done such a thing. *But what was so bad about what I did?* I wasn't quite sure. Did I really use Olivia? *No, she threw herself at me.* Yes, but I could have walked away. I didn't have to have sex with her. I didn't have to lead her to believe that she would see me again, especially when I knew on the first date that we wouldn't last. I shrugged. I did mess up but there was nothing I could do. It was over and done.

I ignored all of Olivia's calls over the following week and soon ended up on a date with Tricia to an artist showcase. As we strolled along,

I remarked, "You walk too slow." Even though I wasn't in a hurry, I was used to a faster pace.

"Sorry, but I can only move so fast in these shoes."

I looked down and smiled at the cute heels she was wearing. "Those *are* nice, but put some pep in your step, damn. I'm starting to feel like I'm standing still."

She gasped at my unexpected comment but wasn't mad. I think she was just surprised. "Forget you. I don't make fun of how you walk."

"That's because there's nothing to make fun of."

"That's what you think," she mumbled.

"Hmph." Feigning insult, I walked ahead of her but heard her giggling behind me. "What the heck is so funny?" I turned to ask.

"You." She laughed. "Do you know you walk like George Jefferson?"

"What? Shut up. No I don't."

"Yes, you do!" Tricia was still snickering.

"To hell with you." I had to smile though. "You're just mad because I said you walk too slow."

She rolled her eyes. I pulled her into a hug and stole a kiss on the cheek. People walked by us but paid no mind. They seemed to be in their own world.

Eventually we ended up at a small Greek restaurant for dinner. She seemed distracted by the time we got to dessert. The playfulness that we'd had earlier was gone.

"Hey, what's wrong, babe?" I asked.

"Nothing."

"You're lying. Tricia, why did your mood change? What's on your mind?"

She sighed. "I don't think you want to know."

"Try me."

To stall for time, she sipped her drink before finally speaking. "All right," she still hesitated. "I'm wondering how much longer I can do this with you."

"Do what?"

"This. Us. Whatever it is that we have, if it is even anything. How much longer can I do it? You've already made it clear that you don't want to settle down."

Totally unprepared for that conversation, I remained quiet; she was right, I didn't want to hear that.

"Well?"

"I don't know what to say. Do you want to stop seeing me?" *Please say no.*

"No."

Whew. "Then what do you want?"

"I don't know. I just don't know. I have so much fun with you. It's just hard knowing that we're only passing time."

I spoke very reluctantly. "Tricia, maybe we should take some space. I don't want to hurt you or confuse you."

She looked down. "But I don't want to be away from you. I want you. Why am I not enough for you, Sadira?"

I could hear her true feelings as she spoke. *Crap, she's hurting. Damn it. That's exactly what I didn't want to happen.* "Tricia I never said that you weren't enough. I just said that I wasn't ready to get into anything serious yet. I'm still not over Jessie." As soon as I the last statement fell from my lips I wished I could take it back.

Tricia just looked at me.

Oh man. "Okay, wait. Let's stop the conversation for a second. Come on, let's get out of here." I signaled the waiter to bring the check so we could pay and leave.

Outside, I hugged her. I really didn't know what else to say. I was not ready to settle down, but what could I do if she didn't want to let me go? She placed her face against my neck as I rubbed her back.

"I don't know what you want me to do, Tricia," I whispered. "I'm sorry."

She kissed me on the cheek. "Nothing, just forget I brought it up."

"Are you sure?"

"Yeah."

"Okay." I shrugged.

Tainted Destiny

That night, I started to think about what I really wanted. I tried to figure out just what it was that I truly needed. A part of me felt as though I were seeing all these different women as a way to make up for all the years I'd wasted with Jessie, but a larger part of me felt as though I were seeing them to keep my mind off her. I knew in my heart that I wasn't ready to commit to a serious relationship with anyone yet. I thought about Jessie too much. I still missed her. Everything was too fresh for me to get someone else's heart tangled in my emotions. It seemed like a lot of time had gone by since our break-up, but it really hadn't. I wanted expedited closure but had no idea of how to go about getting it. It had barely been six months since we broke up. *Bad timing.* A cliché that seemed to have an adhesive on my life; it was always bad timing for me with relationships. And I couldn't be sure Tricia would wait for me.

Tricia wanted more from me than I was possibly able to give at the moment. I genuinely cared for her but thought that it may be best if I left her alone. I just didn't want to. Tears rolled from my eyes when I thought about Jessie and how much I missed her. There were nights when I buried my face in the pillow in hopes that it would force me to stop crying. Anger sometimes substituted for pain when I remembered she was the one who had cheated on me. I thought hard trying to recall our good times but had difficulty. I shook my head in disappointment. The only good thing, as I reflected, was that she was present. *That's dumb.* As thoughts of Jessie resurfaced, I dug deeper inside me to bury them, hoping that one day I'd push them so far down they would never rise again. I hoped.

The next couple of days I only spoke to Brianna. Tricia did eventually agree that we should take time apart, and it hurt me even though I knew it was the best decision. I dared to dream that she'd wait for me rather than move on to someone else who could and would commit to her.

I had more piano lessons and thought they were going well. I started to feel a little better about myself again—or as best as I could feel. One night I decided to go to Piper's open mic lounge. Before I got there though, rain started coming down. Dressed in relaxed jeans, a black polo shirt, Yankees cap and classic Reeboks, I walked briskly from the subway

79

station to the lounge. There were no cabs in sight. I don't know why I didn't think before deciding to go, because if I did, I would have remembered that I risked seeing Olivia there since that was where we had met. Sure enough, when I got inside, she was there. *Aw damn.* I hadn't returned any of her calls and knew she probably wanted to give me a piece of her mind. I couldn't even turn around and leave because she saw me when I walked in.

She walked over to me. "Hi, Sadira."

"Hey."

"So that's it. I thought we could have had something."

"I apologize. I just didn't think it would work."

"Well, did you think about asking me how I felt first?" She raised her voice. "Did you think about that?"

"I'm sorry." *I hope this girl doesn't make a scene.*

"Give me another chance, Sadira. You didn't even get to know me."

I know. That's the problem. "I don't think it's a good idea, Olivia." I had to find a way out of the conversation. "Hey, I'm just going to go. I'm really sorry."

She looked at me with sad eyes. "Please?"

"I can't. I'm sorry." I turned to leave.

She touched my arm to hold me in place. "But you slept with me. I thought because we made love it meant we were exclusive."

What? Made love? "No, I never said that. I never said exclusive." Her eyes narrowed on mine.

"I have to go," I insisted and walked off.

"Fine." I heard her voice behind me.

I moved quickly and hoped she wasn't following me. *Goddamn it.* What a night. I pulled my cap down low over my face and walked back to the subway station hoping that was the end of Olivia.

Back in the comfort of my home I sat down to practice my keyboard using the workbook that Jenny had given me. Then I turned on some music and tried to learn how to play by ear. For hours I sat and tried to match the notes on the keyboard to what I heard and wrote it down. My concentration was broken when I heard arguing coming from next door. It wasn't low enough for me to ignore. I tried to wait a few minutes to see if they would stop, but they only got louder. Aggravated, I went over there. I had to ring Jasmine's doorbell three times before there was an answer. Melissa opened the door with Jasmine huffing and puffing behind her. They both looked like hell.

"Look. You all are too damn loud."

"Well this is my house, and that is yours," Jasmine shot back, pointing. "Why don't you just go back home?"

"Why don't you stop being such a crazy bitch?"

She retorted, "Who are you talking to like that?"

"Stop!" Melissa pleaded. "Stop." For a moment we were all silent before Melissa spoke again. "I'm leaving."

"Where do you think you're going?" yelled Jasmine.

Melissa didn't answer. Instead, she pushed past me and walked down the stoop and out the front gate. Jasmine, not fully dressed, looked enraged. *Psychotic ass.* She slammed the door, and I sprinted to catch up with Melissa. Again, she was in tears.

"Look, it's late. Where are you going?"

"I don't know," she said.

"Why don't you just stay at my place for the night?"

"I can't. Any minute now Jasmine is going be out looking for me. She only slammed the door to go up and get dressed. I need to be gone before she has a chance to find me."

"Damn it, Melissa. Just come back to my place. I won't let her in. She won't be able to bother you there."

"I'm so sick of her shit. This is it. This is the last straw. I have to get out of there now."

"Come on, let's go back."

She stopped and looked at me. She didn't look afraid or pitiful, just tired and angry...like a woman who had finally taken too much.

Cheril N. Clarke

"Okay, but let's walk around the corner and come back around. She's going to follow the way I left, and if we just go back we'll run into her."

"All right, fine. Whatever."

When we finally got back to my apartment, Melissa went in the bathroom to fix herself up and then came back out to talk.

"What is going on with you two? How did you even meet?" I asked.

She spoke with her head down. "We met online. I was living in Kentucky then. That's where I'm from. I came to New York because I got accepted at NYU."

I leaned back in the chair and continued to listen.

"We used to shoot the breeze almost every day, but it was never about being together. It was never about romance or anything like that until after I graduated high school and was getting ready to come up here."

"What happened?"

She sighed and kicked the air. "Maybe I deserve this."

"Don't say that. If you didn't do anything wrong, then you don't deserve to be unhappy. What happened between you two to cause the tone of your friendship to change?"

"I was realizing that I was confused about my sexuality. Even though I had a boyfriend at the time, I knew that I was attracted to women. She was the only other person I knew who liked women. Kentucky isn't a place where people were just out of the closet like they are here.

"I understand."

"So anyway, lonely nights at home led to subtle flirting. My boyfriend in high school went to college in Texas, and we broke up. Jasmine and I chatted every night online, but she was hesitant to show me her picture for the longest time. I sensed something was off but didn't make too big a deal about it. Finally one day I told her she needed to show me so that I could see that she was a woman. She sent me a picture where she was wearing a hat and asked me to give her my phone number so she could call."

"And then what happened?"

82

"Well, I couldn't really see her well in the picture she sent, but when she called she explained how she had esteem issues and since the tone of our friendship was changing she was afraid I would judge her based on physical appearance alone."

"How did you respond?"

"I honestly don't remember, but I'll tell you the first time I saw her in person I was devastated."

Something about the way she said her last statement made me want to laugh really hard, I mean really hard, but I didn't. There was no need to even ask why she felt the way she did. Jasmine looked different, for lack of a more polite word. Her eyes, nose, and head just seemed to be too big. She always wore braids. There were times when she didn't look bad, but those times were always when she had a hat on. I don't know if it was because the hat took attention away from her face or what, but it helped. Her body was okay. She wasn't overweight or too skinny. The best thing about her was her ass, and it was only *okay*.

I picked the conversation back up with Melissa. "So how did you end up in bed if you weren't attracted to her?"

"Guilt. But before the guilt was a chain of events that led to my living with her. School and living here was costing a lot more than I thought, and there was only so much money my father could send me every month. After my second semester I decided to take some time off to work, with the intention of going back to finish."

"And what happened?"

"Jasmine suggested I move in with her to save money. I knew how expensive an apartment was even with a roommate, so I gave it some thought. I went back and forth on the idea for a while before deciding to take her up on the offer. The deal was that I had to pay her grandmother $300 a month for rent, and I could have the extra bedroom that Jasmine has in the third floor apartment."

I ran my hands through my hair. This was quickly becoming a long story, but I was interested.

"There was one thing she forgot to mention though."

"What was that?"

"That her extra bedroom was buried under clothes, shoes, newspapers, old magazines, and mail from as long as five years ago. That room was the nastiest room I'd ever seen in my entire life. And then there was her pet rabbit, Franco, who attracts mice because he's a messy eater. He's in the other room, which wasn't much cleaner than mine. In between the refrigerator and stove, there was a skeleton of what I guess was once a mouse. Can you imagine how long that thing had to have been dead for only the skeleton to be remaining? The place was nasty! It's a bit better now but still not what it should be."

"Damn."

"Yeah. I just got my own room two months ago. It was such a mess that I had to share her bedroom, and *that's* how we ended up in bed together. I was forced. Either I slept in her bed or in a room with mice and God knows what else."

Before I could respond or even fully register everything she had just said, my doorbell rang. I walked to the window and looked downstairs, but I couldn't see who it was. My mind told me it was Jasmine.

"Don't tell her I'm here," Melissa whispered, even though there was no way anyone could have heard her.

"All right."

I went downstairs. Sure enough, it was Jasmine.

"Where's Melissa?"

"I don't know."

"Yes you do. Where is she?"

"I don't know."

Her face contorted with anger. With narrowed, piercing eyes and a strained voice, she spoke again. "I know you know where she is."

"Look, I don't know where she is, but I do know I'm about to close my door now."

She rolled her eyes. "I can't stand you!"

Lunatic.

When I got halfway back upstairs I heard a loud noise, so I went back down to the front door and looked through. Jasmine was just walking away. *Did that bitch just kick my door?* I didn't know if I should laugh or call a psychiatric ward! Back upstairs, Melissa said she didn't want to talk anymore so I let it go.

"Are you hungry or thirsty or anything?" With all the drama I'd forgotten to be hospitable.

"Actually I am a hungry. I have a hard time eating anything that comes out of that kitchen."

"I have some leftover Chinese if you don't mind eating that. It's either that or you can have a sandwich." I decided against asking for more details on Jasmine's kitchen.

"I'll take the leftovers, thanks."

I gave her the food, and we eased into talking again. "What gives you strength? I mean, do you have it internally or are you searching for it?" I asked her.

"I don't know."

"Do you go to church or listen to anything inspiring? What helps you get through each day?"

"I learned how to walk on eggshells. I'm careful about what I say. I've learned the art of keeping secrets and how to say just the right things at the right time to keep her tame. But it doesn't always work. I wouldn't mind going to church again though. It could help."

"Well, this is a black neighborhood. I know there is a church nearby. As a matter of fact there is a gay friendly church down on Lewis Street. It's not far at all."

"Really?"

"Yeah, I've passed by there while walking a couple of times. Maybe you should check it out. I can't remember the name of it, but it's on the left side of the street if you're walking from this direction. You'll see the pride stickers on cars. Just follow the music."

She smiled. "I think I will."

"Good. And listen, you can stay here tonight if you want."

"I can't do that."

"Of course you can."

She looked down at her feet.

85

"It's okay. I don't mind."

She responded softly. "All right."

Trusting her, I left the next morning for work and told her to lock the door when she left. I felt sorry for her. Though I've had my own share of drama in relationships, luckily I'd never truly felt trapped and without money to escape. Melissa was a kept woman, and I didn't know how much I should step in. Her situation reminded me of straight women who stayed with abusive men despite the pain. In this case it appeared to be more of an emotional mistreatment, but a cruelty nonetheless. To me, the people in bad relationships have to want to get out more than they are afraid of leaving. Only *they* can really end their pain. I could only hope that Melissa left sooner rather than later.

I saw her quite a bit more over the next couple of days. That was the only night she spent at my house though. She and Jasmine seemed to merge back into whatever peace they'd had before. Either that or Melissa was doing whatever she had to do to keep Jasmine calm. I wasn't sure which one it was and only wished Melissa would get her life together quickly.

Chapter 9

August tiptoed into September. My conversations with Tricia slowed down. It was too hard for us to talk to each other casually. If we were going to converse, it needed to be about something definite, our status, but I still wasn't ready. Brianna and I were getting along fine though. Olivia, on the other hand, still called me. I didn't answer the phone, but I wished she would give up. I regretted the day I slept with her. Meanwhile my thoughts of Jessie seemed to finally calm down. They were still present, but I was less emotional and my nights didn't seem as agonizing. *I guess time does heal all things.*

I'd been doing pretty well with my piano lessons and was proud of myself. After a few more weeks I planned to play something for Brianna. It would be the first time I played for anyone besides Jenny, my instructor, and I hoped Brianna would appreciate it. We'd recently slept together for the first time. She was like a delicate rose in bed. The exchange of pleasure we shared was slow and sweet, and I felt at ease when we finished. She lay in my arms and we talked. That was when it really hit me that if she got the internship she wanted, I wouldn't see her for months. I would miss her. I wasn't sure if things could go back to the way they were once she left and came back. *Try not to get too attached*, I warned myself. *That's all you can do.*

As fall began to fade and make way for winter, the weather cooled and my conversations with Tricia began to slowly pick up again. She missed me, and I longed for her too. We didn't talk as often and for as long as we did before she decided we needed space, but she did start calling me again.

I was starting to feel like I needed to make a choice. Guilt began weaseling its way into my heart, and I felt bad about keeping Tricia on the edge. Even Brianna. I needed to make a decision, but who and why? I liked them both, but I still did not want to commit to either one of them. I was scared. But I supposed if I had to choose, I would pick Tricia because she and I had a longer history together. Was that a good enough reason?

When I got home one evening, Melissa was sitting outside with Rick. For some reason he'd decided not to leave New York and the last couple of times I had spoken to Melissa she told me that she had visited the church I had told her about. She told me that she connected with two women who took to her instantly. She said they opened their home to her, but she was ashamed to take them up on the offer on a full-time basis. She did tell me however, that she had gotten a job and should have enough money to get away from Jasmine in just a couple of months. I was happy to hear that. The times when she confided in me drew me away from my own struggles and drama but also put a bit of sorrow in my heart for her.

"What's up, Sadira?" Rick spoke first and then Melissa smiled and said hello as well.

"Hey, y'all. What's going on today?"

"Oh, Sadira. I have some mail that came here for you by accident. I'll be right back."

"All right."

As she returned with my mail, Jasmine walked up carrying four pink plastic shopping bags. She looked at Rick. "What are *you* doing here?"

He sucked his teeth and sighed. "Don't start with me, girl."

"I thought I told you I don't like you."

"I thought I told you I wasn't here for you."

"Well, until Melissa pays rent she has no say in who can be here. This is my house."

"Actually it's your grandmother's house. You don't own

88

anything, do you?"

She put her bags down with an attitude.

"And do your glasses work? Because if they did you would know they don't look good on you!"

She stared at him narrowly. "Get the fuck away from my house."

"You make me sick. Thirty years old and still living in your family's house. Please, monkey, you ain't shit! Melissa why don't you just come with me? I'll figure something out for you."

"Monkey? I know you didn't just call me a," she paused. "You know what? Unless you can afford to take care of Melissa I suggest your ass shut up. I don't think your lil' messenger paycheck will cut it. Get the hell off my property, you broke motherfucker."

He was getting angrier. "Look, Jasmine, you're lucky you're a woman or I'd knock your orangutan ass out right now!"

She rolled her eyes. "Oh, I dare you to try it. I *want* you to try!"

"Melissa, come with me," he said again to her, but she sat still.

Jasmine spoke as if Melissa wasn't sitting right there or as though she were up for sale. The whole situation was disgusting. Melissa's face was expressionless. Rick glanced at her with a thin smile and begging eyes before walking out the gate and away from the drama. He said good bye to me. I nodded at Melissa to come to my place, but she still didn't move. She sat there in some kind of zone. I shrugged and then went inside. Before I could put my bag down, my phone rang.

The caller ID said that it was Tricia. "Hey," I answered.

"Hi, Sadira. Are you busy?"

"No, but I just got home."

"Do you want me to call you back?"

"No, that's okay. What's up?"

"Well a friend of mine is having a get-together tomorrow night, and I was wondering if you wanted to go with me."

"What time?"

"Around 8."

I thought about it. "Yeah, sure. Where will it be?"

"Over here in Greenpoint, not too far from me. You can just meet me at my place, and we can go together."

"All right."

Soon after I disconnected with Tricia, Brianna called me. She sounded sad when she answered.

"Brianna, baby what's wrong?"

She sniffled. "I..."

"What is it?"

"I didn't get the internship."

"What?"

Softly, she repeated herself. "I didn't get the internship."

"Oh, Brianna I'm sorry."

"I mean, I know a lot of people applied for it, but I actually thought I had a pretty good shot. I have a 4.0 GPA, I've done a lot of activist volunteer work, and I had four letters of recommendation."

Darn. "I'm sorry. Hey, where are you?"

"I'm at home."

"Do you want to come over? I'll try to make you feel better."

"Yeah," she uttered so softly I almost didn't hear her.

"All right, come on," I said.

"Okay."

Brianna arrived at my house wearing a grey t-shirt and matching sweatpants. Her hair, missing its bounce and shine, was down about her shoulders, and her eyes were red.

"Hey, baby. Come here." I hugged her, and she nestled her face in my neck.

"I know I'm making a big deal, but I really wanted that job. I want a better life. I want to get out of East New York!" she cried.

"Shh." I stretched my arm to push the door closed while still holding her with the other.

Easing out of the hug, I took her hand and led her back to my bedroom.

"Have you watched the news today?" she asked as soon as she sat down.

90

"No, why?"

"There was a shootout around my way earlier today. A four-year-old was hit in the head." She paused. "Sadira, I was getting off the bus when the shots rang out. That poor kid got caught up in some stupid fight. It could have been me who got shot! I hate those fucking projects."

I didn't know what to say. The reason I didn't watch the news regularly was because it was always bad. I could go a month without watching or reading a paper because I knew when I decided to start paying attention again it would be the same: bad. Not knowing what to say to her, I hugged her again. Leaning back on the bed, I pulled her into my arms and stroked her hair.

"I guess I'm so let down because I was hoping that I would get to see something new."

"I understand."

She exhaled.

I kissed her on her forehead, and she put her hand on my stomach. The thought of telling her she could spend more time at my place crossed my mind, but I pushed it away. If she were the only person I were seeing, that could work, but I could see Tricia developing ill feelings if she found out. I felt bad for Brianna though.

"Hey, do you want to go away for a weekend?" I asked the question without even thinking about it first.

"What do you mean? Where to and when?"

What did I mean? "Um, I don't know. I think a break from New York will do you some good."

"Well yes, I would love that. But I have classes and work. "

"What if I take you somewhere not too far? We could go to the Poconos in Pennsylvania."

She smiled.

"Would you like that?"

"I would."

"Okay, let's do some searching online and see what I can put together."

"All right."

Brianna sat beside me as I logged onto the computer and searched for things to do. We decided on a lesbian-owned and operated bed and breakfast in New Jersey instead of the Poconos because it was closer and at least we were sure we could be ourselves.

"I'll get a rental car, and we can drive down one evening after I get off work."

Her spirits had been visibly lifted. "Cool."

We ended up watching television and then falling asleep in our clothes in a spooning position. My alarm clock woke us up bright and early the next morning. I reached over to push the button to turn it off and then kissed Brianna on the back of her neck. "Good morning."

Turning to face me, she smiled and said, "Hey." She moved in closer to me, and we lay there for a few more minutes before getting up. I showered, she freshened up, and we left together. We shared a hug sealed with a quick kiss at the subway station before getting on separate trains.

Later that day I went to the Manhattan Mall to buy an outfit to wear at Tricia's friend's get-together. I didn't buy anything that was much different from what I already had in my closet, but it did feel good to pop the tags off and wear new clothes that night. I wore a raspberry red shirt and black pants. I sprayed a small amount of Giorgio Armani's "Aqua Di Gio" cologne before leaving to meet Tricia.

She looked amazing as usual. She was dressed in all black and wore the sexiest boots I'd seen in my life! Her outfit was accented by a white gold earring-necklace-and-bracelet set, and her hair was swept back in a ponytail that made her look slightly younger.

"Hey."

"Hi, Sadira. I'm just about ready." She gave me a peck on the cheek and closed the door behind me.

"Okay. Damn, you look good."

She gave me a flirtatious smile. "I'm wearing this for you."

"Is that so?"

"Mm hm," she affirmed and walked away.

Yes!

While I was waiting for Tricia to finished getting ready, my cell phone rang. It was Brianna. I debated quickly as to whether I should answer it, and decided not to. I didn't want to make Tricia feel uncomfortable or even disrespect her by speaking to another woman in her house.

"I'm ready," she said when she came out of her bedroom. She smiled at me. Her make-up looked great.

"All right, I'm following you." Looking the way she did I would have followed her to the moon if she had asked me. I was still stuck on those boots!

She turned off the lights in her apartment and led the way. Her friend's house turned out to only be about four blocks away. I enjoyed the short walk on the comfortably cool evening. It wasn't until we got there and she rang the doorbell that I felt nervous about meeting whoever was inside.

A tall man in tan pants and a navy blue golf shirt answered the door. He had the build of a basketball player, a bald head, thick eyebrows, and brown eyes. "Tricia, come on in here, girl," he declared and then grinned at me. There was a strong southern influence when he spoke, stretching the "r" in girl so it sounded more like "girrrl."

Tricia introduced him as Warren. He and his partner, Josh, made a handsome couple. The green in Josh's striped shirt brought out his intriguing eyes. The men led us to a room where four women and three other men were conversing. One of the women looked familiar, but I couldn't place her. She stared at me curiously as I stood next to Tricia. *Have I slept with her?* I didn't think so but couldn't remember.

Brief introductions went around the room and when the woman said her name, I knew exactly who she was. Janae'. She was a friend of Jessie's who I'd met years ago at a party. *No wonder she's looking at Tricia and me like that.* She spoke to me as though it were our first time meeting, and I went along with it. It wasn't the time to dig up how we knew each other, but I had a feeling she would try to pull me aside later in the evening. The room was silent for a second or two before Warren asked if anyone wanted another drink.

93

"I'll take a drink," I said.

"I could use one too," Tricia added. "Let me come in the kitchen with you, Warren. Sadira, I'll bring yours to you."

I smiled. For some reason it made me feel good that she volunteered to bring my drink to me.

Janae' glanced at me quickly as Tricia followed behind Warren, but she didn't say anything.

"So Sadira, how did you meet Tricia?" Josh asked.

"Through her cousin, actually. I work with him at WSOL."

"Devonte'? You're working with him again?" Janae' jumped in.

"Yep." *Was she making a mental note? And so much for her acting as though it were our first time meeting each other.*

Classic R&B songs played softly in the background as Tricia and Warren returned with the drinks and the conversation we'd interrupted resumed. The topic went from teachers being underpaid to a debate on the power of "ethnic" names. Tricia and Janae' went back and forth until finally agreeing to disagree.

"Whew, chile. I think it's 'bout time for another drank," Warren announced with his country accent. It was a perfect diversion from the conversation. "Come on in this kitchen with me, Tricia."

Janae' inched over to talk to me. "So, what are you doing in New York? How have you been?"

"Things changed, and I missed the city." I looked behind me to see if Tricia was watching. She was.

"Where's Jessie?"

"I don't know. Aren't you her friend?"

"We lost contact after you two moved."

I was starting to feel uncomfortable. "Hey, I'm not trying to be rude or anything, but I'm really trying to forget about Jessie, you know?"

She gave me a fake smile. "I understand."

"All right." When Tricia came back, she put her hand on my knee and I placed my arm back around her. I didn't know what my little exchange with Janae' looked like to her, but I didn't want to make her feel funny or embarrass her.

Janae' stood next to Warren across the room.

I wonder how they all know each other. I didn't bother to ask though. Inquisitive thoughts about who Jessie was with and what she was doing crossed my mind, but I pushed them out. It was 3:00 in the morning when Tricia and I finally decided to leave. Josh gave us a ride back to her apartment, and she kept a happy face and attitude going until after we thanked him and went inside.

"What's the matter, Tricia?" I asked. We sat down on her couch.

"You're distracted. You've been distracted. I don't think anyone else noticed, but I did."

I was silent.

"Where do you know Janae' from?"

Here we go. "She was a friend of Jessie's."

"Jessie?" She looked disturbed. "Is she in New York?"

"I don't know."

"Bullshit. She didn't tell you?"

"No! When she brought Jessie up I changed the subject. I told her I didn't want to talk about Jessie."

Her eyes looked apologetic. "Oh," she said softly.

"Tell me what you're feeling, Tricia."

"I feel like I'm setting myself up for a heartbreak by hanging on to you. I know that you don't want to settle down, but I don't want to let you go."

I didn't say anything.

"And I just have a gut feeling that you aren't even totally with me right now. You're thinking of Jessie, aren't you?"

Ouch. She was right.

"Oh, God. I can't do this. I have to stop."

At a loss for words, I could only look at her.

She moved closer to me, and put her head on my shoulder and a hand on my knee. I felt bad. I had to let her go for good if I couldn't give her all of me.

"Sadira." She spoke softly.

"Yes?"

"I've fallen in love with you."

Oh, man. It felt like a trapdoor underneath me had opened and I was freefalling. To be honest, I didn't even know why Tricia's statement surprised me. My feelings for her had grown too, but I had Brianna around to distract me. I brought her hand close to my mouth and kissed it. *Break things off,* I told myself.

"Tricia." I swallowed. "I don't want to hurt you. I really don't, and I think we both know in our minds that we should stop seeing each other."

"What does your heart say?"

"I stopped following my heart a long time ago," I remarked without thinking first. "I follow my mind."

She got off me. "So this is it? We're finished?"

"I don't know. I just want to do what's best for you, and right now I don't think it's me."

Her eyes began to fill with tears. "Why not, Sadira? What is it that you need?" Tricia's words sounded like a plea.

"To get over Jessie, Tricia! I'm not over her. Look, I can't move forward with you, but it doesn't mean that it's because *you're* not enough for me. It's because I'm not ready, baby. I'm not ready." I lowered my voice to a whisper. "You said it yourself; you felt like I wasn't even totally here with you tonight. Could you deal with that every night?"

"No."

"Hey, remember when you said that you wouldn't settle?"

"Yes."

"Well then don't break your rule for me. I won't allow you to do it."

Pain and disappointment streamed from her eyes. "You're right."

It hurt like hell to say the things I did, but I really wanted to do right by Tricia. I pulled her back over to me for a hug.

"I have to leave you alone, Sadira. We can't see each other again after tonight." She sniffed. "I'm not sure I can be friends with you either. As a matter of fact, I'm almost positive I can't be just friends with you."

That was more than I was looking for. "You want to cut off all contact?"

"That's the only way for me."

"Shit." I suddenly felt a bit of regret for pushing us to stop seeing each other. I didn't want us to stop speaking altogether.

She backed out of the hug and looked me in the eyes. "Look, Sadira. I think you are really special…for many reasons, but I know that trying to be just friends with you won't work because we'd lapse back into sleeping together. And I'm not going to be a matter of convenience for you."

Her words reminded me of my own frustration with Jessie when we first started dating. She had made me feel as though I were a convenience store the way she walked in and out of my life. I released a breath filled with pain. "Well, I guess this is it."

"I guess so."

I reached in to kiss her, but she moved back. "I can't."

Tears began to roll from my eyes. I couldn't believe how the evening played out. "Please, can I at least have a kiss good bye?"

She leaned in to kiss me, but I didn't release her. I didn't want it only to be a simple good bye kiss. I held her tightly, kissing her harder. She put her arms around my neck and continued. A few minutes went by before we slowed down. Heart heavy with pain, she gave me another soft kiss before starting to cry. I stroked her hair. *I have to get out of here. I should have left with a simple kiss, now it's even harder.* Tricia kissed my neck and up to my lips. Our emotions eventually led us to a sad exchange of intimacy, if that could be an accurate description. I felt my heart and mind battling as my body mated with hers. My thoughts became whispers from my flesh to hers. With my rhythmic movements I tried to remind her that I *did* want her. I *did* have a desire to love her as she loved me, and I wanted to come back to her when I felt she would truly have all of me. I was too afraid to say the words or even ask her to wait, but I hoped that last night of lovemaking said it for me. Hopefully it would leave such an indelible impression that no one else could compete.

When I left, I could still smell traces of her perfume on my clothes. Fighting back tears, I reminded myself that we did the right thing.

The heartbreak would have only been worse if we had continued. When I got home, I noticed Melissa arriving at the same time I did. She, however, was getting out of a slick black Lincoln town car with a driver who opened and closed the door for her before he said good bye and left. *What's up with this?* I wanted to be nosey and ask what the deal was but told myself to mind my own dreadful business. I saw her look up to the top floor of the brownstone in which she lived. My eyes followed hers. The lights were off up there.

"Hi," she said. Her facial expression refused to give me a clue as to how she was feeling or what she'd been doing.

"Hey, what's up?"

"Not much. I'm just getting in from work, you know."

"Mm hm." Something was different about Melissa. She didn't seem like herself.

"Well, I'm kind of tired so I'm going to go on up."

"Okay, see you around."

"Later." She went inside.

Once upstairs I could no longer act as if I wasn't in pain. I cried and felt an ache for Tricia in the trenches of my heart.

Chapter 10

I felt like a zombie the following days. *What are you doing?* Trying not to think about Tricia was a tremendous failure. And to my aggravation, there were two messages from Olivia on my voicemail. *That girl won't give up.* For a moment my mind even wandered to Jessie to try to escape my feelings. I wondered what she was doing, but mostly, I couldn't stop thinking about Tricia. Abrupt cutoffs in relationships were always hard for me. I always wished I were one of those people who could turn her emotions on and off as needed, but I wasn't. I missed Tricia already.

I wanted to talk to someone and Khedara wasn't available when I tried to call her. The only other person in whom I would normally confide was Devonte', and I was hesitant to call him. I couldn't ask his advice about his cousin. I had a feeling she was still crying over me and I knew that Devonte' would say that we did the right thing anyway. As a matter of fact, I remembered his telling me to leave her alone before I moved to Miami when I was trying to choose between Tricia and Jessie. There was nothing I could do but let time pass and hope that my feelings would sort themselves out.

I turned my television on to a random music channel and regretted it. The instant I heard Norah Jones' bluesy voice I broke out in tears. I laid down on my bed, curled up in fetal position with my face buried in the sheets, crying. I didn't even know why I attempted to listen to slow music when I was sad. For some reason, as I cried, I let it continue to play as if it would pull the pain out of me. I was angry with myself because I still hadn't let go of Jessie. It hurt me to know that I hurt Tricia and made her feel less than enough by not accepting her. I cried until the sheets were soaked. I was a painful mess. Loneliness swept over me like a chilling breeze and I felt like my love life would never work. I was losing myself in self-pity when my phone finally rang and snapped me out of my trance.

I reached over for the phone. "Hello?"

"Can I speak to Sean?"

"Who?"

"Sean."

"You have the wrong number, man." I hung up and straightened out on the bed.

I laid there staring at the ceiling as crystal drops rolled down the side of my face for the next couple of minutes. Even though it was the wrong number, I was grateful for the phone call. *What am I going to do?* Slowly I stopped crying and just let thoughts go through my mind. I still had Brianna but wasn't sure I wanted her the way I wanted Tricia. And what would I do if *she* wanted more, let her go?

Time went by very slowly. I stayed up late thinking, and writing in my journal. Though in pain, I tried to do something constructive rather than sob all night. It wasn't the end of the world, just the end of what could have been a beautiful a relationship. Some time around 4 a.m., I walked to the kitchen for a glass of water and to the bathroom to prepare for bed.

Tossing and turning throughout my lonely nights, I once woke up with dry eyes and a feeling of nagging emptiness. No pain, nothing. I was just numb, not even knowing what day it was. I stretched, yawned, and rubbed my eyes. *Let's make today a better day,* I told myself and went to take a shower. *It's Sunday,* the thought chimed in my head like an old clock going off on the hour. I tried to get myself together while in the bathroom and decided that I'd get dressed and go out to a diner for something to eat. Getting out of the house would do me some good, or at least that's what I thought as I put on a pair of rugged jeans and a white

Polo shirt. I threw on a white Yankees cap and a pair of blue and white Reeboks with the Yankee logo on the side, before grabbing my bag and keys and heading out.

On my walk to the bus stop I saw Melissa coming out of the corner store. "Hey."

"What's up, Sadira?"

"You tell me."

She looked happy. "I'm leaving."

"What?"

"I will be able to move out soon."

"That's pretty fast. What kind of job?"

"A good paying one."

Evasive. "Oh. Well, I'm happy for you."

She smiled. "So am I. Jasmine will be in Detroit for some seminar when I leave. I know that's the easy way out, but I don't want any drama. I just want to disappear."

"Where are you moving to?"

"Either Queens or Harlem. I don't know yet. I just want to move *away* and start over."

"Cool. I'm glad to hear it." I saw my bus go by. *Damn it.*

"Hey, I don't want to hold you up, but I just thought I'd share."

"Okay, and remember in the meantime you're always welcome to come over to my place if you need a break from Jasmine."

"Thank you."

"You're welcome." We shared a smile before parting. I wondered where Melissa was working but didn't ask for any more details. The good thing was that she was getting out. Everything else was really none of my business, I guessed.

Since the next bus wouldn't come for another five minutes, I went into the corner store to buy hot chocolate. It was loud in there. Some guys were speaking another language over in a corner and a couple of kids were playing arcade style video games by the door. I paid for the drink and quickly went back outside.

While I headed for downtown Brooklyn, I got a call from Brianna. I told her I was on my way to a diner.

"You're going alone?"

"Yeah, what's wrong with that?"

She didn't respond immediately. "Nothing, but you could have called me. I haven't heard from you in a few days."

"I'm sorry, Bri. I needed some time alone."

"What's going on with you? You don't sound like yourself."

The bus driver stopped the bus and got off to assist a person in a wheelchair. I sighed. "I just..."

"What is it, Sadira? Is everything okay?"

Remorse slowed my speech. "No, Brianna. Everything is not okay, but it will be."

"Can I do something? What's the matter?"

"I don't really feel like talking about it now, but I'll be fine. I promise." I didn't have it in me to tell her about Tricia. *Some things are better left unsaid.*

"Well, what are you doing tonight?"

"Nothing." I watched the bus driver return to his seat. We were moving again.

"Do you want to see me? Or maybe I should ask if I am welcome to come over? Do you want to be alone...or with someone else?" Her voice softened as she spoke her last words.

I tried not to take too long to answer her. "You know what? I think I do need some time to be alone. I don't want my bad mood to rub off on you."

I thought I heard her gasp before responding to me. "Fine, I guess," she said.

"I'm sorry, but I need a little time to get myself together. Can I call you later on tonight?"

"Yeah."

"Okay." The line was quiet for a moment.

"So I'll just talk to you later on then."

Her statement sounded more like a question but I didn't answer. I

102

simply said, "Yes," before we ended the call.

One part of me wanted to be alone, and the other part wanted to be in familiar arms. I just didn't think I could keep myself together and not tell Brianna what was really bothering me. Her presence would have comforted me, but it was a better decision to be alone. I was sure of it.

I stayed on the bus until it reached downtown Brooklyn. The streets were busy and loud as usual, with people handing out flyers, trying to sell cell phones, slippers, you name it. I stopped to pick up a newspaper before walking into a diner.

"Just one in your party?" the waiter inquired.

"Yes."

His eyes lingered on me for a second before walking me to a booth and bringing me a glass of water. Was I lame because I was eating by myself? *Fuck him.* My paranoia turned into an attitude and I knew I wasn't going to be a pleasant customer. He soon came back to take my order.

I ate while turning to the real estate section of the paper. It was about time I put serious effort into finding another place to live. I don't know why I thought of it then but was glad I did. I sifted through the ads, circling ones that I thought I should look into. Every now and then I glanced up and looked out the window.

"Do you need anything?" The waiter came back by to check on me.

"No thank you I'm fine."

Just as I was about to turn my attention back to my newspaper, a police officer walked in. *Ooh, she's cute.* She had a toasted almond complexion, neat locs, and hazel eyes. *Jesus!* I stared at her, but she wasn't looking my way. *Who is she?* When our eyes made contact I smiled and she returned one of her own. *I should compliment her.* My captivation was put to a halt when my cell phone rang. It was from a blocked number so I ignored it. Still, my fascination with the officer was broken. That's when it hit me. She reminded me of Jessie. Deflated, I gathered my things to leave. Meanwhile the cop took a seat at the counter. *She's still gorgeous, and I wouldn't mind being cuffed to her.*

A part of me wanted to steal more gazes at her as if it would bring me closer to Jessie. *You need to be away from Jessie.* God, Jessie brought out the fool in me. I grabbed the real estate section of the paper, stuck it in my bag, and got up from the table to visit the ladies room. As I washed my hands, I hoped my thoughts would also be rinsed away in the soft warm water. When I went back out to pay, I walked right by the officer and spotted a wedding ring on her finger. *Damn.* I don't even know why it mattered to me. I wanted to laugh at myself. I was a mess!

"Thank you," the cashier said as she handed me my change.

"You're welcome." I walked out. Before I could walk to the next block, my phone rang again. I didn't recognize the number on the caller ID.

"Hello?"

"Hi, Sadira."

"Who is this?"

"Oh now you don't know my voice?"

"Olivia? You've got to be kidding me!"

"What?"

"Are you retarded or crazy? I mean didn't I tell you not to contact me again? For the last god damned time, you need to cut it out, Olivia."

"Or else what?"

"Or else we're going to have a real problem. Get it through your head that I don't want you, we don't click, and there is no us."

"Why did you have sex with me then?"

"Because you were throwing your yourself at me and I was horny, but there is nothing intriguing about you. I can't stand the fact that you even used your energy to find me. You're too needy and I don't care about you. Don't call my damn phone anymore, shit!" I hung up. I knew my words were harsh, but I was fed up with her and had run out of patience. Fuck her.

When I looked around I noticed that I had caused a scene. "What the hell are y'all looking at?" I gave them a cold stare before averting my attention to hail a cab. My phone rang again, and I knew it was Olivia calling me back. I ignored it, but it rang again, and again, and again.

104

"What do you want, girl?" I answered.

"Sadira, don't hang up."

Click.

I turned my phone off as soon as I settled in the taxi. I regretted sleeping with her. The sex wasn't even good. A few minutes into the ride I turned my phone back on and noticed the small envelope emblem on my screen: twelve new messages, the last of which was a text message that said, "You're going to pay for this." I rolled my eyes. *Crazy broad.*

When I got close to home I went to a nearby liquor store to buy a case of Mike's Hard Lemonade to relax with alone. I went inside and turned all of my ringers off, switched on some soulful music, and tried my best to clear my mind. An hour later I found that it worked and I didn't feel annoyed, stressed, or even sad anymore. I felt good just being still. The night came to a somewhat peaceful close.

When I walked into WSOL in the morning, I saw Devonte'. I smiled and he gave me an acknowledging head nod. He was talking to our boss, and I didn't want to interrupt so I went to my work area. While I was sitting in my booth, my phone rang once and then stopped. Afraid it might be Olivia, I didn't bother to check the caller ID for a while. To my surprise I later saw that it was Brianna, but she didn't call back. *Maybe she changed her mind about calling me.* That was the only thing I could think of besides Brianna's dialing my number by accident, which was even more disheartening. I doubted that though.

During one of the commercial breaks Devonte' poked his head in. "Hey, did you hear the news?"

"No, what?"

"Gert is leaving, and we're going to have a new supervisor starting tomorrow."

"Get out of here!"

"Nope, something nasty must have gone down for her to quit on the spot. I don't know. I just wanted to share the news."

"All right."

A part of me worried a little bit because I knew that along with new management came change. I hoped they weren't going to fire any of us.

When I got home, I called Brianna. "Hi."

"Hey, Sadira."

"Hi. Did you call me earlier?"

She didn't answer right away. "Um, yeah."

"What's up?"

There was an awkward silence before she spoke. "I…"

"Say something, Bri."

"I want to talk to you, Sadira. I want to know what's going on and if you are all right."

"Everything is okay, and I'm fine. I was just having a bad day yesterday."

"Are you sure?"

"Yes."

"All right. Well, when are we going to see each other? Are we still going away or not?"

Shit. I'd totally forgotten about it. I responded without alerting her to my bad memory. "Yes, we are. Why don't you come over tonight and we can square things away for this weekend."

She answered without hesitation and probably a smirk. "Okay."

"Cool."

"All right. I'll see you in a few."

"Bye."

I took a quick shower after I hung up with her and put on a fresh set of clothes. While waiting, I got on the Internet to secure a car rental, reserve the bed and breakfast, and printed out driving directions. I didn't want her to have to worry about anything. She arrived about a half an hour later wearing a long honey colored skirt and black sweater.

"Hi." I smiled when I saw her.

"Hey, you." Her dimples dipped into her smooth brown cheeks as she reciprocated a grin.

"Come on inside."

I shut the door behind her and then pulled her close to me for a hug. "I'm glad you came."

"Are you really?"

"Yes, I am. I'm really sorry about yesterday. Come on, let's get upstairs."

"Okay," she responded and grabbed my butt.

"Hey!"

"You know you like it."

I laughed. "Whatever."

"Yeah, yeah."

I was sincerely happy to have her over. "Do you want something to drink, Bri?"

"Yes, I'll have some water."

"Okay. You know I don't know why I'm treating you like it's your first time here. Next time get up and get it yourself." I laughed and walked to the kitchen to pour her beverage.

"Fine. Does that mean I can make myself at home all over your place?"

"Maybe." I responded without effort. *Why did I just say that?*

"What?"

Silence.

I think I surprised both of us with my answer, and I wasn't even sure of what I meant. "I don't know. Never mind." She looked at me as I walked back over to her. "What I mean is you can make yourself at home when you come over...but don't just show up unannounced like a stalker," I said and laughed. I was trying to lighten the conversation.

"Please, I'm not the stalking type, but I suppose I should thank you for bumping me up to be able to make myself at home in your apartment."

"Yeah." I really wanted to change the subject. "Hey, so how is school going?"

"Good, actually. I have another debate this week."

"On gay marriage again?"

"No, thank goodness."

107

I laughed. "Why do you say it like that?"

"Because I hate that debate. I don't even know how I feel about it anymore. All of the back and forth has clouded my stance."

"Oh really?"

"I'm leaning toward it after really thinking about civil unions. I thought it would be fair to argue equality across the board if civil unions were available in every state, but now I'm realizing that's just a case of separate but equal." She took a sip of water and slid her shoes off before leaning back on the sofa. "Nothing will satisfy everyone."

"Of course not. That would make life too easy."

"Well, if you take out the option of having a civil union, which is what was done in one of my classes, I have no choice but to be for marriage because without it there is no option for us to get tax breaks, insurance, and inheritance rights, or even hospital visitation, and that's not even a complete list."

"Tell me about it."

"The problem is someone always throws a religious spin on it and says gays are damaging the institution of marriage."

"So tell them it's untrue. I don't think most gay people are looking for Christian approval anyway. We want equal rights and recognition of our commitments."

"The word marriage will always have a Christian foundation in this country and people hold it dearly. They're afraid we'll tarnish the institution."

We? She said we. "I don't mean to shift the topic, but are you still going to go back in the closet?"

"I have to, Sadira. That's the only way I'm going to get ahead in my career."

I was quiet.

"Things would be great if it didn't have to be that way, but I'm black, a woman, and a Republican. Adding the lesbian factor doesn't seem to be the smartest decision."

"I understand, believe me I do. But on the other hand, it's people like you who can make more of a difference by being the agent of change

108

you want to see in society. You follow me? If more professionals were out, then fewer people would think that we're all freaks who only party and have sex."

She sighed. "I wish I it were so simple, Sadira, but the timing just isn't right. I'll hit prejudice from the gate if they know I'm openly gay."

"So you're going to date men to cover?"

"I'm not going to date anyone for as long as I can so I can stay focused."

I sensed she didn't want to talk about it anymore. "Come here," I said and pulled her in my arms. We'd said enough on the subject, and I didn't want to get her upset.

She put her arm around me and I reached for the remote. "Are you up for some TV?"

"Sure."

We finally just settled on a PBS documentary of all things. It was on the history of New York, so I figured it wouldn't be bad. "Is this too boring for you to watch?"

"Nope, I like history too."

"Good." I kissed her forehead and adjusted so I could sit comfortably holding her.

We watched the special for at least an hour and a half before becoming drowsy. It was a good documentary but long. I glanced over at the clock to see that it was still quite early in the day. *I'm tired though, damn.*

"Hey, I don't know about you, but I could use a nap." I told her.

She yawned. "That's not a bad idea."

"Come on." I got up and walked toward my bedroom, and we both laid down.

We didn't have sex at all that evening. Instead we slept and held each other. It was 1 o'clock in the morning when I woke up, after she'd slipped out of my arms to go to the bathroom. I smiled when I saw her walking back over to me in bed. Her hair was out of place, but she still looked cute.

"It's late; I better get going," she said.

My smiled faded. I didn't want her to go. She felt good, and I would have enjoyed holding her until morning. "You should have just brought a change clothes so you could spend the night."

"I'm sorry. I didn't think about it. I wish I could stay, but I have class in the morning and my books are at home."

"It's okay." I sat up and reached out for her. She walked into my arms. I rested my head against her womb and felt her hands rub against the back of my neck. "I enjoyed tonight," I told her honestly.

"Me too," she said and ran her fingers through my hair.

I got up to give Brianna a full hug and a kiss on the neck before she eased out of the embrace to gather her things and call car service.

"Hey," she announced before walking out the door, "don't forget about our weekend getaway. I'm looking forward to it."

"I won't, and make sure you call me when you get home tonight."

A car pulled up and honked twice outside.

"Okay," she said.

"All right." I kissed her and she walked out.

Chapter 11

Having Brianna around the previous evening kept me from feeling depressed. I needed to see her again so I asked her to meet me at the subway station near my job. When she arrived, we went to pick up the rental car before going to Central Park together. We stopped at a sidewalk cafe to buy two franks and drinks. *There's nothing like street hot dogs!* I savored the taste in my mouth as I ate.

It was a warm day for late-November, comfortable enough to walk outside with only a light jacket. Brianna and I walked and talked, and it reminded me of the first time we met in person at Ft. Greene Park in Brooklyn. This time though, she told me that she was thinking of changing the program she was enrolled in so that she could take a semester off to work and save money since she didn't get the internship. She badly wanted to move away from East New York, and I couldn't blame her. As we strolled through of the park, a man with a thick salt and pepper beard and foreign accent offered to draw a picture of us for $10.

"Do you want to?" I asked her. We'd finished eating by then.

"Sure, if you do."

"Okay."

We sat down for about 20 minutes as the street artist sketched our picture. I was impressed with the finished product and let Brianna keep the picture.

"I need to pick up the clothes I packed for the weekend," she said.

"Okay, but you're going to have to guide me a little bit because I don't know the street names in your neighborhood."

"No problem."

When we got to the projects, I followed her through a courtyard that led to her building. She stopped to check her mail before we took the stairs four flights up. The elevator was out of service. Brianna began sifting through her mail as we exited the stairwell on her floor, and stopped when she came to an envelope. I almost walked into her.

"What is it?"

She didn't say anything. She just stared at it for a second longer before tearing it open.

I looked at her expectantly. "Well?" I saw her eyes scan the first few lines quickly.

"Oh my God." She smiled broadly, and her eyes widened. "I got the internship!"

"You what?"

She read over the letter, looking as if she wanted to jump up and down. "A position opened up, and I was selected."

"That's great, baby." I hugged her.

We walked a few more feet to her apartment, and once inside she read parts of the letter aloud. "A part of your duties will include keeping Senator Chase and his staff updated on the latest news by compiling print, television, and radio stories and tracking important issues." Elated, she put the papers down without finishing.

"Congratulations! When does it start?

She had the biggest grin on her face.

"In January. I'm to call immediately if I can't accept."

"Oh," I said and smiled. I was happy for her, but a selfish part of me didn't want her to go. I'd already lost Tricia. Now Brianna was going to leave too. Damn it.

"I have to call my mother and tell her!" She picked up her phone and dialed.

As I listened to the one-sided conversation I tried to not be bothered. It was an incredible opportunity for her. She wanted to be out running political campaigns, writing speeches, lobbying, and stuff like that. I couldn't think of a better way for her to have an impressive résumé when she finally graduated. I still wished that I didn't have to lose her in the process.

She hung up the phone after several minutes and said, "My mother is coming downstairs." She paused. "My grandmother too."

Uh oh. I got nervous.

"Don't worry, it'll be okay."

"But I'm not ready to meet your folks yet." I panicked.

"Just relax. It'll go smoothly. They're so excited for me, they won't bother with you too much."

"I hope so."

Pretty soon there was a knock on her door. I rubbed my perspiring hands on my pants and sat up straight. Brianna opened the door and her mother and grandmother came inside, beaming.

"Brianna, baby, come give your grandmother a big hug! I'm so proud of you." She was thin and short, with long gray hair. She wore a black shirt, red skirt, and black flat shoes.

Her mother spoke to me first. "Hello."

"Hello, ma'am, how are you?"

Brianna interrupted before her mother could respond. "Mama, this is my friend, Sadira."

"It's nice to meet you," her mother said.

Her grandmother looked at me inquisitively. "Is this the young lady you were talking about, Bri?"

She told her grandmother about me? I fought my almost natural response to widen my eyes in surprise.

Brianna looked at me with a hint of apology before responding to her grandmother. "Yes, Grandma, this is she."

"You must be special then," the older woman said to me. "Brianna smiles real big when she talks about you...her eyes light up. And well, I guess I can only be happy someone is putting a smile on my baby's face."

113

Nervous and unsure of what to do, I thanked her respectfully. Brianna was right, they were so excited about her they really didn't pay much attention to me or ask many more questions. I was relieved. Looking at them comparatively I noticed that all three of them had beautiful smiles and dimples. Brianna looked strikingly like her mother, except her mom was a bit heavier and a shade darker. Their facial features were the same though.

About an hour later or so, they left and the two of us sat alone in her small apartment. The walls were thin, and I could hear lots of outside noise. A look outside the window and down into the courtyard revealed a bunch of people just sitting around. Some were playing Dominos, and others were standing around talking and smoking in their sagging jeans and Timberland boots. I heard music and smelled fried chicken coming from another apartment too.

Her place was sparsely decorated. I sat on the small love seat looking at two shelves that were full of books. Photos were on top of the shelves. Her apartment was very clean, the floors shined, and I supposed she did the best she could with what she had.

"Well, let me get my things. That is why we came here in the first place."

"Did you tell your mother you were going away with me?"

"Shit, I didn't!"

"You're an awful child."

"Shut up."

I laughed. "Well don't you think you should let them know?"

"Of course. I'll call up there now," she commented. She was so happy, and despite my selfishness, I was too. *Wow, the Capitol.* And if she made a good impression she could have so many opportunities.

"Be sure to do a hell of a job on all assignments and network your ass off," I said as we drove back to my apartment.

"Oh, I will. I'm so excited! I'm going to miss you though."

"Yeah." I would have to make the best out of this weekend with her just in case things got busy and I didn't get to see her much before she had to go. "So, how much are you going to go back in the closet."

114

She thought before answering. "A lot."

I wanted to pout. "Oh."

"You understand, don't you?"

"Yeah."

There was silence.

I slowed to stop at a red light. "So where does that leave us?"

"I...I don't know. I don't want to stop seeing you." She sounded unsure.

"Will you call me often while you are away?"

"Yes, I mean if I can."

"Or will you fall in love with some woman in D.C.?" I joked.

She smiled. "No, I don't think that will happen. I won't even be in any lesbian environments in D.C., much less dating."

"I guess we'll see, huh?"

"Don't worry," she assured me.

Yeah right. I was insecure but shut my mouth because I didn't want her to know it.

We eventually subsided into silence for a few minutes before I found a parking space on my block. Upstairs, I could hear faint noises coming from Melissa and Jasmine's place so I turned on music to drown them out.

"Let me use your bathroom for a sec," she said.

"Go ahead."

When she returned, I slipped into the bathroom to freshen up quickly. She'd dimmed the lights by the time I had come out, and in my bedroom we kissed. I enjoyed her entire body that night and felt myself getting more attached to her. The intimacy was pleasant and deliberately slow, as was our weekend getaway, which started the next day. We talked all the way down to New Jersey as I drove, and once there, we spent time exploring. We stayed up late familiarizing ourselves with each other over and over again. It was fun but had touches of bitter sweetness to it, as the reality of another woman leaving settled in my mind.

115

Chapter 12

I went on acting as if it didn't bother me that Brianna was leaving soon. I missed Tricia too, but didn't call her. Since my personal life had slowed down, I felt depression every now and again. Thoughts of Jessie slithered into my mind daily. Constantly. I had no more women to distract me from my memories of her. Jessie's presence crept inside me, and my misaligned heart and mind couldn't protect me. I *needed* someone or something to help me move beyond her. That much I knew to be true. I took to my keyboard and banged out melodies that reeked of my feelings.

I'd slowly stopped attending my lessons with Jenny but had learned quite a bit during my stint with her. I tried to push my heartache and loneliness out in the form of song. In a modest attempt to give Brianna a piece of me, I decided to hook my keyboard up to my computer to master a song for her. It had no words; it was just an instrumental, but I hoped she would like it. I also planned on buying her going away gifts. She deserved it. My phone rang, interrupting my thoughts. I ignored it, but five minutes later it rang again, and again.

"Hello?" I was annoyed and knew it had to be Olivia calling even though the ID said it was a private number.

"Hi, Sadira."

"Stop calling me!" I said and hung up. Regret couldn't even describe how I felt about sleeping with her. I wished she would just disappear! Without hesitation, I turned the ringer off and looked outside the window to make sure she wasn't out there.

I didn't see her, but I did see Jasmine pacing back and forth. I waved my hand in annoyance and went to sit down at my computer. When I logged into my e-mail I saw something from Olivia. *Why?* Reluctantly, I clicked on it and read it. She was going on and on about how I wasted her time and took advantage of her body, which she considered sacred and blah blah blah. It didn't even dawn on me that I had never given her my e-mail address. I felt myself getting angry. She ended her note demanding an apology for all the wrong she claimed I had done to her. By then I was so upset I responded with one word: **NO!** Little did I know she was online and got my reply immediately. An instant message box popped up with a screen name I didn't recognize saying: What do you mean, no?

To which I responded: **NO!!!**

I changed my privacy settings to block all messages and e-mails from her, wishing I could erase the day I met her. *What did I get myself into?* I spent hours on the Internet until my eyes couldn't take the computer screen anymore. During my time online, I sent my sister a lengthy letter to update her on my life. I missed her. And as the hours wore on I began to think of Jessie. Images of her sank into my mind. *Her smile was so beautiful,* I thought, melting in a memory.

Elapsed time still couldn't extinguish the fire. It had simply reduced the flame to a flicker with lingering potential to reignite. Even a dose of infidelity could not dampen my desire for her. It only confused me. I wanted to be rid of her, yet simultaneously yearned for her. I remained a hostage. Her gaze pinned me, leaving me to forever crave her. With her there was no such thing as time—moments, maybe—but not time, calculated and passing, that would one day run out. My feelings for her were infinite. *Her blue-gray eyes were spellbinding.*

It felt good when Jessie and I had first met and exchanged contact information. On a grubby city subway I found beauty. She radiated. Her distinct features were piercing, branding me with her splendor. *Now **that** was an instant attraction.* I felt as though I could live on her smile alone.

117

Her touch was orgasmic. It felt like heaven the first time we were intimate. *She had the softest and warmest skin.* I was losing my damn mind! Jessie was a cheating bitch. *To hell with her,* I thought. Her eyes were so captivating they disabled me. *She never gave you all of her.* I would try to rationalize that what I got from her was all she knew how to give. *She used her prettiness to reel you in, and then she crushed you, squeezing the very life from you as you patiently waited then begged her to open up to you.* But when she finally opened up, I'd been smitten with another woman. Jessie was poison. And I was one thought away from being as crazy as Olivia…no wait, that was going too far.

Between Olivia's harassment and my relentless musings on Jessie, I was fit to sink into a state of helplessness, giving way to sharp blades of pressure cutting me from within. I didn't cry. I was still, waiting for things inside me to calm down. The day felt like a month.

The next morning the sun rose with a blazing glow stretching across the city. Before I knew it, Brianna was getting ready to leave. It was a cold evening when I went to help her finish packing some last minute things. Though I didn't get a chance to play the song I'd written for her, I put it on a CD and gave it to her. After we finished getting her things together, she made dinner and then I gave her the gifts: a black pantsuit, navy skirt suit, leather bound journal, and a gift certificate to a department store where she could buy a new bag or briefcase, whichever she preferred.

"Oh, thank you, Sadira!"

I smiled. "You're welcome. I wanted to give you going away gifts that you could use."

"You've given me plenty, thank you so much." She beamed. "This is such a surprise."

"No problem."

Brianna climbed on top of me. "You are so thoughtful."

"Am I?" I leaned in to kiss her and she placed her arms around my neck.

We continued kissing for some time before slowing to a stop. She shifted positions so that she was sitting on my lap, and her back was against the arm of the small sofa. Brianna and I talked for at least an hour. I loved my conversations with her. She was so full of life, hope, and energy.

By the end of the night, all of her personal belongings were ready to go. Her mother would move back down into the apartment, and her grandmother would live alone again.

The day she left wasn't totally sad. I was happy she had the opportunity, but it wasn't completely joyful either.

"I'm going to miss you," I said.

"Me too."

We shared an intense stare. I didn't want her to go. "Come here," I told her, and she did.

Tears were building up in her eyes as she took the few short steps toward me. I opened my arms and we embraced. "I want you to stay in touch, but I guess I understand if you don't."

"I'll call you, Sadira."

Unable to think of more to say, I hugged her tighter. After we released each other and kissed for the last time, Brianna left and I was alone again.

Winter glistened across the city. Tricia and I didn't speak, and Olivia's phone calls became less frequent. The only consistency in my life were my late lunches with Devonte'. I decided to start attending more spoken word events as well as go out to local jazz bars to try to maintain some kind of a social life. For the most part though, it was just me. I heard from Brianna, but it was never a long conversation the way we used to have them. She called and e-mailed me when she could. I missed her but didn't want to sulk about it. *Let her go,* I told myself, and eventually I did.

Coasting through the weeks working on music, poetry, and photography, I built an amateur portfolio of art and sound. My black and

119

white pictures were the ones of which I was most proud. And the songs that had my heart carved into them sounded the best to me.

I noticed that I wasn't the only one who was going through changes. One afternoon when I got home, I saw that Melissa was moving out. A lanky guy with stringy blond hair was helping her load things into a red pickup truck. She was all smiles and moving quickly.

I spoke to her first. "Hey, I see you're finally getting out, huh?"

"Yeah, I have enough money to get away from her for good."

"Where are you heading?"

"The Bronx."

"Why so far? What's up there?"

"A place I can afford. And the farther the better."

"Gotcha. Well, congratulations. I'm really happy you're leaving Jasmine. How is she taking it?"

"She doesn't know. She's not even in New York. I plan to be gone without even a note by the time she's back. She can have a nice life."

Coldblooded. I wanted to laugh, but I didn't. "Hey, you've got to do what you've got to do. Who's that?" I motioned to the guy putting her boxes in the truck.

"He's just some guy I'm paying to help me move."

"Oh. Well, I'll let you get going. You do have my number right?"

"Yes."

"Cool. If ever you need someone to talk to, just give me a call."

"Thanks, Sadira."

"No problem."

Good for her, I thought. I went upstairs to settle in and check my e-mail. There were responses to some of my poetry and audio files as well as notes from Khedara that included pictures of her and her boyfriend. She looked so happy I almost envied her but chastised myself for the thought. *It can't always be about you.* I had to be happy for her. I was. To not drag her down with my tattered love life, I only responded to her with glee about her newfound joy. I told myself to call her soon.

120

Days went by with a deep yearning to belong or be loved. On those days I *was* lonely and *did* feel lame for eating alone. It was different this time around because I wasn't choosing to go out alone; I had no one else to go with. But in the instant of a breeze it seemed as if things changed. One day while I was in Burger King and scanning the restaurant for an empty table, I noticed a familiar and distinct tattoo on the lower back of a woman bending down to pick up her keys. The rich skin and shoulder length locs made me stop and stare. *Jessie.* My eyes widened in shock, and my stomach felt like stone. I knew it without having to see her face. My heart began to pound at a dizzying pace. I wanted to turn and walk out unnoticed, but I couldn't. Caught off guard, I stood completely still, frozen, with perspiration forming on my hands.

When she stood up and turned around, our eyes locked. Her lips parted slightly and her eyes became fixed on me, penetrating me in their surprise. She mouthed my name in disbelief. I didn't hear her voice, but I could read her lips. Neither of us moved. Emotions ran through me like water churning over rapids. Anger was first because a quick flash of the night of infidelity played in my mind, but I wanted to play it cool and act like I was getting along just fine without her.

"Sadira?" she repeated. Her eyes narrowed on me as she stared and walked over to me. "What are you doing here? I thought you were in Atlanta." She reached out to touch me, but I flinched as if it would hurt and she pulled her hand back.

I hadn't stopped staring into her eyes since I locked on them and didn't answer her question.

"Well, aren't you going to say something?"

I swallowed and spoke slowly. "I didn't like it there. What are *you* doing up here?"

"My mother is sick. I moved back up here last month to take care of her." She sat down and motioned for me to do the same. I did.

"Oh." My anger began melting to a mixed feeling of betrayal and sadness. She was back in my life. *She's back.* The words echoed in my head.

A pause in our conversation felt awkward. I rubbed my chin and then placed my hands on the table. My food was growing cold, but I'd lost my appetite. Jessie looked at me with a painful smile and bit her bottom lip. "How have you been?" she asked.

I rubbed my hands together. "Pretty good."

Again, there was a piercing silence. I decided to leave. It felt too funny, and I definitely wasn't ready to idly chat with her. "Jess," I began and paused, "I'm sorry to hear about your mother and hope whatever is wrong can be fixed. I can't talk to you right now though. I have to go."

She hesitated before speaking. "Okay."

I got up and walked toward the door. I'd only gotten a few feet away from the exit when I felt her presence behind me.

Her voice was almost a whisper. "Wait."

Stopping in my tracks, I turned around to face her. "What's up?"

"Will I see you again?"

My words followed a sigh. "I don't think so."

She nervously jingled her keys. "Maybe we can just be friends?"

"Jessie, I'm not ready for that."

"What if you are ready in a few months? How will you know how to find me if we don't exchange info now?"

Before I could respond, a crowd of teenagers came loudly through the door. I moved back to allow them to pass, and thought about her suggestion. She looked at me with expectant eyes. "I'm not sure that's a good idea. Things are still fresh for me."

"Oh," she paused to gather herself, "Okay, well maybe I'll just see you around."

I shrugged and turned to walk out.

"Sadira," she called.

I stopped but didn't turn to look at her.

"Do you remember the screen name I used online when we were together?"

Still, I didn't face her or speak, but I knew the name she was talking about. How could I forget when I had spent so much time chatting with her in the early days of our relationship?

"Well, I never deactivated it."

I walked out of Burger King and headed home. As I neared the subway station, thoughts of Jessie overwhelmed me. I wished she hadn't told me about her screen name. I couldn't settle my thoughts no matter how hard I tried. I could hear Jessie's voice inside my head. Visions of her eyes haunted me. All of a sudden I was very concerned with how she was doing and wanted to talk to her immediately. I had to repeatedly tell myself not to add her to my buddy list. *Don't do it.*

When I got home I tried to take my mind off her by pulling out my keyboard, but it worked against me. My fingers only touched keys whose sounds were anchored with sadness when combined into chords. Frustrated, I turned the keyboard off, pulled out a notebook, and started writing. At the end of an hour I had seven pages and my hand was hurting.

The only good thing about that evening was a call from Brianna. We weren't talking long before she asked me why I sounded so distracted. Not wanting to lie, I told the truth and was met with a hurtful silence. Maybe it wasn't a good thing that she called.

"How do you feel about her, Sadira?"

"I'm not completely over her."

"Does that mean you are going to try again with her?"

"No!"

"Are you sure?"

"Yes." *Am I sure?*

Brianna was silent.

"How are things going for you?" Desperately, I tried to change the subject.

She didn't follow my lead. "I'm uncomfortable now. You still love her, and now she's within your reach."

"What do you want me to do?"

Brianna's voice went from concerned to flat, as if she'd turned her emotions off. "Do what you think is right, not what I want you to do."

Ouch. She was right, but damn, she could have sugarcoated it. "Okay."

"So what are you going to do?"

"I don't know. If you're asking will I contact her, no, I won't." I tried to convince both Brianna and myself with that statement.

I heard her exhale. "I have to go now. You should think about what you want to do. The last thing I need right now is a broken heart, and the truth is, Sadira, I love you."

"You—"

"But I'm not so in love with you that I will let you hurt me. I can't take that right now. I need to be focused."

"I realize that, Brianna. And I wouldn't hurt you. At least not intentionally."

"I have to go, Sadira."

"Okay."

She hurried off the phone without saying when I would hear from her again. Why did she wait until she was out of state and resigned to go back in the closet to tell me that she loved me? That wasn't fair to *me*! Did she expect me to wait for her? "Women." I threw my hands up in aggravation. My conversation with Brianna left me exasperated. I'd already lost Tricia because I was unable to get over Jessie. Where the hell were all of these women *before* Jessie? Why did they have to rain down on me after I'd just been trapped in a thunderstorm?

My thoughts were interrupted by a knock at the door. When I asked who it was I got no answer. I looked through the window and to my dismay saw Olivia. I panicked. "Oh God, why?" I said under my breath. *What is she doing here?* I was sure she saw my shadow when I looked out, and if I didn't answer she would keep knocking.

I went down and opened the door. "What are you doing here?"

"I wanted to see you."

"No, no, no. I don't think so. You cannot see me. There is nothing for you to see!" I shut the door.

She knocked again, calling my name this time. "Sa-dir-aaaa."

I covered my face with my hands. *This is sooo embarrassing.*

Again, I opened the door. "Look, you can't come around here with this drama. I don't know how you found out where I live, but you better forget it. Now get away from here!"

124

"Damn, Sadira." I looked next door and saw Jasmine was sitting on the stoop.

I ignored Jasmine and refocused my attention on the problem at *my* doorstep. "Olivia, get out of here!"

"I want to talk. You hurt me. You broke my heart, Sadira."

What kind of thin line between love and hate fuckery is this? I thought, remembering the crazy character Brandy Webb in the movie with Martin Lawrence. "Look Olivia I may have hurt you, but I damn sure shouldn't have been able to break your heart."

Anger boiled in her eyes, but I didn't give a damn. I just wanted to get her away from me.

"You took advantage of me!"

I slammed the door.

For the next 10 minutes she continued to knock and call simultaneously. I ignored the racket until she left. *Why didn't I move already?* I'd been skirting around the issue of buying an apartment, but it was really time to stop bullshitting. I needed to relocate ASAP. I logged online and filled out a form to have a realtor contact me the next day.

My head was aching after Olivia left. Too much was going on; the women were literally starting to drive me crazy! All I wanted was quiet. Stillness. I didn't want to be bothered by my thoughts, feelings, or Olivia. I wanted everything but me to pause, like it happens in movies. *Dream on.* I went through my nightly routine, adding two Advil pills before getting ready for bed.

I had so much difficulty sleeping that night that I decided to take the next day off. I was exhausted. Agonizing memories of Jessie made sleeping feel like trying to swim in sand. We always seemed to be in a constant state of departing and arriving, whether in thought or physically. Good byes were never truly good byes. She was always around me in some way or fashion. And there was an antonymic feel to our interactions making joy and pain fuse into one. When she'd go, I wanted her to come. When she came, I wished she would leave. She was an ocean, forever going and coming and never being completely still. Though I hated to admit it, there was a tiny piece of me that was glad to know that she wanted to be around me.

Chapter 13

My emotions were the worst they had been in my entire life. How dare Jessie come back into my life! Thoughts of her ran rampant in my mind every night, but it was getting much worse than before. Her being closer, more accessible, and available made everything ten times more difficult. I still had a lot of anger inside me about what happened in Miami, but the pitiful thing was that I still loved her and was tempted to contact her. Something in me *knew* that she was yearning for me. I could feel it. Despite all the events, the pain, and the drama, there was something there. I was sure of it.

I thought about calling Khedara or Devonte' for advice, but I knew both of them would tell me to steer clear of Jessie. There was no one I could talk to. I didn't think anyone could possibly understand my attachment to her. It was so unconventional, and I knew that anyone would tell me to run away from her and never look back. That was more easily said than done. Countless times I'd told my heart to rid its feelings of her and my mind to demolish thoughts of her, but they never cooperated with me. They only flip-flopped liked two sides of a possessed coin, but again, I would try.

I threw myself into my music and poetry, organizing compilations I'd made. I went out by myself to find distractions, figuring if I ignored my feelings long enough they'd go away. Adding a drink or two to my evenings made them fade out more quickly too, but when I looked in the mirror I saw self-destruction looking back at me. One night I couldn't even remember how I'd gotten home from a bar, but thanks to Olivia, even in a non-sober state, I didn't bring anyone back to my place for a one-night stand. Never again.

It was 3:00 in the morning when I broke down and added Jessie to my buddy list. *To hell with it.* I was lonely and depressed, and talking to her would make me feel better. Less than a minute after I added her to my list, I saw the icon next to her name light up. *She's online!* I felt a rush but kept it in check. While waiting for her to speak first, I checked my e-mail. Khedara had written me. Even though I knew how she'd react about the resurfacing of Jessie, I responded to her, telling her about everything, from Jessie to Olivia to Brianna.

I looked at a few message boards and then began searching for a porn site—hey I was lonely. That search frustrated me because I was too lazy and cheap to pay for any adult movies and got stuck looking at cheesy sites riddled with annoying pop-up advertisements. *How long is Jessie going to make me wait? I need her.* Seeing her available and fighting the urge to speak to her first was torturous.

A half an hour later, I got up to use the bathroom. I came back to see a dialogue box flashing back and forth between orange and gray. Jessie finally spoke, and like magic, my frustration vanished. My face softened with a smile.

<pre>
Jessie: i just wanted to say hi.
Sadira: Hello.
</pre>
There was a long silence.
<pre>
Jessie: so...
Sadira: Yes?
Jessie: ....you contacted me.
Sadira: That's what you wanted, right?
</pre>
As if I didn't already know it, my last statement reminded me of how I'd always given her what she wanted.
<pre>
Jessie: yes, i did want it.
Sadira: Why?
Jessie: because......
Sadira: Because what, Jessie?
</pre>

128

```
Jessie:     i guess i miss you.
Sadira:     What?
Jessie:     i miss you, Sadira.  i'm lonely.
            i hate to admit it, and can't
            believe that i am...but i've have
            turned over a new leaf.  i'm no
            longer hiding my feelings... i've
            been so alone without you......
```

What I needed to do was what she had done, turn over a new leaf and no longer act the way I used to. I needed to think rationally and abandon my misleading feelings. *You can do it, Sadira. Just get rid of her.* I talked to myself as if I were split in two, one half patient and the other half therapist. I knew I had a problem if I were still desiring her—a glutton for pain, but Jessie was encouraging me so it couldn't have been all in my head... or could it? I was confused.

```
Sadira:     I'm tired.  I'm going to go to
            bed.
Jessie:     *sighing* okay.
Sadira:     Bye.
```

I took note of how she typed her action within the asterisks, and then I logged out of the messenger but stayed online. *Who does she think she is? I like her nerve just trying to casually get close to me again. It's her fault we broke up. Miss me? Yeah, well good!* Instead of feeling sorry for myself for pining for Jessie, I channeled my thoughts into putting the blame on her. I'd rather be angry than a whining baby. I needed to build my self-esteem back up, and her confessing that she missed me was a helpful first step, at least I thought it was.

The next morning I gave myself a pep talk and rules to follow. I was going to go out and construct a social life. So what that Tricia and Brianna had left me, and Olivia was crazy. I had to meet new people.

My journal pages filled up quickly as I wrote my feelings down every night. The days passed slowly. I went out to bars and lounges, but they didn't help. Refusing to sleep with random strangers, Jessie kept penetrating my mind when I returned home alone. I felt like a smoker dying for a cigarette.

I logged onto the messenger on another evening and there she was again. Instead of talking about us, we talked about Jessie's mother, who was battling cancer. By the end of the conversation I felt numb. I was unmoved about her mother and unsure of what to think or do about Jessie. She wanted to be friends. "At least that much," she said. I acted like I wasn't interested, but I was. My longing for her was a quickly becoming a raging fire, consuming me. I needed a distraction so I went out to a lounge in Brooklyn.

It was there that I saw Tricia, with red eyes, sitting alone. *What happened to her?* I walked over to her. "Tricia, what's going on?"

She looked startled and didn't speak immediately.

"I didn't mean to startle you, but I can tell you've been crying. What happened?"

She shook her head negatively, not wanting to talk, but I sat down next to her anyway.

"Say something, Tricia." I didn't have much patience for silence. I needed to know what was going on with her.

"It's over," was all she mumbled.

After thinking about it for a few seconds, I assumed she was referring to a short-lived relationship.

I tried to give her a hug, but she pushed me away. "No. You can't do anything for me. You've already proven that."

What? There I was trying to console her and she told me to leave her alone. *Well, I'll be damned.* I stared at her for a few seconds. She was wearing a ginger colored fitted button-down shirt and black pants. *This might be an opportunity,* I thought. Tricia was a woman for whom it was worth getting my act together.

"Tricia, I'm not leaving you here like this."

"What do you care?" She looked me directly in the eyes.

"I care a lot." She could only use her hurt to fight me for so long. We didn't work out because I was honest, not because I'd betrayed her.

130

She just stared at me, pain piercing through her weighted brown eyes.

Just then a group of men came in. They were all loud, ugly, and vulgar. "Tricia, let's get out of here."

She looked over toward the guys who walked in and then back at me before getting her purse to leave. They looked like trouble. All I could hope was that we didn't run into any problems while walking by them. To my relief, they were too busy arguing with each other to notice us slip out behind them. Outside, it took me several minutes to hail a yellow taxi. Finally, one stopped. I gave the driver directions and settled into the back seat. It had started drizzling when we got in the car. "What happened with you, Tricia?"

"I walked in on the woman I was seeing…with a man."

Oh shit. "When? Where did all of this happen?"

"This morning. I went by her place because I thought I'd left my purse there and he answered the door. I asked who he was, and he said he was her husband. It hit me like a ton of fucking bricks. Apparently he had been away for some time and came home early to surprise her."

What a surprise.

Tricia continued speaking. "I wanted to beat the shit out of her, but what could I have done? He beat me to it. I stood there pissed off, hurt, and embarrassed. There was nothing I could do so I left."

"Damn."

"And that's not all. Before I left her street, I saw her husband throwing a half-dressed woman out of their place. I guess he caught them in bed."

"Geez." I knew my one-word responses weren't helping, but I had no clue what to say.

"I took today off from work and already called out tomorrow. I can't face anyone right now. I don't even know why I couldn't see that she was a liar. She came off so smooth, so sincere, so I don't know…just trustworthy. And I'm usually good at spotting bullshitters a mile away."

"Sometimes one always gets by you," I told her and then spoke to the driver. "It's the house coming up. Just stop by that black truck."

"Why are we at your apartment?" Tricia questioned.

"Because this is where I live. Would you rather go to yours?" It was late, freezing, rain had started coming down harder, and thunder shook the sky.

"No," she sighed. "I'm tired. Let's just go inside."

"Come on," I told her and she followed me.

I gave her a set of dry clothes and changed myself. Neither one of us had an umbrella, and the short time it took to get from the cab to my front door had us dripping wet. Once we settled on my couch, she cried for a little while. I held her, thinking that she wouldn't have been hurt if I'd taken her off the market sooner. Now I'd have to heal the damage someone else did if I really wanted her, and I did.

"At least I found out sooner rather than later," she said in between sniffles. "I'll be fine. I just need to take better care of my heart."

"What if you had help, Tricia?"

"What?"

I swallowed. "I'm saying..." *Do it.* "What if I said I wouldn't allow you to feel this way ever again?"

She looked at me and rolled her eyes. "How can I trust you when just months ago you said you were still in love with Jessie? This is too much too soon. I don't want to be bothered right now."

"Fine." I didn't want to press her but would bring it up again another time, because I wanted her and wasn't going to let her slip away this time. Not again. "All right."

We didn't talk much more that night. Tricia fell asleep before I did. It was a good thing too because my cell phone rang in my pocket. Even though I didn't recognize the number, I picked up and it was Jessie. I didn't remember giving her my number but realized it could have happened the night I was drunk and on the Internet with her. I couldn't recall anything we had said at that point and very well could have done something that stupid. Moving away and speaking in a whisper, I lied and told her I had a date and I would speak to her another time. She surprisingly acted as if it didn't bother her, and that was the end of that conversation. It affected me, but I ignored my feelings and coerced Tricia

132

to move from the couch to the bed to sleep comfortably. It took me a few minutes to wake her up, but she finally moved. I wondered how much she'd had to drink. She didn't appear drunk, but once she hit the bed she was out cold.

The next morning Tricia looked as if the sleep had helped her. Talking with her made me late for work, but I didn't care. I told her she could stay at my place until I got back if she wanted to, and she accepted the offer.

All day my mind kept racing back to Tricia. I wanted to be with her and couldn't wait to leave. Things at work were changing and everyone was in a sour mood. A number of people were fired to cut costs, and since some people had worked there for over 10 years, it didn't go over too well. A family-like environment had been forcefully broken up. None of the DJs or sound people were terminated, just some janitors, doormen, and secretaries.

I pulled Devonte' aside. "Hey, I'm bailing out of here, man."

"Where are you trying to rush off to?"

"Home."

"Why? Do you have some girl laid up waiting for you?"

"Not exactly." I cleared my throat. "I mean yes, but I wouldn't say it quite like that. She's not just some girl."

"A new one, Sadira?"

"No." I took sip from my glass. "Tricia."

His facial expression soured. "I thought you two broke up. She called me yesterday, but I didn't get a chance to call her back. What's going on?"

I didn't know if I should tell him her business or not. "She's going through some stuff right now. She's hurt, but it's *not* my fault. I'm just trying to pick up the pieces."

"What the hell you mean she's hurt? Damn it, now I feel bad for not calling her back sooner. Tell me what's going on, Sadira."

"Calm down, Devonte'. She's not physically hurt, but she found out that some chick she was seeing is actually married to a man. Tricia thought she forgot something at the woman's house and went back to get it, and he answered the door."

His eyes narrowed. "Did that motherfucker touch my cousin? Because if he did, I swear to God I'll…"

"No! I said she wasn't physically hurt. It's just her feelings."

"And what about you? What is she doing at your place if y'all broke up?"

"I ran into her at a bar last night and told her to leave with me. We didn't sleep together or anything like that, man. I care about her and didn't want her to be alone."

He looked as though he were trying to figure out if I was lying.

"Trust me. I've always had her best interest at heart, Devonte'. You know that."

"I know. I know. Let's go."

"Where?"

"To your apartment."

I didn't question him. Instead I got up and followed him out of the radio station.

On the train, he said that he knew if it were truly only her heart that was broken she'd be fine in time, but he wanted to see for himself that nothing was physically wrong with her. I assured him she was okay and told him that I thought I was ready for her, but now the timing seemed to be all messed up.

"I didn't even know she was seeing anyone after you."

"I don't know what to tell you. Neither did I."

Before he could say more, I saw Olivia's familiar face at the other end of the train. *Shit.* I tried not to make eye contact with her, but she saw me and walked over.

"Sadira, hi."

"Go away, Olivia."

Devonte' looked her up and down. He knew of her, but not what she looked like. She said nothing to him and proceeded to talk to me. Trying to ignore her didn't work. Then the train slowed to a stop in the tunnel. *Oh this is just great. Just freaking great!*

134

Aggravated, Devonte' glared at her before speaking. "Get the hell out of here!" he said loudly enough for other passengers to hear. He was generally an intimidating guy standing at 6'2" and 220 pounds of muscle.

"And who are you?" she asked. She rolled her eyes, dismissing him.

I saw him exhale to restrain himself.

"Olivia, enough of this shit. Go away, god damn it, just go **away**." I told her.

Olivia put her hand on my shoulder and my tolerance for her immediately went to zero. I turned around quickly and pushed her. "Look you crazy bitch, I told your ass there is no us. Do not call me. Do not think of me. I can't stand you. Back the fuck up, and don't touch me again unless you want to get your ass kicked, shit!" *Why do I always end up causing a scene with her?*

"Sadira!" She yelled.

"What?"

"Why are you doing this? That whore you were with last night doesn't want you. *I* love you."

What? I hadn't a clue as to what she was talking about. The train was moving again and wasn't far away from where Devonte' and I needed to get off.

"I know you hear me talking to you, Sadira."

I ignored her. I was sick of her. A bunch of people were staring at us and whispering. By then I was too angry to be embarrassed. I could feel sweat rolling down my back and building on my forehead. This kind of drama was the last thing I needed Devonte' to witness. *That whore you were with...* was she in the bar or was she hiding outside of my apartment? How did she know I was with someone or was she bluffing?

"Do you think I'm scared of him?" she asked motioning toward Devonte'. "I'm not afraid of him. You're really going to regret what you did to me." She tried to rush me, but she bumped into Devonte' and he held her back.

"The *only* reason you're not on the floor is because you're a woman." He held her wrist. "But I will shake you until your unborn kids

135

come out with a speech impediment if you don't knock this shit off!"
There was a thick vein bulging in his neck.

The train finally made it into the station. We got off, with everyone staring at us. Things were happening too fast. Devonte' let Olivia go and we walked out of the car, but that didn't get rid of her. She ran out just before the doors closed and took a swing at me. Quickly, I ducked and missed it. She lost her balance and fell on the platform.

"Stay the hell away from me, Olivia!"

She didn't get off the floor; she just stared at us.

"Come on, Devonte'." I was so annoyed.

He was fuming. "Sadira, you better fix that fucking problem. It took all of my strength not to smack that girl. Fix it!" He sounded more like a scolding father than a friend.

"I will. I will."

We walked up the stairs of the subway station. It wasn't until we exited the turnstiles that I realized we weren't even at the stop closest to my apartment. *Damn.* We went above ground and I hailed a cab home. A feeling of worry started to surface as we rode the short distance. Olivia was obviously psychotic. She was following me—she was stalking me!

"Which house?" The cab driver interrupted my thoughts.

"It's coming up on the right hand-side. You can stop right here." I paid him, and we got out of the car. Jasmine was sitting outside on her stoop. *Great, here's another crazy fool. I should hook her up with Olivia so they can stalk each other.* I walked by her without speaking.

I was disturbed by my run-in with Olivia and didn't know how things would play out inside with Devonte' and Tricia. However, Tricia wasn't there. Instead, there was a note saying she'd gone home around 1:00. *Thank you for getting me out of that bar last night. I don't know what I was thinking. I'll be fine soon. I just need a break from dating and some time alone. Thanks again, I appreciate it and am sorry I was nasty to you.* I stared at the note for a second before putting it back on my desk where she had left it. After I told Devonte' what it said, he looked relieved.

"I'm going over to check on her, Sadira. Good looking out."

I wanted to see Tricia too. Not only see her, I wanted to hold her and console her. I didn't want to run from my feelings anymore. I wanted Tricia, but I decided to let Devonte' go alone. I owed it to her not to confuse her at the moment and wanted her to know that I was coming straight from my heart, not lurking around for vulnerability. I was ready for her whenever she was ready for me. When I walked Devonte' to the door, I was horrified to see Olivia sitting on my stoop.

"Oh my God, Olivia this is fucking ridiculous now. What the hell are you doing here?"

She got up, looked at me, and smiled.

"Do you think this is a game?"

She laughed.

The bitch was scaring me.

I wasn't afraid of her physically, but I had no idea of how mentally disturbed she just might have been. She walked up a step closer to me, and Devonte' stood between us.

"Move, motherfucker this doesn't concern you." She glared at Devonte'.

He ran his hands over his head, took a deep breath and let out an exhausted laugh.

"Move!" She was no longer giggling or smiling.

Devonte' stood still. Smile erased. Jaws clenched.

"You, move!" I couldn't stand there and take her shit any more. I walked around Devonte' to face her. Fear or no fear, I needed to put her in her place. "*You* back up. *You* get off my damn stoop." My eyes locked on hers in a stare of pure hatred and disgust. I stood so close to her I could feel her breathing. "Leave," I said, spewing abhorrence and probably spit. "Leave, you crazy bitch!"

Jasmine walked outside and sat on her stoop like it was a fucking movie or something.

"I will not leave. No. Not until you apologize to me." Olivia pushed me.

A gust of frigid air passed over and chilled me to the bone, but I was so upset I remained focused on Olivia. "I'm not playing with you!" I shoved her back hard and she stumbled down the slippery steps, falling on the cold concrete. She got up and in my face. I pushed her again. "I told you to leave me alone. But you just keep fucking with me." Just as I was going to grab her by the neck, I felt Devonte' yank me back by the collar of my jacket.

"Don't do it, Sadira." He held me in place as she stared at me. "Keep your cool."

I wanted to choke her, but I felt like a dog on a leash they way Devonte' restrained me. "Stay the hell away from me, Olivia!"

"Oh, you've done enough, Sadira. You've done plenty!" Olivia flashed a deranged grin and slowly backed out of the gate.

"Why didn't you let me go, man?" I spoke to Devonte'.

"Because, Sadira. I know her type. It's better that you don't hit her."

"Whatever." I was pissed. I looked over to see Jasmine on her stoop looking like the mascot for El Pollo Loco with a bright orange and yellow outfit and a matching hat and gloves. "Take your bulging eyes off me. There's nothing to see here!"

Devonte' laughed. "Sadira, man I'm out of here. I'm going to see my cousin."

"All right."

"You be easy."

A glance in my mailbox revealed no mail, which I thought was strange since I only checked it once a week or so. *There's always something in there.* I brushed it off and went up to my apartment. I was exhausted and felt slight pains in my chest and had difficult breathing. Stress. I reached into my nightstand for my inhaler. It helped. If Olivia showed up again, I decided that I'd call the cops on her. I should have done that earlier, but it was too late at that point. Next time.

138

Chapter 14

A nightmare about Olivia, sitting in a giant moving tree, with binoculars woke me out of a snooze later that evening. I felt sweaty and clammy. The entire situation made me debate getting a restraining order against her. On one hand I felt as though it would be taking a punk way out, but on the other hand I really didn't want her just showing up whenever she felt like it. Who knew what her crazy self was capable of doing?

I got on the Internet to get more information about getting a restraining order against her and I saw that Brianna had logged online. I hadn't heard from her in a few weeks and accepted the fact that she would probably fade out of my life just as easily as she had come into it. My messenger status was set to invisible so she couldn't see me, and it didn't take me long to decide to leave it that way. She was sweet, but I felt it inside that our relationship wasn't meant to be long-term. Plus, there was no need to bring her back into my thoughts when I knew I wanted Tricia. I wasn't trying to play games. All I needed to do was kick Jessie out of my mind and I'd be set.

I got up to walk to the kitchen and I thought I heard tapping on my door. I was paranoid. After pouring myself a glass of water I went back to finding out about a restraining order. When I went to the website the search pulled up, I read a page describing how to obtain the order. A protective order, I learned, was the correct name. I downloaded the forms I needed and printed them out. I vowed to take care of that the next day. I hoped the judge would grant me an immediate order but wasn't sure. It was worth a shot.

I sat and stared at the paperwork for a while, wondering how I had gotten myself into this mess in the first place. *Careless sex. You live and you learn.* I didn't have the energy to reprimand myself.

I turned on the television. It was set to the Home and Garden Channel and I knew Tricia must have been watching it while I was at work. I restrained my impulse to call her. *Give her time.* I forced myself to wait so she wouldn't misinterpret my presence as taking advantage of her vulnerability. Before I could think too much about Tricia, I thought I heard a sound coming from my window but looked and saw nothing. Olivia had me on edge. Was I imagining things?

Both Tricia and Olivia consumed my thoughts at work the next day, and I could only halfway pay attention to Devonte's morning show. I wanted to get close to one and far away from the other. By the time my break came around, I couldn't take it anymore. I called Tricia but got her voicemail. Undeterred, I left her a message saying I wanted to see her that night. During a commercial break I pulled Devonte' aside.

"How was Tricia last night when you went over there?"

"She was crying off and on, but she'll be okay."

I didn't say anything immediately.

"Are you trying to get with her seriously now, Sadira? Make up your mind, and don't mess with her feelings."

"I've never messed with her feelings, D. All I did was protect them from me. It's not my fault someone else hurt her, but to answer your question, yes, I'm ready to step to her now. I want her."

He ran his hand over his mouth. "Look, I'm already in her business more than I would like to be, but I just have to say be sure that you're sure this time. I really don't want you pressing her right now, but if you're going to do it anyway, then be sure you're going to be good to her."

"I'm positive."

"Okay then."

"Hey, look I have to get out of here, but I'll catch up with you, all right?"

140

"See you," he replied.

I left the radio station wondering what my life would be like with Tricia as my exclusive girlfriend. Tons of ways to put a smile on her face crossed my mind. But before I could get to any of that, I had to get the protective order against Olivia. She had left several messages on my voicemail saying how she was going to pay me back and I'd be sorry for hurting her. *See what people like you need to know is that everyone isn't like you. You can't just use somebody and expect them to take it as a part of life. You're stuck with me, Sadira!* I saved all of her messages so that I could prove she was harassing me. Since I got off work before the close of normal business hours, I had time to go to the courthouse to file the paperwork.

When I got there, however, I was disappointed to learn that I couldn't obtain an order. I had misunderstood the forms that I saw online, and was told the only way I could get one was to press criminal charges against Olivia. I sighed. Pressing charges was farther than I wanted to go, so I decided against it. I left, annoyed at the system, and went to the gym before going home. There was a message from a realtor on my home voicemail. With so much going on I'd forgotten that I had requested to be contacted. I decided to return his call after trying to reach out to Tricia one more time. I couldn't wait any longer to speak with her. This time she answered.

"Where are you?" I asked.

"I'm still at work, why?"

"I want to see you tonight. Let me come over, Tricia." God, I sounded desperate. "Please."

She didn't respond right away.

"Tricia?"

"I'm here."

"So how are you feeling? Can I come by tonight?" I kept trying.

"I'm fine. A little better but not at all back to normal."

"What about my other question?"

She spoke softly. "You can come over."

"Seriously?"

141

"Yes."

A big smile crossed my face. "What time should I come? When are you leaving work?"

"I'm actually going to leave now. I was only working late because I didn't want to go home and be alone."

"You sound like you need a hug."

"I need more than that. I need a break from liars, cheaters, and lunatics."

Tell me about it, I thought, after hearing her last reference. I would have to tell her about Olivia soon too. "All right, I'll let you go now. I'll give you a call when I'm on my way over."

"Okay. See you later."

Flowers. I should bring her flowers, I thought after hanging up. The problem was that there were no damn flowers for sale in my neighborhood. If I were lucky, I could buy some cheap corner store roses, but that wasn't what I wanted to give her so I took the train to a real florist and spent $65 on a dozen yellow roses.

When I finally got home, I showered, brushed my teeth, and changed into a fresh set of clothes. I was ready to see Tricia. She had been floating around in my thoughts all day, and I found myself even reaching for her—not physically, but mentally and emotionally. I craved her. Oddly enough it reminded me of the hunger that I'd had for Jessie so long ago. *Don't think about Jessie right now.* I picked up the phone to let Tricia know I would be there in a half an hour.

"Okay, I'll look out for you," she told me.

She was surprised to see me show up with the roses, and I was glad I had decided to get them.

"Thank you." Her smile came naturally, almost as a sign of relief that I was there. "Come inside."

I followed her in and thought about making myself comfortable on her couch as she put the vase on her dining room table, but I stood still instead. There was a tissue box on the small end table next to me, and two laundry bags in a corner. I walked up to her and asked for a hug.

"I'm sorry the place is kind of a mess."

142

"Shh. I don't care about that. Give me a hug," I persisted. That was all I wanted—to feel her in my arms and nothing more.

She gave in. I could feel her hot tears trickling onto my shoulder and melting on my skin. Running my hands carefully up and down her back, I tried my best to comfort her. After a few minutes we released each other and walked over to her couch. I was still fumbling for words. What can you tell a person whose heart has been broken, besides the trite *everything will be okay*? I wished I'd never let her go. "Tricia, I'm so sorry you're hurting right now. I really am." My thoughts gave me guidance.

She didn't say anything.

"And if I could go back in time, I would have never let you go. I would have kept you as my own and cherished you the way I want to do now. I..." I swallowed and moved closer to her.

"What are you telling me?"

Taking her hand, I said, "I want to pick these pieces up and make sure you never feel this way again."

She looked away. "I can't take this right now."

"You need this right now. You need me. You've always wanted me, but now more than ever you *need* me. And I'm here for you." The words were flowing out of my mouth before I could think about what I was saying. I wiped the single tear that was rolling down her cheek. "Give us a try." I hoped I didn't come off arrogantly.

She shook her head negatively.

"Please?" It was time to plead. "You can't tell me that you don't still have feelings for me."

"No, I can't say that, but I can say that I don't want what's left of my heart to be shattered again."

"Come on now, I've always looked out for your heart. Don't go being afraid of me now, Tricia. I know you've been hurt, but trust me; I can take care of you."

Her eyes told me that she believed me but was still afraid. I didn't say anything else and waited for her to speak again when she was ready.

When I heard her voice, she looked me directly in the eyes. "Let's just take it slow. I don't know what I want right now, but I do need a friend—a familiar one."

"I'll be your friend," I told her and kissed her on her forehead. "When you need someone to talk to, just call me. Even if you only want company to escape loneliness, all you have to do is let me know and I'll come to you wherever you are. I promise."

She smiled, and I returned one of my own. She opened up. "I just feel stupid, you know? I've never been played before."

"We're all a fool for someone else at some point in our lives."

"Yeah, I guess."

"Hey, at least you didn't invest years with this chick."

"I wish I could have invested an ass whooping to teach her a lesson."

I laughed. "You're too cute to be fighting. And you're too old too."

"I know. I know, but still." She leaned closer so I could put my arm around her.

All I wanted was to be around Tricia, take things at whatever pace she felt comfortable, and work towards building a relationship with her. I had hope, and I really thought we would work if given an honest chance.

Chapter 15

Tricia and I saw each other over the next couple of days. I loved being around her and also saw that being with her cheered me up. She always followed through when she said she was going to call or meet me somewhere and I appreciated that. I was so glad she gave me another chance that I pretty much had a surprise for her every time I saw her. Flowers, a poem, a love letter, a puzzle that read something special when put together; I was creatively romantic to make her days memorable. I still thought about Jessie every night, but not as much as I did when I was spending my evenings alone.

The good buildup with Tricia was unfortunately brought to a screeching halt one morning when the police came knocking at my door. Olivia had pressed charges against me and the detectives came to get my side of the story. Apparently they had already spoken to Jasmine, whose story was in line with Olivia's. Lies. She said that *I* had picked a fight with her, pushed her down the stairs, and caused her to bang her head on the concrete. I told them what really happened and informed them that I had a witness of my own.

"She's been stalking me for a while now," I said. "I can prove it. I have a lot of messages of her harassing me on my voicemail. Yes, we got into an argument, but I didn't assault her. I was defending myself."

When I finished saying what I had to say, they still asked me to go to the precinct with them.

"Why? I didn't do anything wrong." I was scared.

145

"We just want to ask you some more questions."

I cooperated, putting on my coat and hat before following them to the police car and getting in. I wanted to cry as I sat there behind the plexiglass divider feeling like a caged animal. Everything felt so surreal. Sweat began to stream down my face and stomach. The only noise was chatter coming from the police radio. Looking out the window, I saw so many people going on with their normal lives. Crossing streets, going in and out of stores, laughing, smiling, waiting for buses, I paid close attention to the normalcy I always took for granted. I couldn't believe the situation I was in.

At the precinct, I was told that I could call my lawyer if I had one. I didn't have one. I never needed one. For the next forty-five minutes the detectives questioned me, asking me about my past, if I'd ever had charges pressed against me, misdemeanors, or anything that had involved the police. I told them *no*. Never. One detective kept firing questions at me without giving me a chance to respond. She was pissing me off. I tried not to lose my temper, but she kept hassling me!

"No, damn it. I told you that I've never been in fucking trouble before!" I banged my fist on the table, accidentally knocking over the cup of water I'd been given. It spilled on the officer who was interrogating me and onto the floor, but I didn't apologize to her. Fuck her. "This is some bullshit."

"It is," she said, and then told me I was under arrest.

"What!" I couldn't fucking believe it. The bitch had deliberately pissed me off! "Under arrest? No, no, I was just…" I tried to take my anger back but I couldn't. I didn't know if she was having a bad day or what, but I was stuck. She read me my rights and cuffed me. I was under arrest for assaulting Olivia. *What a load of shit*, I thought. The officer arrested me because I pissed her off. She knew it and I knew it, but I didn't want to aggravate her anymore. Now in cuffs, I kept my mouth shut.

The next thing I knew I had been fingerprinted, photographed, and given a number before being put in a holding cell. I fought back tears and rage. Jail. I was in fucking jail thanks to Olivia! There were a two other women in the small cell. I wanted to call Tricia so badly but I couldn't do so until the police allowed me to. I had to sit there with a couple of real criminals. One woman smelled like piss and pickles. She was ashy, had nappy hair, and was wearing dingy undershirt, a too-tight jean skirt, and a raggedy pair of flip-flops. I just wanted to die. *What in the fuck did I do that was so wrong to land me here?* I kept to myself, and hoped no one bothered me. If anyone did, I decided that I might just have to act crazy to get rid of them—just start talking to myself or something stupid like that. I didn't know. I'd do anything to be left alone. I wasn't trying to make any friends or talk to anyone. I wanted to go home.

At some point I did get to make a phone call to Tricia. I got her voicemail and gave her the short version of what happened. It felt awful to say where I was. It felt worse to know that she couldn't call me back, and I didn't know when or if I'd be able to make another call.

Hours later, I was transferred to Central Booking in downtown Brooklyn. They took all of my personal belongings and put me in a cell with a lot more people in it. My palms were sweaty, my head was aching, and my nerves were going crazy. And if that wasn't bad enough, Mrs. Pissy Pickles was smiling at me. *Oh my God!!!* I had to get out of there!

When my arraignment finally came up, an officer took me out of the cell, cuffed me, and led me to the courtroom. I was beyond relieved to see that there was a Legal Aid representative there to help me. I pleaded not guilty and the representative was able to convince the judge to release me on my own recognizance. The judge, however, still issued a temporary protective order against me for Olivia, as if I wanted to be anywhere near her! A court date was set and I was brought back to the cell in handcuffs until I was entered in the system. Finally, about an hour later I was free to go. They gave me back my belongings and I saw that Tricia had called my cell phone three times.

Chapter 16

That whore you were with doesn't want you. Olivia's voice ricocheted in my head. I called Tricia back and told her I was on my way to see her. She kept asking me to tell her what had happened, but I didn't want to discuss all of my business in the back of a cab.

"I'll be there soon, baby."

"Hurry up!"

"Okay. Okay." I hung up.

How was I supposed to explain all of this without freaking her out? After everything she'd been through with the last person she had been seeing I knew she didn't need to deal with *my* drama! When she opened the door, her eyes were full of questions.

"Come in," she beckoned, and I did. We sat down on the couch. "What is going on, Sadira?"

"I was going to tell you about her sooner."

"Who? Why were you in *jail*?"

"It's this girl named Olivia. I was talking to her a while ago. I realized that it wasn't going anywhere and broke things off."

"And?"

"And she's crazier than a motherfucker! She's been stalking me. And I think she has seen me with you."

"What?"

148

I told her everything.

"Did you see her today?" she asked when I finished.

"No. I don't know how she looked when she went to the precinct, and though she did fall on the ground, she didn't bang her head on the concrete like she told the cops. At this point I know she's crazy enough to inflict pain on herself and say I did it."

"Is she too crazy to know that *I* will inflict pain on her if she doesn't leave you alone?" Tricia was pissed.

"But Devonte' was there and he saw everything. Yeah, Devonte' was a witness, but so was lying ass Jasmine, my next door neighbor. According to the police, her story agrees with what Olivia said. They're lying about me."

Tricia sighed. "So what happens now?"

"I have to go to court. And baby, I know we just got back together and this is a lot to ask," I paused, "but will you come with me?"

"Yes," she said.

I hugged her. "Thank you."

"You're lucky I never stopped loving you," she said and kissed my neck. "Otherwise I wouldn't put up with this at all. You know that, right?"

I smiled. "Yes, I know."

Leaning back, she looked at me and shook her head. "How did you get yourself into this? Jail, Sadira? God."

"I-" Damn, I didn't want to answer that question, but I did anyway. "I was careless, Tricia. For the first time in my life I just did what I felt like doing without thinking of another person's feelings. I did it to the wrong person."

"Mm, hm."

"So you're sure you'll you go to court with me?"

"Yes. And I'll help you find a lawyer too. Maybe Josh can help you. He's a criminal lawyer. You'll need one to get out of this."

"Thanks."

"You're welcome. Come here," she said, and I did.

We shifted positions so that she was stretched out on the couch, and I lay on top of her kind of curled up, resting my head on her stomach. "I'm hungry. What do you have to eat in the kitchen?"

"Not much, I haven't gone grocery shopping lately. Shit, I haven't even washed the dishes. This place is a mess."

"You don't have any leftovers or anything? I haven't really eaten all day." I looked up at her.

"Right. You were locked up." She smirked. "There's a little lasagna from my order last night. Do you want that?"

"Sure," I said and laughed.

"Okay, I'll get it for you, but why don't we just lay here for a few minutes like this? It's comfortable."

"It is." As I lay on her, I closed my eyes and relaxed. In the midst of silence the only movement was the slight up and down of her abdomen as she breathed. It felt good to be close to her—really good. Tricia soothingly ran her hand over my head. At that moment I really appreciated her more than ever.

I couldn't wait to get the hearing over with and pick up the pieces of my life to move on with Tricia. Besides Olivia, there was only one person I needed to get rid of, and that was Jessie. A part of me unfortunately enjoyed her attention. I knew I should just tell her not to contact me anymore, but I kept procrastinating about doing it. I told myself to get rid of one person at a time, with the first one being Olivia. She was more of a pain in the ass.

When I finally got around to calling the post office to find out about my missing mail, I was informed that a change-of-address request had been filled out. But because of a privacy act I couldn't get any more information over the phone and would have to go to the post office with ID to straighten things out. *Olivia, the fucking nuisance.* It had to be her. I was told, however that a confirmation of the request should have been sent to me.

After hanging up, I went to the local post office to fix things and sure enough when I returned home I saw the confirmation notice in my

150

box. My mail was being sent to the Bronx—to Olivia's home. I showed the notice to my lawyer and played the messages for her too. Josh couldn't help me, but he referred me to a colleague of his. It was when I met with her that I saw pictures of Olivia with a big knot on her head, a bruised up face, and a fat lip. She looked a hurt mess all right, but I didn't do it. My lawyer told me that though I had the confirmation for my mail being forwarded, it would be hard to admit as evidence because we couldn't prove that Olivia did it.

"Even though it's going to her address?" I asked.

"You would think it's that easy, but unfortunately it's not."

I was disappointed. Even worse, without voice analysis, Olivia's phone messages were going to be tenuous evidence because she never said her name in them. Though my lawyer said to trust her, suddenly things just didn't look too good for me.

Chapter 17

On my court date, Tricia had taken the afternoon off to be with me. Devonte' promised he'd meet us there. On the way, I noticed a difference in Tricia's demeanor. She had on a charcoal pantsuit that complemented her body very well. Each thread seemed to be sewn together to fit her perfectly. It wasn't as though I'd never her seen her dressed for business before, but there was something different about her aura that I couldn't put my finger on. I dressed in a pantsuit as well.

At the courthouse, the elevator ride stopped on the second floor and a couple of men got on. They smiled at Tricia, but she didn't respond. On the next floor, a fat guy wearing a plaid shirt and dark pants and sporting uncombed hair walked on whistling. The elevator stopped two more times and the chubby man whistled during the entire ride. *What an irritating asshole.* I and sighed loudly. My nerves were getting the best of me.

When we finally got off, I saw Olivia walking in another direction. Tricia and I proceeded to the room in which the hearing was being held. My attorney was already there. Olivia didn't come inside until a few minutes later and I didn't see Jasmine or Devonte' at all. A few minutes went by before our case began.

After the jury was picked and formalities were finally over with, our lawyers made their opening statements and it was time for the witnesses to be called to the stand. Olivia went first and told her side of the story, totally omitting the incident on the train. She pretty much lied from start to finish about what really happened, sticking to her tale when my attorney cross-examined her. She was a great actress. The same couldn't be said for Jasmine though. She was called after Olivia stepped down.

"Yes I was there. I saw the whole thing." She lied. Jasmine didn't come outside until after Olivia and I were already arguing.

"Will you tell me the events that occurred that day?" The prosecutor continued.

Jasmine barely spoke any truth. She made it seem as though I went crazy on Olivia, hitting her and pushing her down the steps onto the concrete. She told them that she thought I was on medication or needed medication because I was shaking.

"Thank you. Is the person who assaulted Olivia in the courtroom today?" asked the prosecutor.

"Yes." Jasmine pointed at me. "Her, in the blue shirt."

I bit my bottom lip to suppress anger. After they were finished, my attorney began to cross-examine her. "So, Ms. Jackson, you say that you saw everything?"

"Johnson. My last name is Johnson." She seemed annoyed at my lawyer immediately.

"Of course. What is your relationship to my client, Ms. Johnson?"

"She's my next door neighbor."

"Are you two friends?"

"No. I mean, we *may* say hello in passing, but I would not call her a friend," she paused, her right hand nervously tapping the stand. "Sadira irritates me."

"Thank you. So could it be that you are testifying today not as an honest witness, but as someone trying get back at Sadira for…irritating you?"

A gentleman in the jury cleared his throat.

"No," Jasmine responded. Her face showed slight signs of anxiousness.

What a dummy, I thought. The questioning went on in a manner that took a blow at Jasmine's credibility. She fell into my attorney's trap and began to look stupid on the stand. She responded emotionally rather than staying calm.

"Was it cold that day, Ms. Johnson?"

"What?"

"The weather. You know, the temperature. Was it cold outside that day?"

"Yeah, it was. Of course it was cold. It's winter."

"So is it possible that my client was not shaking in the manner of nervousness, but just cold?"

"I guess." She sighed.

"Generally speaking, do you tend to remember things better right after they happen or after a few months have passed?"

"Um, right after things happen. I mean, whose memory wouldn't be fresh right after something happened? Yes. But I also have a good long-term memory..." Jasmine's eyebrows furrowed as she rambled on. The jury took it all in, glancing at me and glancing at her.

"So would you agree that what you told the police on the day of the incident in question was the truth?" My attorney continued.

"Yes."

"Did you tell the truth today?"

"Yes."

"Was what you said today the same as you told the police regarding the day in question?"

She thought. "Yes!" Her eyes widened as she exclaimed her answer. You'd have thought she was on the Price is Right game show. Jackass.

"No further questions."

When my attorney was done questioning Jasmine the judge allowed her to step down. The police officer who took Olivia's complaint took the stand next. The questioning of the officer was brief on both sides. It was then that the photographs of Olivia came into play. The cop confirmed that that was how Olivia looked when she came in to press charges.

After the police officer's testimony, Devonte', who had finally

154

arrived, was called next.

"Mr. Parks, on the day in question, did you see the defendant?" asked Olivia's lawyer when it was his turn to question Devonte'.

"Yes." He looked the attorney in the eyes.

"Where?"

"At work. We work together, and on that day I went home with her. We also have mutual friends."

"Have you ever had a romantic relationship with the defendant?"

"Negative. Absolutely not."

I found his answer humorous despite the seriousness of the courtroom. I was pleased with how it went with him though. When Olivia's attorney tried to reverse his words, Devonte' listened carefully, corrected him, and kept his composure. Devonte' was patient and clear when most would have been eager and perhaps displayed difficulty while trying to expressing themselves.

"Your Honor, if I'm supposed to tell the truth then it requires more than just yes or no," he said after Olivia's lawyer tried to force a one-word answer out of him.

After thinking for a moment, the judge allowed Devonte' to fully explain what he saw. Devonte' told the court that the drama began before we even got to my house and how Olivia was on the train harassing me. After Devonte' stepped down, I was asked if I wanted to take the stand. Legally, I was told, I didn't have to. But I wanted to, and I told the truth.

"I even have most of the messages she left on my phone, Your Honor. She's left numerous messages saying that I'm going to pay, and that I haven't heard the last of her, not to mention she's been following me around and lurking in the shadows outside of my residence at night. I'm telling you, this woman is unstable." I decided to give my evidence a shot anyway.

Olivia interrupted me. "That is untrue, Your Honor. I only asked her to apologize to me! She has been stalking *me*!"

The judge pushed his glasses up. "Ms. Bartlette, please. Let Ms. Cooper finish. You've had your turn."

Bingo. She admitted to leaving messages. Well, sort of. Olivia gave me a dirty look as I continued to speak. "*She* is lying. On the recordings that I have she is harassing me. I feel threatened by her. I don't know if she's sitting in front of my house with a butcher knife or peeping through my window. I—"

"That's not true!" Olivia interrupted me again.

"Ms. Bartlette!" The judge warned. "Need I remind you that this is a court of law? One more outburst like that and I will hold you in contempt! Are we clear?" The judge raised an eyebrow and gave Olivia an intimidating glare.

"Yes, Your Honor." Olivia was beet red with rage. I fought the urge to smile at the fact that she was not able to control the situation.

"Objection, Your Honor," injected Olivia's attorney. "Not only is the defendant's response leading to speculation, it's irrelevant."

"Sustained. And please control your client. Now," the judge turned his attention to my lawyer, "were these recordings admitted as evidence?"

My attorney told him that they were not and then requested that the evidence be admitted and the judge allowed them! The judge then looked directly ahead and spoke. "For the record of the court, this will be exhibit A for the defendant."

"Objection, Your Honor." Olivia's attorney interrupted again, complaining about the evidence was inadmissible.

"Overruled. Objection noted. I want the jury to hear this."

The bailiff took the mini recorder and walked it over to the court clerk for identification. He then gave it to the judge who pressed play. Immediately, Olivia's voice came from the recorder. "You're not going to get away with this. You think you can sleep with me and then throw me away like I'm nothing? You're going to pay, Sadira! You're going to pay!" The recording went on with more messages Olivia had left.

My attorney pressed stop and began questioning me. "When were these messages left?"

"On various days over the past five months. As you can see, I am not the one stalking her. She has been threatening me non-stop!" Disgust

156

spilled out of my voice. I was getting angry again but held it in.

"No further questions, Your Honor." My attorney was shutting me up.

After being cross-examined, I stepped down and my lawyer was allowed to recall Olivia to the stand.

When asked about the recordings, Olivia admitted, "Ok, I did leave those messages. Clearly, that is my voice. But, those were left after the FIRST time we were intimate!"

"Exactly how many times were you intimate?"

"*Lots.*" She spoke matter-of-factly. "We were in a relationship for a month or so more recently. Those messages were left before we began a relationship. But back then I was upset because she was ignoring me. We later made up and started spending a lot of time together."

This can't be real.

Olivia continued telling her story without so much as a stutter. "Once I started noticing disturbing behavior patterns in her, I started to rethink our relationship. She would get very violent in bed, so I decided to leave her and then she became my worst nightmare!" Tears began streaming down her cheeks.

I can't believe this!

She wasn't even finished speaking. "She's been showing up everywhere I go and watching me. She's only doing this to try to hurt me. She knows I'm no threat to her. She's a threat to me!" She wiped her face with her hands and sniffled.

The judge motioned to the bailiff to give her a tissue and he did. A woman in the jury who previously looked unmoved by Olivia's testimony suddenly looked concerned.

What is this? Why are they sympathizing with her? I'm the one in danger here! I wanted to know why they were even letting her go on with the charade. I wanted to interrupt and tell them how everything she was saying was an outright lie. But I remembered how upset the judge got at Olivia for interrupting me, so I decided to remain quiet. I'm sure a flawless picture of disbelief was displayed on my face. Members of the jury looked glanced at me. One woman, middle-aged and thin with wavy

157

dark hair, looked sympathetic while others appeared indifferent. A younger woman looked thoroughly entertained at my expense. She had to know Olivia's testimony was a lie. I was sure at least *one* of them had to deal with someone who was a nuisance.

"Do you have anything else you'd like to add, Ms. Barlette?" the judge asked.

"Just that I am a very sincere person and just want to be left alone by Sadira. I've moved on and so should she. This whole thing is unnecessary," Olivia managed to say through her sniffles.

My skin had turned hot and my stomach tightened with anger. "Everything she just said is lie. She's crazy!" I exclaimed, not being able to hold myself back any longer.

"See, Your Honor? She is the one with the horrible temper!" Olivia pointed at me.

"Sadira." My lawyer looked at me with disapproval.

"That's enough! Both of you!" the judge demanded.

After my outburst, I stopped paying attention for a few moments. I snapped back to reality when my attorney asked the judge to dismiss the case, but the motion was denied. Both attorneys made their closing arguments and Olivia's lawyer had the last word. It was finally down to the wire and up to the jury. I paced while waiting for them to deliberate, hoping they'd see that Olivia was a lying lunatic and that I was the real victim. I wanted my record expunged and I wanted a protective order against *her!*

My palms were sweaty when it was time to hear the verdict. I knew in my mind that I should be found not guilty, but Olivia's theatrics could have either worked for or against me. Seconds felt as if they were dragging by. When it was time, my attorney and I stood up and the jury foreman started speaking. I tapped my fingers against the table in anticipation. My ears perked up when I heard, "…finds the defendant not guilty."

Yes! I won the case. Olivia gave me a disgusted stare and turned to walked out. *Good riddance.* I saw her exchange fierce glances with Tricia, but they exchanged no words. I gave my attorney a firm handshake, thanked her, and got ready to leave.

"Let's get out of here," I told Tricia and Devonte'. By the time Tricia and I got back to her place I felt drained. Tricia's expression was unreadable though she asked me questions.

"Everything Olivia said about you was untrue, right?" She needed to be reassured that everything Olivia said was a lie.

"Of course. You can't really believe I'm violent, Tricia. I was just angry and fed up with her in there. I was never overly aggressive."

"And you two never had a relationship?"

"Hell no."

"All right," she answered in a voice that warned if she found out it were a lie, I'd be in trouble.

I just wanted Olivia to be gone for good this time.

Chapter 18

After things with Olivia were finally laid to rest, I felt better. She had been a nuisance in my life for far too long. I got an order of protection against her and got my mail situation fixed.

Tricia and I got closer. If she wasn't at my apartment on the weekends, then I was at hers. We talked to each other every day and even hung out a few more times with Warren and Josh. Eventually I gave her a section of my closet. We were having a good time with each other and building permanent memories. I don't think I'd ever smiled so much in my life than when I was with Tricia, but there was one problem, Jessie.

I was ashamed to admit that I had never cut off the *just friends* status with Jessie. With so many other things going on that limited my times talking to Jessie, I never bothered to cut her off completely as I'd told myself I would do after Olivia. The week after my trial, Tricia had to travel on business and I wanted someone to talk to. Jessie was available when Tricia wasn't. I told her all about the drama and eventually the conversation turned to us, Jessie and me. All of the feelings that we had never actually spoken to each other were finally put out in the open. Like our early days, we chatted online via instant messenger and caught up with what we were doing, seeing, and feeling.

As she poured her heart out to me about how she felt after our breakup, thoughts of her began to overpower me. It felt as though all of the feelings that I'd been trying to either bury or rid myself of returned with the force of an avalanche. Bits and pieces of our conversations stuck out in my mind long after I signed off the Internet.

> *Jessie: sometimes i thought i saw you in the corner when i turned my head too fast. the worst were the clothes and bed linens that smelled like you no matter how many times i washed them. i had to burn that stuff. the flames still didn't help the way i felt because i knew deep down it was my fault.*

Indeed it was her fault we ended the way we did, but it was my error for us allowing us to last as long as we did. Chatting with Jessie again made pain and pleasure indistinguishable. I knew I wasn't truly over her, but I didn't want to wait around forever, so I moved forward with Tricia.

She made me remember the woman in Miami, how I lusted after and even kissed her. I recalled the feeling of drowning agony that I experienced the night I found out Jessie had slept with her.

While I was sickened with Jessie for what she had done, I was still glad she had come back. I didn't know why. All I knew was that I was smack in the middle of an emotional storm. I was still entangled in Jessie's world, but I refused to let her get in the way of my relationship with Tricia. As a matter of fact, I told her about it. Jessie didn't make it obvious that she was bothered. Instead, she told me about some girl named Lisa that she'd started seeing about a month before we ran into each other. *Since we'd both moved on...we could just be friends.* At least that's what she suggested and I went along with it. Jessie didn't seem to be a threat to my developing relationship with Tricia, so I didn't bother to tell Tricia at all. Jessie remained in the background, invisible as far as Tricia was concerned.

The night before Tricia's birthday, she'd planned a surprise for *me.* I was so busy trying to make sure she had a great birthday, I didn't notice that she had a little plan of her own. I'll never forget that weekend.

We went out to the Four Seasons restaurant for dinner. Tricia had told me that she'd made reservation weeks before. It took her a little over two hours to get ready. I was getting impatient waiting for her until I saw her. She looked stunning in a ruby full-length satin dress accented by a thin necklace that had a small heart pendant on it and a dainty white gold watch that had tiny diamonds in it. Her make-up was soft and gave her a glow. Everything thing was beautiful, her eyes, her lips, her skin…she looked gorgeous. I wore a tailored black pantsuit that I'd bought some time ago but had never gotten a chance to wear. Tricia gave me a manicure and persuaded me to wear light make-up. We both looked very feminine in our own comfortable way.

Tricia and I were blown away by the romantic ambiance in the restaurant. From the moment we were escorted to our table, I was in awe. We were seated near a white marble pool, beneath a canopy of trees. I even drank wine that night. Everything from the food to the service was topnotch. We enjoyed each other's conversation and savored moments when our eyes locked and stared in a loving gaze. My stomach tingled with excitement and my skin warmed to the pleasure of our date. I felt *loved.* I began to appreciate the culture to which Tricia exposed me. Everything that I was used to was average compared to what I did with her.

After dinner, we were chauffeured over to a theater to see "Beauty and the Beast" on Broadway. Tricia had secured a car for the entire night. It was my first time going to a Broadway show and I was captivated by this timeless story of a developing love.

When the show was over, I used Tricia's pocket-sized digital camera to take a couple of photos of her and she took some of me while we were near Times Square. Our driver offered to shoot us together, which allowed us to really get good pictures and capture the evening. I was on a natural high. The evening was one I never wanted to forget. And the best part about it was that it was only the beginning of my life with her. As our date wound down and we were on our way back home, I said flat out, "Tricia, I'm so in love with you."

For the longest time, I'd told her how much I cared and looked forward to seeing or talking to her, but I'd dodged the L word. I couldn't deny it anymore. I'd fallen in love and was scared to death. There were butterflies in my stomach.

She beamed. "I love you too. I've loved you for a while now, Sadira."

We were silent for a few moments after my revelation, as the driver carefully drove through the busy streets. For a second I remembered the first time we'd had a serious talk in the back of a car. Only then it was about sex and this time it was about love. True love. Unsure of what to say next, I took a sip from the bottled water provided by the car service.

Eventually the driver stopped in front of Tricia's home. I was feeling so…so unlike I'd ever felt with anyone else before. Inside Tricia's apartment, I pulled out the camera again. I loved her in the dress she was wearing.

"Pose for me," I said. "I want to save every bit of this night." I took a lot of pictures until she finally stopped me so she could set the timer to take another photograph of us together. I hugged her from behind as we smiled for the camera.

"All right. I think we have enough for one night," she said and smiled. "Plus my feet are starting to hurt and I want to get out of these shoes."

"What? I love those shoes. You should wear them to bed."

She laughed out loud. "Bed? You are insane!"

"Hey, I like your shoes."

"And you get overly excited every time I wear a pair of sexy heels. Hmm…"

I chuckled. *Dang, maybe I have a fetish.* I laughed at myself. "Okay, okay. Let's change into something comfortable and I'll give you a foot massage." *Ha! She's right.*

I rubbed her feet and then massaged her entirely. I appreciated every inch and sophisticated detail of her body, and I did it slowly. Tricia had set the mood with a playlist of love songs. With my eyes closed and our raw emotions being exchanged through the passionate colliding of our bodies, I felt as though the planets were perfectly aligned. Everything was in my favor. As soulful music swept through the room, every kiss and touch that I shared with Tricia took me to another euphoric height. Our passions seemed to stretch time. Hours after we climaxed we stayed up talking until the sun crept into the sky. It was her birthday.

I went into the living room to get her gift out of my bag and returned to the bedroom. "Here you go."

Her eyes widened when she tore the paper off and opened the long box. "Wow."

"So…" I'd bought her a bracelet.

"It's beautiful, Sadira." She stared at it and smiled endlessly. "Thank you, baby."

Our bodies got the best of us once the gift excitement died down. We bundled up under her thick comforter and drifted off despite the bright sunlight peeking through her blinds.

The next week went by quickly and before we knew it we were at a party at Warren and Josh's place. There were at least five other couples there and everyone was having a good time. They had food catered and Warren was the bartender as usual. Janae' wasn't there, which was a relief. I didn't know if she and Jessie had gotten in contact again, but that would have made the night uncomfortable for me. I hadn't spoken to Jessie in two weeks and was quite okay with that. Tricia was keeping me very happy and I hoped things would continue that way.

Laughter filled the room. Warren was the life of the party, as he always seemed to be. Every story he shared had the words, "Ooh, chile I was good and liquored up that night. Let me tell you…" We all had a great time though. I didn't drink too much that night, because I wanted to remember it. Tricia and I clung to each other so much that others commented on how in love we looked. Love felt great.

Chapter 19

Devonte' and I didn't have nearly as many after-work lunches since we'd both gotten serious with our significant others. I thought about Tricia all the time. She made me smile and want to tell the world about her. *I ought to e-mail Khedara and see how she's doing with her boyfriend.* Since Tricia and I had gotten so close, the time I spent online had been cut in half. My sister and I did talk by phone sometimes to fill in the gaps. She knew about everything with Olivia and my progressing relationship with Tricia. *I'll log online tonight.*

Tons of e-mail, mostly junk, littered my inbox when I finally sat down to check my messages, but there was one note from my sister and another from Jessie. In fact, Jessie was online. It took me a half an hour to get through all of the mail I had. Everything I wanted to know about Khedara's life was written in her e-mail. She was doing great and was very happy. I smiled. She was considering staying in Bermuda because she loved it there so much. "You've got to come visit me," she said. I definitely wanted to.

I sent her a long message to catch her up on my life and then opened Jessie's e-mail, but it didn't say anything; it was just blank. *Maybe she recalled the message after sending it out?* I saw that she was still online and logged into an instant messenger but didn't speak to her. Instead, I visited a couple of message boards to see if anyone had responded to the stuff I had last posted. There were a few comments from members and two anonymous comments that praised my work. Still, my

eyes kept shifting to the icon next to Jessie's name...*available*. She soon
spoke to me.

```
Jessie:    hey you...
Sadira:    Hi.
Jessie:    i listened to some of your
           poems...it was interesting to
           hear your thoughts and feelings.
Sadira:    What are you talking about?
Jessie:    i don't remember the name of them
           now, but i came across audio
           files that you put on a message
           board.  it was clear that you
           wrote them about me.
Sadira:    Oh.
```

Duh. I decided to end our conversation. I wasn't in the mood to
talk about us and didn't want her melancholic mood rubbing off on me.

```
Sadira:    Hey, Jess.  I have to run now.
Jessie:    okay, i'll see you around.
Sadira:    Later.
```

I closed our dialogue box and signed off the Internet.   Actually, I
was quite surprised Jessie wasn't acting like the typical person after a
breakup. She made it obvious that she was thinking of me even though
she told me she was seeing someone. But, she didn't say she wanted
another chance. She just wanted to be friends, or so she claimed. She
wanted to hang on to a thread of me if that was all she could get. Oh well.
That's all she would get.

I remembered the poems she was talking about. I had named them
"War" and "Translucent Love." They were created out of pain, frustration,
and my desire to move beyond the damage that had been done. I put my
pummeled soul into those poems as well as the music that accompanied
them.   They were slow and dragged out, placed on top of a bluesy melody.
I wasn't going to dwell on them or Jessie for too long though. I had a new
and better woman in Tricia who made me feel good all over. I didn't have
to beg for her to show affection, and more and more I liked the person I

was turning into because of Tricia. She had to be the one for me.

The next time I saw Tricia was at a karaoke bar in Manhattan where we met up with Josh and Warren. I got tipsy from one too many apple martinis and ended up on stage singing Prince's "I Wanna Be Your Lover." Off key and off beat, I butchered the song, but I didn't care.

"Miss Girl you know you tore that song up!" Warren said laughing.

"Literally," added Josh as he sipped his beer. He smiled at me.

"Heeey." That was all I could say. I had way too much to drink.

Tricia touched my hand. "Sit down, baby."

The small room was dark and the stage took up more than half of it. We stayed to watch other people do a few more songs before leaving to get something to eat at a nearby pizzeria. It was almost 3 a.m. by the time we split up. Tricia and I went back to my apartment. By then I was beginning to sober up, but Tricia still made a pot of coffee and made me drink some.

"I hate coffee," I protested.

"Oh, you hate everything. Too bad, drink it."

"Why? I'm already home."

"Just drink some, Sadira, and stop whining."

"Fine," I pouted.

She smiled. "You're such a big baby."

"Hmph. Breast-feed me then."

She shook her head and laughed at me. "What am I going to do with you, huh?"

"Awe, just love me." The coffee did help me.

"I plan to."

Our casual talk in the late night hour was sweet, and I was thankful she was there with me. It would have been torture to spend the night holding my pillow instead of her.

The next day I went home with her, and we made it a lazy Saturday. As she lay in my arms on the couch, our conversation went from our current feelings to a direct focus on my past. She and I talked about the issues that I thought might have been the downfall to my old relationships. When I told her about my fear of abandonment, it led to a long dialogue explaining my childhood. Tricia gently nudged me enough to willingly go back in time and share with her events from deep in my past

"I don't recall much."

"That's probably because you don't want to and you've blocked out a lot of things, but try to relax and think back. Tell me your earliest memories."

"Hmm." I closed my eyes for a few seconds but thought of nothing. I felt her touch my hand and I opened my eyes. In the midst of the silence I gave it my best shot to think back to when I was child. Still, I drew a blank. Rubbing my chin and softly biting my bottom lip, I relaxed for a few more seconds before speaking. Memories *were* there.

"My earliest childhood recollection is of my dad…his smell. He always smelled good and I loved being in his arms to inhale the scent. For some reason, I equated it with strength and thought he was the strongest man alive and would always keep me safe. I was more of a daddy's girl than Khedara."

"Really?"

"Yeah, but I really don't remember too much. My first day of kindergarten is a blurry memory in my mind too. I remember running back to my father and wanting to go back home, while nerdy Khedara started making friends."

Tricia laughed. "You said it like you're still bothered that she went off and made friends!"

"No, no," I chuckled. "I didn't mean for it to come out like that."

"What about your mom?" asked Tricia.

"My mother was a woman of few words. While my father joked around a lot, she only spoke when it was necessary. She could cook though. I always wanted to be in the kitchen when she was baking. When I think about my mom, I think about Thanksgiving."

"Because of her cooking?"

"Well yes and no." As my mind moved through time, I became saddened at my next patch of memories. "I remember one year when my mom and grandmother made all of the food and my father took pictures of it. I probably only remember that weekend because of the photos I held on to for years afterwards. Khedara still has one that she's managed to keep in good condition. Mine got lost somewhere along the way."

Tricia rubbed my hand and listened intently. "You should ask her to have a copy made for you."

"Yeah, I think I will." I paused to think of what to say next. My memories were so jagged I didn't know how to piece them together in my explanation. "That holiday season was a good one. The day after Thanksgiving we went to Walt Disney World." I smiled a little as an image of an old photo popped into my head. It was a Polaroid picture of Khedara and me sitting next to a Christmas tree with gifts all around us, a bittersweet recollection.

Feeling tears coming on, I fought them off wishing that I had never lost that picture. Tricia shifted positions so that her back was against the arm of the sofa and then she pulled me to her. I lay in between her legs with my back touching her chest and my forehead at her chin.

"It was the following summer that our parents died. Khedara and I were away at a summer camp for girls in Augusta, Georgia when it happened. We were doing arts and crafts that day. We'd..." I paused and sighed before continuing. "We'd made these cards out of colorful paper and a necklace out of macaroni that was supposed to be for our parents. All of the kids made something because we it was supposed to be the last week of camp."

I kept speaking as memories trickled back, painful and vivid pictures in my mind. "Early the next morning our grandmother and Uncle Kirk came to pick us up. Khedara and I didn't know what was going on. And I don't remember much else of that day besides the bad news that our parents wouldn't be home when we got there." Tears streamed down my face.

Tricia held me tighter and kissed me on my head. "It's okay."

It hurt to dig up my past. I tried to blink back the tears as if it would stop them from flowing but they continued.

"Sadira, you can cry. Go ahead and let it out, baby."

169

I exhaled and tried to continue telling more. *I might as well get it all out.* "Apparently the power in Miami was out for days after the hurricane. Well, my parents were using a generator to manage but left it on while they were sleeping one night, and they died from inhaling carbon monoxide."

"Where was your grandmother?"

"She wasn't with my parents. As the story goes, she refused to leave her tiny home in Ft. Lauderdale."

"She lived alone?"

"Yeah, my grandfather had passed years before and she was a stubborn woman. She didn't want to move out of the house that she'd shared with him."

"Oh."

I cleared my throat and thought a while before speaking again. Tricia hugged me but didn't say anything. Eventually I took a deep breath and began talking again. "I don't remember the funeral, and I don't remember the condition of my parents' house when we finally saw it. Ultimately we ended up going to live in Ft. Lauderdale with my grandmother. But two years later she died."

"My God."

"Yeah."

She sighed.

"And then we thought we were going to live with our Uncle Kirk, but he didn't take care of his own children and was a useless alcoholic. With no other family available to take us in, we drifted into the foster care system."

"You only had one uncle?"

"Only one that we knew of and that was my father's brother. We didn't know anyone from my mother's side of the family as she hadn't talked to them since she left Trinidad."

"I didn't know you were Trinidadian!"

"Yeah, partly, though I've never been there and don't know anything about the country."

"Wow."

170

My tears had subsided and I was actually feeling drained, perhaps from our conversation. I yawned and stretched.

"Tired?" she asked.

"Yeah."

Tricia sighed softly and kissed me on my head.

"We can talk about this some more another time. I mean, I just think I've had enough for tonight."

"All right."

We stayed on the couch a few minutes longer before retiring to her bedroom. After changing into pajamas and climbing into bed, I ended up breaking down and crying again. It was the first time I'd ever talked about my feelings or memories. Khedara and I both said we'd put it behind us and not bring it up. And we didn't. But when I opened up to Tricia, it was if the dam had broken and I cried painful tears as the horror of my childhood came back to me. Not only did the tears flow, my body shook in exhaustion. I'd been carrying that baggage for far too long. I felt like a big baby for bawling.

She, too, cried as she held me. "It's okay," she said repeatedly. "It's okay, baby. It's all right."

Comforted in her arms and by her voice, I began to talk again despite my decision to stop earlier. The floodgates were open, and I had to let the painful rush continue to flow out. "You know, after Khedara and I were placed in the foster care system, we bounced around Miami from one home to another to a bunch of strangers."

"Different homes, different schools, weird people, and mean classmates. We felt unloved, disconnected, and abandoned. The houses never felt like a real home, and sometimes we'd catch nosey neighbors pointing and whispering about *those* foster children, like we were on display or something. And this went on for years, as if losing our parents wasn't traumatic enough. Not only did we have to deal with the shock, we had to deal with feeling unwanted." I paused as she ran her hand against my body to soothe me. "We were too young to have to have felt some of those things and we damn sure weren't prepared for all of the drama after

171

we were ripped from our normal lives. Khedara and I both sometimes wished we would have died along with our parents."

"No," she said, cutting me off. "I mean, I understand how you could feel that way, but I am so thankful it didn't happen. Sadira, you are such a gift. I'm just glad both you and your sister turned out to be good adults."

I hugged her. "I'm happy to be alive now, and I wouldn't want that wish to come true today. But back then there were some times we were in homes with five other children, and all of us would have to share two bedrooms. When we were first put in the system, Khedara and I at least had each other. Being together helped us cope with all the changes that seemed to be happening so fast. Every time we switched schools or moved to a new neighborhood, we remained together, which seemed to be the only thing that was consistent. But by the time we were eleven years old, we had been split up. Social workers thought it was in our best interest because there were too many children in one house for the caring family to handle. Why they chose to split up twins rather than send another child away I have no idea."

"I don't understand splitting you two up either. It just doesn't seem to make sense."

"Yeah, tell me about it. There were some kids there who didn't have any brothers or sisters. They could have sent them off instead."

"That's crazy. Well, what happened after they separated you and your sister?"

"Khedara was ended up living on the other end of the county, while I was sent to live with a woman named Esther who I despised. She beat me whenever she felt like it, and if I didn't have her house clean, including her bedroom and bathroom, she'd only feed me enough to prevent me from passing out. I hated her and thought about poisoning her. She kept a nasty house, always leaving dirty dishes on the table when she finished eating, and *I* would have to go behind her and clean up...fucking bitch." I was getting angry just talking about her. "I'm sorry, Tricia. I'm sorry." For some reason I felt bad for my foul language, but the years I had spent with Esther were the worst times in my life.

172

"Go ahead, I understand. Curse, cry, get angry, and do whatever you have to do to face all of the things you feel."

Tricia shook her head in shock as I continued. "I remember being whipped with an extension cord because I didn't finish the one meal she gave me on one day. The meat wasn't cooked all the way so I didn't eat it, and she got upset, called me ungrateful, and went into a rage. I couldn't walk straight for days afterward. Just my luck that that was on a Friday night, and the bruises were gone by the time Monday rolled around. And what's worse was that she would take the phones out of the house when she left and only allowed me to talk to Khedara when she could listen in on our conversation."

"I can't even imagine living like that, Sadira. I'm so sorry you had to go through so much."

"Yeah, but luckily it didn't break me. I'm damaged but not broken beyond repair."

My abandonment issues stemmed from my childhood, and I probably wouldn't have had them if I'd done this kind of talking before or at least gone through counseling. I could have gone on and on about my traumatic childhood experiences, but I didn't say much more that night. I did tell Tricia that what saved me from running away or ending up in a worse situation was that I took a liking to music and wanted to be in my high school band. The grade point average requirement gave me an incentive to want to apply myself in class and be friends with people who could help me study and catch up. I even signed up for additional tutoring outside of normal school hours so that I could show I wasn't a damn retard. When I started to do better on tests and show improvement, it made things worse at home because it messed up Esther's plan. I got beatings for that, and as punishment, she wouldn't allow me to practice on my trumpet at home. That actually worked out fine for me because it gave me an excuse to stay at school longer and to be away from her. Eventually she just stopped caring. She had a new kid in the house who she could profit from. Wanting to be in band is what saved me. Once I stopped acting like the dummy I'd been labeled, I realized that I did like what was being taught in class.

Khedara didn't have it as bad as I did in the last couple of years of our childhood. She lived with a good family who showed her love, while I was stuck in hell with Esther.

When the new kid came into Esther's house, Esther stopped watching me so hard, which allowed me to connect with Khedara again. The family that she was with wanted us to remain in contact and was supportive of trying to arrange visits. Esther wasn't because she said it was too far away, but we at least were able to speak on the phone. Many nights Khedara cried for me because she felt guilty for being in a better situation.

By age eighteen, I joined the Air Force and Khedara went off to college in Atlanta. Joining the Air Force was one of the best things I could have ever done. Being in the military helped me feel a sense of belonging and purpose.

Chapter 20

Thin layers of dried tears were impressed upon my face from the night before, but I felt lighter in emotional weight and closer to Tricia, different from how I felt with Jessie. Things felt genuine and tangible with Tricia, whereas with Jessie they could have been my imagination mixed with a desire so intense it drove me to do things based on false emotions. I had been in love with a fantasy based on a woman, not the real woman. It was all in my head, and I knew it by then. Tricia was *real*.

Tricia made a big southern breakfast for us. After filling myself with grits, scrambled eggs with cheese, bacon, biscuits, and fresh fruit, I was ready to go back to sleep. We didn't stay inside though. By the afternoon we were walking around in a park looking at ice sculptures. We had an early dinner at an Italian restaurant, before going back to my place. It felt like I hadn't been home in a long time. I was spending more and more time with Tricia and it was seriously making me think of how much money I was wasting on rent for a place at which I rarely spent time. On the other hand, it was nice to always have my own apartment, just in case. I just got lazier about seeking another place to live.

I was practically dancing around my apartment the following morning because I felt so good. When I got to work, Devonte' immediately asked me what I'd been up to.

"What did you get into this weekend? You look like Cupid shot you in the ass. "

"Man, he did." I smiled.

"What?"

"Tricia."

He laughed. "Yeah, she told me you two were spending more time together, but I wanted to stay out of her business so I didn't say anything to you. I was waiting to see how long your punk ass would wait to tell me."

"Punk?"

"Yep."

"Whatever, Devonte'. I love her, man. I'm *in* love with her."

"Damn. You sound like you're ready to be my cousin-in-law, girl."

I laughed. "Shut up."

He looked at the clock. "It's almost time to start my show."

"I know. Let's get to it."

Devonte', too had fallen in love. He often went on and on about his girlfriend, and I was happy for him.

"For real, Sadira. I don't know what it is she has, but whatever she put on me has me wanting to settle down."

"Say what?" I laughed.

"I'm serious."

"Damn, it's really like that?"

"I'm afraid so."

"Well good. It's about time someone was able to tame your ass. Treat her good, man."

"Go to hell. Ain't nobody taming me like I'm some animal."

We talked a little while longer before parting. Tricia was working late that night and to channel my longing for her into something productive, I pulled my keyboard out of its case and started working on a song for her. Surprisingly it came to me very easily, and after a couple of hours, I had a verse and the chorus done. It was about the way she made me feel, how the sincerity in her eyes and the familiarity of her touch and voice comforted me. It was a melodious transcript of what I felt inside when I thought of her. Sort of a fusion of classical and R&B with the

176

heavy strings. I wanted it to have soul *and* show serious musicianship. I didn't take all those piano lessons with Jenny for nothing.

It wasn't until I was finished with my music that I remembered to check my voicemail. There was another message from a realtor following up on my previous request for information. I wanted to stop procrastinating about moving but felt as though I should discuss it with Tricia first.

She called me when she got in from work. "I am so tired."

"When will you start getting off at five o'clock when you're supposed to?"

"Ha! Not for a while. I want to prove myself so I can move up the management ladder. If I leave when everyone else does, then I won't stand out as someone who is willing to go above and beyond—the type of person they promote from within when a higher position opens up."

"Yeah, yeah."

"Hey, everyone can't work for six hours a day like you."

"Mm hm. So anyway, listen I wanted to talk to you."

"About what?"

"Well, it's time I move into a new place. I don't want to rent another apartment though. I want to buy one and stay put."

"So…"

"So I want your input. What do you think?"

"I don't know, Sadira."

There was a pause in our conversation before I spoke again. "I'll stay in Brooklyn. I don't want to be too far away from you."

"Well, do you want me to help you look for a place?"

"Yes." I answered more quickly than I wanted to. I wanted to spend all of my time with her, but I wasn't mentally ready to give up all of my freedom by living *with* her. "Would you come with me when I start looking?"

"Of course."

"Cool."

177

I wondered if she were pondering about us living together too but resisted suggesting it. She exhaled. "Sounds like a plan. Look, Sadira, let me unwind a little bit and then I'll call you back."

"All right."

We did speak again later that evening, but didn't see each other. It was so cold that neither of us wanted to venture outside. A conversation with Jessie almost started online, but as soon as she sent me an instant message, she said that she had to go because her girlfriend Lisa showed up unexpectedly to surprise her. *Yeah, so what.*

The later it got, the lonelier I felt. I wished I hadn't been lazy and had gone to Tricia's place to spend the night, but by then it was definitely too late to go out. I felt a little jealousy about Jessie and her girlfriend, but I ignored it. *My relationship is better.*

I made it through the night alone and told myself that I wouldn't go through the torture again the following evening. Tricia was working late again so I lounged around and watched television until I heard from her. All I knew was that I needed to avoid another lonely night or I might be tempted to reach out to Jessie. That nagging voice of reason in my head telling me to let go of Jessie was so loud it would give me a headache that aspirin couldn't cure if I didn't listen.

"Okay," I mumbled to myself. "I won't give Jessie an opportunity to entangle me in her web again."

Since I knew that Tricia was the better woman for me and deserved to have all of my attention, I deleted Jessie from my online messenger list so that I wouldn't see when she was available for a chat and I wouldn't be tempted to contact her. Unfortunately, I wasn't strong enough to block *her* from seeing me or change my phone number, which would really end all contact. I tried to, but I couldn't bring myself to do it. *Always wanting to leave a window of opportunity,* I thought. Dumb, I know but that's how it went because I couldn't let go…even when I wanted to, I stood in my own way.

As the clock ticked on I got more bored. I decided that I would go back out to kill time. Though it looked dark out, it was still relatively early.

Tainted Destiny

Dressed in relaxed jeans, a tan sweater, and brown shoes, I sprayed a little cologne on before grabbing my wallet and cell phone, putting on my coat and gloves, and heading out the door. I called Tricia's cell phone and left her a message to let her know about my plans. I had no idea what time she'd be leaving her office. I asked her to give me a buzz when she was calling it a day at work. On my walk to the subway I thought of different places to go keep me preoccupied until Tricia left work. I figured I would find somewhere in the Village or close by that had live music or poetry.

I ended up at The Cage, a tiny brick building on the Lower East Side of Manhattan that was hosting an open jam session with the house band. The place was packed with an energetic bunch of music lovers. A guy who reminded me of Bo Bice from American Idol was on stage singing with the band when I arrived. I maneuvered my way over to the bar to order a drink. The Asian bartender had a gorgeous set of dark brown eyes. I couldn't help myself and complimented her on them. She smiled and winked, but the bar was too crowded for friendly flirting. I left her a tip and found a corner where I could hear and see who else would go on stage.

I'd consumed two drinks by the time I felt my cell phone vibrating in my pocket. *Tricia*, I thought and was right.

"Hey, hold on a sec, let me go somewhere quiet," I answered and then quickly made my way to the exit. It was freezing outside. "Hi, I'm back." I tried to button my coat up while talking to her. "Are you at home already?"

"No, but I'm getting ready to leave now."

"Oh."

"How long will you be out?" she asked.

"Not long if you say I can spend the night with you."

She laughed. "You are so easy."

"What?"

"Of course I want to you to come over. I hate sleeping without you."

179

Her statement made feel warm inside. It felt so good not to have to beg her to share her feelings and know that she felt the same way I did. "What time should I come?"

"Whenever you want. I'm taking car service home so it shouldn't take me too long."

"All right. I'll be over in an hour or so." It was getting too cold to stand still so I started pacing.

"Okay, and by the way, I have a surprise for you."

"You do?"

"Yes, so hurry up."

I began walking to the nearest subway. "I'll be there soon. As a matter of fact I'm going to start making my way back to Brooklyn now. I'll call you back when I'm closer."

"All right, talk to you later."

"Bye."

I picked up a bouquet of flowers from a corner store after I hung up and quickly moved through the cold night air to get to Tricia. When I got to her apartment, she took a long time to open the door for me and had a silly grin on her face.

"What is up with you?" I asked and laughed.

"Nothing. You got here faster than I thought and I was running around making sure the place was clean. Are those for me?" She smiled broadly at the flowers in my hand.

"Yes they are." I handed them to her. "And as much time as we spend with each other, you shouldn't still be trying to impress me...well..." I smirked.

"I know. I know. Anyway, hurry up and come inside." She stepped aside so I could walk ahead of her.

"Mmm. You smell good. Are you wearing a new perfume or something?" I took off my coat and gloves.

"Thanks. It's not new, but I haven't worn it in a while. It's actually scented oil."

"Oh."

"So what's your big surprise for me?"

"I'll tell you soon enough; just relax for now."

"Fine." I was anxious to know what she had but obeyed her wish. *Why did she rush me over here and then make me wait for my surprise?*

She made two cups of hot chocolate and put whipped cream on the top. We watched television cuddled up next to each other on her couch until she finally excused herself to get something out of her bedroom. "I'll be right back," she devilishly declared.

While she was away I felt my cell phone vibrating in my pocket, but when I reached for it I noticed it wasn't an incoming call but a text message. I didn't recognize the number and the message only said, "Expect the unexpected." *What?* I didn't understand it and hurriedly put the phone back in my pocket when I heard Tricia coming back out of the bedroom.

She had a nervous smile on her face and was holding a small white envelope. My curiosity was truly piqued. "Come on give it up. What's my surprise?"

"Okay, okay." She took a deep breath, sat beside me, and then handed me the little package, which felt padded.

Wasting no time, I opened it up to see a key. "Is this what I think it is?"

"Yeah," she nodded affirmatively. "It's a key to my apartment."

Tricia brought us to another level. "Wow," was all I could say. I don't think I should have been surprised but I was.

"I want you," she announced, taking my hand and looking me directly in my eyes, "to be able to come and go as you please and feel comfortable here as if it were your own home. Even though you don't live with me, I've started thinking of it as our home."

Still in shock, I smiled and hugged her. I was happy and nervous at the same time. Her giving me the key felt like a subtle invitation to move in, but I wasn't sure if that was just my interpretation.

She broke my thoughts. "This way I don't have to hide a key in a secret place or something if you want to be here before I get home."

Well that makes sense. "Thanks." Grinning, I felt those mushy in love feelings rapidly returning. "Thanks!" My excitement was delayed, but it was there.

She laughed at me.

"What?"

"Nothing. You're so cute."

"I am, am I not?"

"And arrogant too. I love it."

"I love *you*." I kissed her passionately, pulling her body closer to mine. She moaned and ran her fingers through my hair as she kissed me back. Sliding my hands up and down her back, I kissed her a bit longer before slowing out of it and gazing into her eyes. Tricia made me feel so good and had me at a loss for words. I stared at her, feeling my heart filling with fascination and love. She just smiled.

"Tricia. I don't know what to say. I mean, thanks for the key. I didn't expect it."

"Neither did I, but I was taking a walk on my lunch hour the other day and passed a shop that copied keys. I thought about you and had an extra made."

"Mm hm."

"Yeah."

"Well cool. I'll have a copy of mine made for you tomorrow."

"Okay. Hey, what about your moving anyway?"

"Nothing. I just dropped the ball. My neighbors don't make all of that noise anymore because the young girl left."

"So does that mean you're going to stay there now?"

"I'm not sure. The downside is that I'm still renting." I paused and thought for a moment. "I need to get out of there and buy something."

"Okay."

I looked at her and she looked at me, but neither one of us said anything. I'm sure both of us thought of moving in together but didn't speak up about it. I'd thought about how nice it would be to have her around all the time but told myself that we weren't ready for that just yet. In the midst of silence she tapped her finger on the couch.

182

"So…" I tried to pick up our dialogue.

"Um." Now she tapped her foot a couple of times as if it would give us a push. "So when is the last time you've felt the way you do now?"

"Never," I answered without hesitation.

"Me either, Sadira. There is something special about you. I've never felt this way or wanted anyone around me as much as I do you, and I have *never* given anyone a key."

I absorbed her words. They seemed to seep into my mind and heart effortlessly and make me look at her in amazement. It was the first time I'd felt reciprocal wholehearted love.

"Come closer to me," I told her, and she did.

Tricia reached for the remote and changed the channel to a music station before speaking again. "Sadira?"

"Yeah, babe?"

"I've been thinking…"

"About what?"

"Well, I want to get away—take a vacation you know? We should go away together."

"That sounds nice. Where do you want to go?"

"Anywhere as long as I'm with you." She smiled at me with the most loving eyes I'd ever seen.

I felt as though I were falling in love with her all over again. A flutter of exhilaration made itself at home in my stomach, and I returned her happy gaze. "What about the Caribbean or Hawaii? I'm just throwing ideas out."

"Not the Caribbean," she said and stopped to think. "Well, as long as we can go somewhere and be comfortably out of the closet. I want to be able to hold your hand in public without having to fear for my life."

"I agree. How about this? You pick wherever you want to go and that's where we'll vacation. I'll leave the destination up to you."

"Okay!"

I kissed her on her shoulder and chuckled.

"What are you laughing at?"

183

"Nothing. I'm just…this feels so…I don't know. I'm happy."

"Me too."

Okay this is getting too mushy. "Come on let's go to bed."

She exhaled with a soft moan. "Yes, let's go." Seduction was in her voice.

"Well, all right now." I followed her to seal the evening with ascension to a realm so pleasurable we did it again and again and again until we were simply spent.

As sunlight crept into the bedroom, I got out of bed and got dressed for work.

"Baby," I whispered.

She stirred but didn't open her eyes. "Hm?"

"Hey, I'm leaving for work now." I kissed her on the cheek.

She smiled at the feel of my lips on her skin. "Oh okay. Call me to wake me up at 6:30."

"All right." I gave her another quick peck on the lips before heading out.

Chapter 21

Tricia had me feeling extremely romantic. I bought her a new dress and a necklace with a small diamond pendant. There was no special occasion, I just wanted to see the smile on her face as she unwrapped all that I'd bought for her. Instead of going out to a restaurant, I told her I wanted to spend a romantic evening at home. Besides, she had to go on a business trip for a few days afterwards and I wanted to enjoy my short time with her.

I'd ordered four dozen roses to help set the mood. After arranging them and putting them in a vase on her table, I went back out to the nearest grocery store to buy ingredients for a seafood dinner, shrimp and scallop scampi over linguini.

By the time Tricia got home I had showered, changed, set the table, lit the candles, and poured the wine. I hadn't put the food on the plates yet but did so after greeting her with a hug and kiss. She was pleasantly surprised with the initiative I had taken.

"Look at you in here cooking dinner for me. I sure could get used to this." She smiled and looked at me with a trace of lust in her eyes.

185

"Mm hm." I winked at her and turned to go back in the kitchen. "Go change into something comfortable and then sit down so I can serve you."

"I'll do that," I heard her say.

"Wouldn't it be nice to come home to each other every night?" Tricia blurted out over dinner.

Of course it would be nice, but I was afraid. I didn't respond immediately.

She continued to speak. "No pressure, Sadira. I'm just saying it because I've thought about it. Have you?"

"Yes."

"And?"

"I don't know." We'd finished eating by then so I motioned to go sit on the couch to finish our conversation. Tricia followed me.

She began to massage my shoulders and seemingly went in for the kill. The more relaxed I got, the sweeter her words sounded and the more places her hands seem to wander on my body.

"I could take care of you better if we lived together." She kissed my earlobe.

Without giving a response, I closed my eyes and enjoyed her attempt at seducing me to move in. When my hormones began to rise, I finally spoke. "I'll think about it," I said. "But in the meantime why don't you uh…get ready for the rest of the night while I clear the table and clean the kitchen?"

She kissed me and then smiled. "All right."

It seemed like a logical choice to move in with her, but still I was apprehensive. I couldn't think of a single reason not to move in with her except that I would lose some privacy. But I hated sleeping without Tricia and was wasting a lot of money on rent. *I guess I'll tell her yes but not right now.* I exhaled as I finished the dishes and dried my hands on a towel. I was really going to do it.

The sound of the shower turning off cut through my thoughts like a falling blade. My mind instantly switched to excitement about being romantic with Tricia that night. I was craving her. I wanted to enjoy

186

Tricia's body and make love to her from top to bottom. I also wanted to let her do whatever she wanted to me. She emerged from the steamy bathroom wearing a peach silk gown that gave her an aura of regality. The soft color looked deliciously attractive against her warm skin. Her eyes beckoned me to her. I turned off the lights and only left the burning candles on the table to illuminate the room. Tricia stretched her hand for me to take it and follow her into the bedroom. I complied.

I deliberately undressed slowly and she lit a couple of candles that she kept in the room. I had another surprise for Tricia that night. Her eyes widened after she turned around to see me clad in a black lace camisole and boy shorts set.

Oh my God, I read her lips as she mouthed the words while looking at me in awe and with intrigue. She'd told me more than a few times that I should show off my body more, but I never listened. One day though, I bought that lingerie set with the intention to surprise her one night and this was that 'one night.' Tricia looked as if she wanted to devour me.

For quite a while we alternated being passive and aggressive in bed, she on top of me and vice versa; there were no roles and no femme or stud that night. We exchanged our feelings of mutual love and desire for each other without the hindrance or strain of keeping a who-should-do-what mentality. Dominance and submissiveness comfortably passed between us with one following the other's lead for a sensual exchange of passion. After we reached our climaxes, I got up to blow out all of the candles and returned to bed where Tricia snuggled up in my arms. We floated into a peaceful slumber.

Hours later I was annoyed out of my sleep by the faint but apparent sound of my cell phone ringing in my pants pocket on the floor. I looked at the clock on the nightstand to see that it was one o'clock in the morning. Tricia didn't wake up, but she stirred. *Who the hell is calling me?* The phone stopped ringing before I could get to it, but a few seconds later it rang again. I got up as quickly and gently as I could to answer it, and I froze when I heard the voice on the other end of the line. It was Jessie.

I tiptoed out of the room. "Jessie, what are you crazy?" As the words fell from my lips I questioned if *I* were crazy. I shouldn't have even answered much less walked out of the bedroom. *Damn it!*

"I'm sorry, Sadira. I didn't want to bother you, and I don't mean to disrupt your life, but I'm alone and I'm scared."

"What the hell are you talking about?" I looked to make sure Tricia hadn't stepped out of the bedroom.

"My mother passed away."

Whoa! I sat down at the dining room table. "I'm sorry to hear that." I'd met her mother in the past, around the time that Jessie's brother had died. "I'm sorry, Jess."

All I could hear was her crying on the other end of the phone. She sniffled and spoke again. "I know we aren't supposed to be speaking and I know it's late, but I just need someone to talk to."

I sighed. "Okay."

Just then I heard the door creak and saw Tricia step out of the bedroom. "Sadira, who are you talking to?" She crossed her arms and looked at me expectantly.

"Hold on," I said into the phone and then turned to Tricia. "It's Jessie."

In less than a second the expression on her face changed to a mix of shock and anger.

"Wait, no it's not like that. Her mother died."

She stared at me.

"I'm serious," I said.

Dropping her arms to her side Tricia's demeanor changed. "Fine," was all she said and stepped back into the bedroom leaving the door open. I knew she was bothered.

I rubbed my forehead and then turned my attention back to Jessie. "Hello?"

"I'm sorry, Sadira. I didn't even think about the time and that you might not be alone. I was just going through my phone list trying to find someone to talk to. I knew for sure that you would be there for me."

"How did you get my number?"

"That time you called me and changed your mind…I saved your number. I'm sorry."

"Oh," I paused. "Well, I am here. Go ahead and say what's on your mind." I needed to tell her that I wouldn't always be there, but right then just didn't seem to be the right time.

Ten minutes went by before I found myself easing out of the call with Jessie. She'd cried and talked about losing her mother to a battle with cancer. I felt bad for her, but there wasn't too much I could do besides lend an ear. And I knew that I couldn't be there too much for her without making Tricia feel disrespected. It truly did hurt me to know that she was in pain but my hands were tied. Before hanging up and going back into the bedroom where Tricia was wide awake, I told Jessie that I'd pray for her.

"I'm sorry about that, Tricia."

"You mean to tell me that you are the only person she could think to call?"

"I don't know, baby. Her mother died. She probably didn't know who to call and contacted me because I was familiar and I'd met her mother."

"Look, I guess under the circumstances I can understand her calling you…once. But I can't say that it doesn't make me uncomfortable. I don't want you talking to her while I'm gone."

"I won't." I couldn't say I faulted her for her insecurity, and I honestly wanted to do right by her. "Don't stress it, baby."

"Just do not allow her to drag it out, Sadira. She can talk to a pastor or get a counselor."

"All right, baby." I kissed her. "Okay. Let's get back to sleep."

"Good night."

"Night."

Five minutes hadn't passed before she spoke again. "How did she get your cell phone number anyway, Sadira?"

Her question was like a blow to the stomach, and I was ever grateful that she couldn't see my facial expression in the dark. Slowly, carefully I tried to choose the right words to respond to her. Blank. I couldn't come up with an excuse quickly enough.

"Sadira?"

"I um. I gave it to her a while back…before you and I got serious." In the midst of terrible discomfort I bit my bottom lip and intertwined my fingers under the sheets. "It won't happen again." Finally, I seemed to get myself together. "Don't worry about it, baby. I promise I won't allow her to drag it out nor will I converse with her."

"You better not." A trace of bitterness laced her voice.

"I won't." My heart was pounding. Nervousness.

Neither one of us were able to get much sleep that night. I could feel our chemistry slipping off track even in my subconscious state, and I tossed and turned throughout the remaining hours before dawn.

The following day, the only thing I could think of to do to lighten the situation was to tell her that I'd decided to move in with her. *That ought to shift things.*

"Hey," I said.

"What?"

I smiled. "Don't answer me with that attitude. I have something to say that I think you'd be happy to hear."

"And what would that be." She had a smirk on her face.

"I've decided to…"

"Well?"

"I'm ready to move in with you."

She didn't expect me to say that and it showed. "What? Are you serious?" A full-blown smile was forming on her face.

"Yep. I've made up my mind, and I think it's the right decision."

"Oh that's great!"

And with that declaration I got the shift in mood I wanted. I didn't think she had forgotten about the whole Jessie situation, but at least it wasn't the focus of her thoughts. All I had to do was keep control of the situation and hopefully we'd live drama-free.

The next morning she rose early with me to do some last minute packing. I put some Pop Tarts in the toaster for a quick and easy breakfast after I got dressed. "What time is your flight again?"

"Ten o'clock."

"Okay, well make sure you call me if it runs late or anything. And let me know when you touch down too."

"Of course I will." She forced a smile.

"Come here, babe," I told her, and she walked toward me. "Listen, don't worry about Jessie."

"I trust you to handle this appropriately when I'm gone."

"And I will."

The toaster popped and broke our conversation. "Here, have one of these and relax," I said.

After eating quickly, I hugged and kissed her. "Remember to call me," was the last thing I said before walking out the door. Halfway to work I was already dreading spending that next couple of nights without her.

I thought about Jessie and hoped she was feeling better but I didn't call her. I would have sent a condolence card if I'd had her address.

I spent that night in my own apartment figuring I wouldn't be constantly reminded of Tricia. She called me as soon as she landed and it felt good to hear her voice. I spoke to her again later in the evening. I think it comforted her that when she called I wasn't on the phone with anyone else.

But the night before Tricia was due back in New York, Jessie called.

"Hello?" I answered.

"Hi," she said softly.

"Hey, Jess." I reclined on my sofa.

"I just wanted to say thank you for being there for me…the other night. And I'm sorry I called you so late. I wasn't thinking about the time. I don't even think I was in my right mind, and I hope I didn't get you in trouble."

"I'm not in trouble, and you're welcome. Are you doing better now?"

"I don't know. I guess so. The pain comes and goes."

191

"I'm sorry."

"Well, I only called to tell you thanks and I appreciate your being there for me."

"All right. Just…just pray for peace or maybe see a therapist if things feel like they're too much to bear."

"Yeah. I could use a hug from a friend though."

"You know maybe this is an opportunity for you to reconnect with your sisters." I didn't want to acknowledge her last statement. And she and her sisters hadn't spoken in quite some time because they assumed Jessie thought she was better than they were.

"They can't stand me."

"Well then church. You can always count on the church to help you get through difficult times."

"I suppose. Okay, well I'm going to let you go now."

"All right, Jessie. Be strong."

"Bye."

"Good bye."

Replaying everything from the first night she had called up until then told me that I'd already made several mistakes. Yet the fact that Jessie had surfaced again was enough to throw me out of my comfort zone with Tricia. I realized that I'd only been suppressing my feelings, and all it took was the sound of Jessie's voice to take me back in time…or to remind me that I had never truly moved on.

A phone call from Tricia severed my thoughts.

"Hey, baby," I answered.

"Hi, I can't really talk long. I stole a moment just so I could call you. I miss you."

"Me too, sweetie. Tomorrow can't come fast enough."

"Are you okay up there all alone?"

Something about her question told me she was asking in a roundabout way if I'd talked to Jessie. "I'm fine. I wish you were here, but I'm okay."

"Me too. I have to go now, but I'll call you back later on tonight."

"Okay, I'll be waiting."

"I love you," she said.

"Me too." We hung up.

The hours following our brief conversation were filled in with movies that I watched one after another while planted on my couch. It was about 2 a.m. when my phone rang and woke me up.

"Yeah?"

"Hey, I'm sorry I'm calling so late." Tricia's soft voice floated through the line.

"It's okay. I'm glad you called. It's hard being without you."

"Aw, you miss me."

"I sure do."

"You sound so sexy right now."

I laughed. "Yeah?"

"Yes you do, and trust me, being without you is difficult for me too."

"Don't worry, when you get back I'll give you some good loving."

I could hear her trying to hush her amusement on the other end of the phone. She spoke in almost a whisper. "I'm going to hold you to that."

We continued to talk with longing and naughty undertones, which led to a session of steamy phone sex.

"Now that was pleasurable. I can't wait to have you back in my arms so I can hold you afterwards," I said.

"Soon, speaking of which I should get off this phone to make sure I have all my stuff packed."

"All right. Call me in the morning, baby."

"I will."

The next morning, I told my landlord that it would be my last month renting the apartment from her. I also logged online to chat with Khedara. Her boyfriend, Lance, surprised her with a trip to Europe where she got a chance to visit France and Italy. She sent me a link to an online photo album that had beautiful pictures of them looking like the happiest

193

couple on Earth. He was handsome with dark skin, a low haircut, and goatee, accented by a charming smile. I was thrilled for her.

I really wanted to visit her so that I could meet Lance and she could meet Tricia. I told her that I'd be sure to bring the idea up to Tricia and try to plan on visiting in the spring. I also told her that I'd finally managed to get rid of Olivia for good and that Tricia and I were doing great. When I mentioned the resurfacing of Jessie, however, I knew she wasn't pleased. Khedara reminded me to keep things in perspective and remember who should stay in the past and with whom I was trying to build a lasting relationship with now. Don't blow this, Sadira, she typed, and I assured her I wouldn't. We ended our conversation with a promise to talk to each other more often as well as plan a vacation together.

Tricia's flight ended up being delayed, and idly waiting for her was driving me nuts. To kill time I did some grocery shopping. While I was putting things away in the refrigerator, my cell phone rang. When I looked at the screen I didn't recognize the number, but I answered it anyway.

"Hello?"

"Hi."

"Jessie?"

"Yes."

"What are you doing? Where are you calling from?"

"I'm at home. I've never called you from this number before, but I can't find my cell phone and wanted to talk to you."

I glanced at the clock, wondering when Tricia would be showing up. "Okay…"

"Well," a pause with an air of uncertainty crossed the line before she finished her sentence. "I know this may be pushing it, but I was wondering if I could see you."

Oh hell. "That's *not* a good idea, Jessie. I'm in a relationship."

"So am I. I'm just … I want to at least be friends with you."

"I can't," I said softly. "I'm sorry for what you're going through right now, but I just can't do that."

A few seconds went by before Jessie finally spoke. "I understand, but if you change your mind or if you're going through something and just want to talk, then just dial my number. I'll *always* be here for you."

"Okay…I have to go now."

"Bye."

Always, the word echoed in my head as if it were an empty hallway. I wished Tricia would hurry up and come home to save me from myself! Long after disconnecting with Jessie, thoughts of her rushed me. I pulled out photos of Tricia and me to help me combat my state of mind. I needed Tricia and I needed her badly. It felt like forever, but I finally heard from her.

"I'll be there soon. The driver is putting my bags in the car right now."

"Great. I can't wait to see you! You're not allowed to leave me alone again. This is torture."

"Aw, don't worry I'm on my way."

"All right. I'll see you when you get here."

While preparing myself for Tricia, I gave myself a pep talk. I hoped she wouldn't ask about Jessie but was almost certain she would. I decided not to lie to her and fess up that we'd spoken again, but I would tell her that was the end. I would, however, lie to myself. And fib number one was that I did not give a damn about Jessie.

I noticed the sky was dark and without a star as I kept looking out the window for Tricia to arrive. She didn't waste time after settling in to ask, "Did you speak to Jessie while I was away?"

I hesitated, "Yes."

Her eyes widened.

"But I told her that I am in a relationship and that I can't be there for her. I told her that if things got too hard for her that she should see a therapist."

"Okay. You know I don't believe in being friends with exs, right? Especially not her."

"Yes."

"People in your past belong in your past. And I won't compete with an ex either, Sadira."

"I know that. You've said it before, and I know."

"So long as you're aware."

"All right all right. Let's change the subject."

I told her the truth. Most of it, at least. I omitted the part about Jessie wanting to see me. I figured she'd flip, and I didn't want to deal with that. I'd much rather spend the night getting reacquainted, which we did.

I spent the next couple of days packing my things up to prepare for moving in with Tricia. My computer would be the last thing to be put in a box. To break up the monotony of gathering my belongings, I ventured on the Internet and was eventually spotted by Jessie when my instant messenger automatically logged on. I didn't know that she was online because I'd taken her off my friends list, but I never actually blocked her so that she couldn't see me. About a half an hour after I'd been on, a dialogue box popped up with a message from her. After she said hello, a snippet of our last phone conversation replayed in my mind. When I said I was in a relationship she said, "So am I." I thought about it for a few seconds before bringing it up...

> Sadira: Why did you call me the other night if you're in a relationship? Why didn't you call your girlfriend? What's up with that?
>
> Jessie: well, we're on again and off again. she'd broken up with me right before my mother died and wasn't returning my phone calls.
>
> Sadira: Why? Did you cheat on her too?
>
> Jessie: no! i've changed so much since you and i were together, but Lisa doesn't seem to think so.
>
> Sadira: I don't care what her name is.

196

Jessie:	....
Sadira:	What is it you want from me? Why do you want to be friends with me? We've both moved on.
Jessie:	i don't want you to be gone from my life forever. i know that i messed things up with us, but i know that you don't hate me for it. i'm not trying to break up what you have with...
Sadira:	Tricia.
Jessie:	i just know that there is still a bond between us and don't want to let it go. why should we...from the very beginning of our meeting each other our connection has been quite unexplainable.
Sadira:	And?
Jessie:	and i want you to be happy even if it is not with me, but i want to still feel you. that connection made me feel alive...and right now i need *something* to make *me* feel alive.
Sadira:	As always, it is all about you...
Jessie:	but it's not. i know in my heart that you desire the same...to have a piece of me.
Sadira:	I'm happy with my life and with my girlfriend. I love her.
Jessie:	but you didn't deny that you have the desire.
Sadira:	Look, I have to go.

I exited the messenger before she could respond. The whole conversation felt like a hallucination. I had three feelings for Jessie: allure, deep resentment, and tenderness where I neither loved nor despised her but just craved her presence. It made me feel safe that she could always be around. Everything rotated inside me like a thunderstorm interrupting a beautiful day. "Shut down" I commanded the computer. I'd had enough and was wondering what I had gotten myself into by allowing her to stay in my life.

Chapter 22

You should come and visit. And you can bring Tricia if you want. I can't wait to meet the woman who has you so sprung. A distant memory reminded me to talk to Tricia about going to Bermuda to visit Khedara and Lance. A vacation sounded like paradise at the moment. It would be good to get away. When I brought it up with Tricia she responded enthusiastically.

"I'd *love* to go."

Her excitement warmed my heart. I could only imagine how great two weeks away with her would be.

"Great. I'll let my sister know and then start making plans."

"Ooh. I bet the beaches there are beautiful."

I smiled. Bringing up the vacation was a great idea. To get a better picture of what we could look forward to experiencing in Bermuda, we got on the Internet and visited a bunch of sites that outlined all the lovely attributes of the small country. It *did* look gorgeous.

When I spoke to Khedara and told her we wanted to visit, she was happy too. We hadn't seen each other since I the short period when I lived with her. And I was a depressed mess during those three months. It would be good for her to see me happy, and vice versa. The more I thought about it, the more excited I got about the idea.

I made travel arrangements for us to fly to Bermuda and stay for two weeks. But as days went by, Jessie floated into my mind, sometimes staying with me for hours at a time. I didn't say anything about it to Tricia or reach out to Jessie. I kept it all inside hoping the obsessive thought patterns would disappear.

Unfortunately things didn't turn out that simply for me. In time, Jessie and I did speak again on the Internet through instant messenger. It didn't even bother me when she mentioned her girlfriend. I knew they wouldn't last. Jessie did tell me that she took my advice and was seeing a counselor to help her deal with the loss of her mother.

I started to wonder how long I could be discreet about our conversations. I didn't live alone anymore, and that made things difficult for me. It bothered me on one hand because I wasn't cheating, but on the other hand I knew I had to be careful because Tricia would be upset if she knew Jessie and I were in contact, even if my intention wasn't to step out of my relationship with Tricia. I knew I was wrong for doing it, but I couldn't help myself. I was addicted to Jessie.

Chapter 23

Warren and Josh were having a get-together at their house again and Tricia asked me if I wanted to go.

"Sure, we can go," I said with a smile.

"Good. Start getting dressed."

I followed her lead and soon we were heading toward their house. I tried my best to hide my nervousness. *Please don't let Janae' be there.* My prayers were answered when we arrived and it was only Warren, Josh, and three other people whom I remembered from the time they'd previously had a get-together. Hors d'oeuvres, wine, hard alcohol, and stories were all in abundance. The night was passing by smoothly until the doorbell rang and Josh got up to answer it.

"That's probably Janae' coming up in here all *late.*"

My heart stopped. She walked in with someone I didn't recognize, which was a good thing for me. My fear of being found out had me thinking that somehow she and Jessie had linked back up and were going to appear. Janae' and I exchanged glances and said hello, but I refused to be alone with her for too long. It would have been awkward, and we had never told Warren or Josh that we knew each other before their first party.

The evening concluded with a pleasurable uniting of bodies between Tricia and me. Thoughts of Jessie crossed my mind as I held Tricia, but I did not let on. Somehow I managed to present myself as being totally into Tricia when parts of my brain wandered to Jessie. I did

201

remember, however, to turn my cell phone off so that there could be no chance of it ringing in the middle of the night. The last time Jessie and I spoke we'd agreed not to call each other, but I just wanted to be sure.

In the morning, I kissed Tricia before going to work.

As Tricia and I got closer, my friendship with Jessie began to get stronger. Despite our agreement to only speak online, the next time we engaged in conversation was on the telephone, but using landlines instead of cells. My paranoia and fear of getting caught prompted me to use something that would prevent Tricia from easily looking at the bill and seeing the list of numbers coming in and being dialed out of my phone. Our last conversation got deeper than I wanted. She revealed that her girlfriend had broken up with her after overhearing Jessie on the phone with me. I asked about what had happened.

"She got fed up with me," Jessie responded. "All along she thought she was different from anyone that I'd ever been with, but the story of you and me was too familiar for her. She said she realized that she was no different at all and broke up with me that night, again. She'd called things off before but she always came back. That night seemed final though…"

"Oh."

"She told me she couldn't find a single reason to stay. After all, look how you and I ended," she sighed. "Anyway, how are you and Tricia?"

"So I cost you your girl?"

"Well, not exactly. I fought for Lisa to stay with me. It was one of the scariest things I've ever done. I sat outside of her house until she would talk to me."

I stopped paying attention to our conversation for a minute. I was angered at her statement. How could she go through all that for someone when it was so damn difficult for her to give me what I wanted? *Well, I'll be damned. She truly has changed. Isn't that a bitch?* I felt myself getting upset but held my emotions back and listened.

"If my best isn't good enough for her, then I just have to deal with it. It's probably payback for what I did to you. I want it to work though. I

202

think she's the next best thing outside of you."

"Really now?"

"At least you have Tricia. It seems like she really loves you, and I'm happy you got to experience the love you so badly wanted. Well, I feel torn. I wish I could have given it to you years ago. Where is Tricia tonight anyway?

"She's working late."

"Does she come home late a lot?"

"Off and on."

I didn't want the conversation to veer off too much on Tricia so I eased out of it and told her good night.

I got used to talking to Jessie once a week or so and went so far as to buy pre-paid cell phones so that there would be no record of calls to her. That was easier than trying to use e-mail or instant messengers all the time. I only had a few hours to myself in the afternoons before Tricia got home.

I felt guilty but was getting in deeper. I wanted to see Jessie, and the feeling was mutual. I knew it wasn't my imagination because she said it in a way that almost got me busted. One night Tricia and I were at the movies and I felt my cell phone vibrating. It wasn't a call but a text message sent from the Internet...*Just one night...I want to make the sweetest love to you in a way that brings you into a realm of ecstasy where only I can take you... I'd never tell a soul...damn, I want you.*

The message caught me so off guard that I reacted verbally. Softly, but still, I said, "What?" I was in disbelief.

"What is it?" asked Tricia.

Shit, was my second thought. I quickly deleted the message and pretended my phone was malfunctioning. "I don't know. It keeps vibrating, but it's not ringing and there aren't any messages. Maybe I dropped it too many times."

She took my statement at face value and let it go. "Oh."

Whew. "Give me some popcorn." Ha! I held a grin back and laughed at myself inside.

After leaving the movies, Tricia suggested we go up to the Village to shop. At that time of night I knew the only shops open in the Village were adult pleasure stores. She told me to go browse in the video section while she picked up a few things.

"Okay," I said. I felt like a pervert but did as I was told. Even though I looked at porn from time to time, it was in the privacy of my own home, not browsing aisles and aisles of it like I was shopping for a sweater or something.

Tricia came to get me, and we stopped at the counter to pick up the bag of nasty goodies she'd bought. I was intrigued and excited. "What did you get?"

"Don't worry about that. You'll see soon enough."

"Hmph."

"Oh hush," she told me. "Just hail a taxi and stop being a brat."

I laughed. "Fine."

"Where to?" asked the driver when we got in the car.

Tricia spoke before I could. "The downtown Brooklyn Marriott on Adams Street."

I looked at her confused, and she winked at me. That's when a full smile crossed my face. *What kind of kinky night is she turning this into?* I had no idea, but I couldn't wait! The element of surprise and spontaneity was enough to get me aroused. I was ready to attack her right then but decided to hold on and not have another taxicab love scene.

When we got to the hotel, she pulled a $20 bill out of her purse and gave it to the driver. I walked behind her into the building where she asked for a suite and slid her debit card across the counter. The young Indian woman working at the front desk was very attractive herself. For a second, my mind conjured a scene with the two of them in bed with me, but I quickly shook it off when Tricia grabbed my hand.

"What's up with you tonight?" I asked once we were inside the elevator.

"I don't know. I just felt like doing something different."

"Mm hmm. So what's in that bag?"

"You'll see," she whispered with an evil laugh.

Before I knew it, we were on the top floor and walking down the hall looking for our room. It was the last room and looked great inside.

There wasn't too much time for me to admire it though as Tricia promptly told me to go take a shower.

"Yes ma'am." She didn't have to tell me twice.

I went into the bathroom, stripped down, and showered thoroughly and quickly. Without a change of clothes I just sat on the bed naked.

She looked at me devilishly, licking her lips. "I'll be out soon," she told me before going to shower. She took the bag into the bathroom with her. It seemed like she was in there forever, but she eventually emerged dressed in a patent leather outfit, with furry handcuffs in one hand and a blindfold in the other.

"Damn," was all I could say. My eyes widened as I looked at her from head to toe. She had on a pair of heels that made me want to get down on my knees and kiss her feet.

"Dim the lights and sit at the foot of the bed." She spoke with authority, and without questioning, I obeyed.

She stood in front of me. "Touch me," she said. "Glide your hands up and down my body and worship me."

As I let my hands pass over her leather-clad figure, I closed my eyes to submerge myself in the moment. A second later she began talking again, in a stern, powerful voice. "I know you like what you're feeling, what your fingertips are touching, and the reaction it's causing in your own body. You see Sadira, most of the time at home you run things. But tonight," she turned around and pushed me back on the bed. "*I* am in charge and *you* are a submissive bottom."

I coughed. "Me?"

"Yes, you. Lay down." She threw the blindfold at me. "Put that on."

Oh no, she's going to turn me into a bitch tonight, was my last though before laying on my stomach and feeling a smack on my behind. But it wasn't her hand. It felt like a tassel or something like that. After the slight shock, I found that I liked it.

Tricia continued to talk, and I felt her climb on the bed. "Put your arms above your head so your wrists are close to each other." She handcuffed me. That was certainly a position I did not expect to be in.

205

She moved her finger from the base of my neck all the way down my back. With the blindfold on, I remembered the image of her in the outfit, and just then she turned me around so that I was on my back. I wished I could see her. I wished I could touch her, but I couldn't. I had to lay there as she kissed, groped, and took advantage of me in a way that felt teasingly good. She kissed me and softly bit me everywhere. Tricia sucked my breasts and kissed down my stomach, over to my sides and back up to my neck. I moaned, and after what seemed like hours, she finally took the cuffs and blindfold off.

"Don't move." She moved down and pushed my legs apart before taking me inside of her mouth. I exhaled loudly as the feel of her warm and wet tongue pleasured me. Riding a wave of elation from heights of intense passion into the depths of cataclysmic bliss, I soon reached a strong climax.

"Oh my God," I said softly. Tricia came up to lay in my arms and I kissed her on her forehead. Spent, I told her to give me a few minutes to enjoy the feeling of sexual release before I would take care of her. I really wanted to hand her a vibrator to take care of herself so I could roll over and go to sleep, but I couldn't that. Not only did I owe her, I needed to remind her who was in charge of the bedroom.

Before I got too relaxed in my post-orgasmic state, I turned to undress her. I peeled the sexy outfit off her and went straight to her center, deliberately forgetting about foreplay. I couldn't be gentle with her after she had me cuffed and screaming like a bitch. Fuck that. Down I went to taste the essence of her womanhood. I held her hands down by her side as I used my tongue to bring her satisfaction. She tried to wiggle free, but I continued and kept her in place without losing my rhythm. Uninhibited, Tricia screamed. She wrapped her legs around me and moved her center upward more into my mouth. She had penis envy, and I could feel it as her rising mound grew hard and titillated in my mouth and against the flicks of my tongue. To please her mentally as well as physically, I moved my head up and down as I sucked her. Managing to free a hand, she placed it on my head pushing me further into her.

"Yes, baby yes. Don't stop!" The way she was moaning, yelling, and carrying on had me on the verge of another orgasm, but I slowed down to keep both of us under control. Down to a few kisses, I eased out and got on top of her at full length so our bodies touched. Soon the only sounds in the room were the bed banging against the wall and Tricia's pleasure-filled screams. Now with her hands free she grabbed me. Her nails scratched my back as our bodies collided.

"Give it to me, baby. Bang me, Sadira. Oh, yes take it."

I began to feel sweat building between our bodies as she talked to me. I closed my eyes, fucked her harder, and joined in the dialogue. "Whose is it?"

"Yours, baby."

"Whose is it? Say my name."

She moaned but didn't say it.

Sweat was dripping from my body as the bed continued to bang against the wall. "Say my damn name."

"Sadira!"

Now *I* had penis envy and she knew it. My eyes were closed and I was gone. "Shut the fuck up, and just let me take you," I said, then held her right arm down above her head with one hand and covered her mouth with my other one. She held on to me with her one free hand.

All I could hear were her muffled screams and the sound of the bed as I rammed my body into hers. I was on the edge of another climax and her body told me she was too.

"You like this shit, don't you? You like the way I fuck you don't you, Tricia?"

"Yes, baby, yes! I'm about to…oh, Sadira…I'm, oh baby!" She yelled as I released my hand from her mouth and she climaxed. I reached my second shortly after. Tired and drenched in sweat, I collapsed on top of her. She hugged me and brushed my hair away from my face. What a night!

We woke up with just about an hour to spare before it was time to check out of the hotel. I could not stop smiling. The thrill of the evening still had me in a good mood. Before we walked out of the room we shared a long, sweet, sensual kiss.

"I love you," I told her.

She smiled and touched my hand softly. "I love you too, Sadira."

We gazed into each other's eyes as emotions tingled inside of me. I really did love her.

Chapter 24

A couple of days later I was alone and my hormones were raging. Tricia was working late, and Jessie and I stole the moment to talk online. Our conversation began to shift and an added visual made it arousing. Turning on her webcam, Jessie reminded me of the body that I once used to make shiver at my touch. The enchanting eyes that used to look so deeply into mine and the long legs that used to wrap around my neck as I pleased her were on display.

I watched her as she reclined in a chair and unzipped her top to reveal her deliciously looking breasts in a black lace bra. She got out of her chair and took a step back. My eyes ventured lower to her pierced navel. My attention was drawn further south when she placed her hands about her center to form a V. She was wearing jeans, but I'd already been in those jeans and knew of the sweet treasure that was hidden within.

"I miss you, Sadira," she said, grabbing my attention. She had a mic attached to her somewhere.

I looked back up at her, but I didn't say anything. I couldn't say anything.

"I'm trying to get over you, but it's so damn hard." She continued to speak and slowly unzipped her jeans.

I took a deep breath and swallowed. "Shit," I said softly...and slowly.

"What? You wish you could touch me, don't you?"

I laughed nervously as she touched herself and moaned my name in a way that reminded me of how many times we'd made love until sweat dripped from every pore in our bodies. As the memories poured into my mind, I loosened up, feeling my body liquefying in response to the visual of her undressing for me.

"Can you honestly look at me and tell me you don't want me, Sadira?" She had slid out of her jeans by then.

Of course I wanted her. There was so much different about her. She was so free, so tempting, so irresistible. "Jessie…" was all I could get out. I found myself touching the screen as she walked closer to the camera.

"I know you love Tricia, but I also know that no one can make you feel the way I do."

"Yeah…" I pulled my shirt off. It was hot.

She backed away from the camera again and lay down on a bed behind her. I could still hear her voice clearly though. "I know you miss the way a certain part of my body hardens under the feel of your tongue. Oops. Did I say that out loud?" She continued to talk to me.

I unzipped my jeans, and my hands wandered. She was wearing black matching v-string panties and her locs were swept up in a ponytail. Her skin looked enticingly smooth. I began to get lost in the field of pleasure she was luring me into when I heard keys jingle at the door. *Oh shit. Tricia's home!* I closed the window that was showing Jessie live on camera and quickly told her I was sorry, but I had to go. She'd understand.

I logged out of everything, grabbed my shirt, and signed off the Internet with just enough time to slip into the bathroom before Tricia got inside. I needed a second to gather myself before I could face her.

"Hi, baby," I heard her call from the living room.

"Hey, what's up?" I put my shirt back on.

"Hurry up in there, I need to use it."

"Okay." I flushed the toilet I didn't use, splashed some water on my face to help me transition for a night with Tricia, closed my eyes, and took a few deep breaths before I dried my hands and face. Properly

210

dressed again, I walked out of the bathroom.

Smiling, she strode into my arms. I hugged her, kissed her on her neck, and told her I missed her.

"I missed you too. Let me use the bathroom, and I'll be right back."

"Okay."

Tricia was so overwhelmed by her job she didn't notice the subtle differences in my behavior. The one time she asked me if I was feeling okay I told her yes. "I just can't wait to go on vacation with you," I said with a smile. And with that, the topic of discussion switched to envisioning the good times we'd have on the pink sand beaches of Bermuda.

The next day I went to the gym to work off my excessive thoughts. It was like walking a tightrope above a fire pit. I had to back away from Jessie for a couple of days because I felt my urge to talk to her getting stronger than it should have been, and I needed to make sure that I didn't behave in a way that would alert Tricia to something being off between us. Our vacation was right around the corner, and I had to be on my best behavior.

I talked to Khedara but didn't tell her about Jessie. I was ashamed and tried to keep our conversation on her and her beau. When she asked about me, I told her how wonderful Tricia was and how happy she made me. "I think she's the one," I said. It wasn't a lie; it just wasn't the whole story. At work I chatted with Devonte' when we had free moments. I assured him too that things were just swell between his cousin and me.

Jessie and I spoke only once more, but it wasn't a sexually charged conversation like our last one. She told me about a painting that she'd done after we had broken up.

"It's hard to describe," she said. "I'll have to e-mail a picture of it to you so you can see. I'd named it 'Pandemonium' at first, but last night I decided to call it 'Tainted.'"

"Tainted," I repeated softly. The word hit me. "Why don't you send me the image tonight? I'd like to see it."

"Okay," she said.

I didn't check to see the image at that moment because I knew Tricia would be arriving soon. Instead, I started cooking dinner to help shift my thinking to Tricia and *our* relationship. Things went by without a problem, and I began to think that balancing Jessie and Tricia might not be as hard as it seemed.

Tricia and I spent the next night packing. Finally our long awaited vacation had arrived. She was excited, filling more bags than I thought could have possibly been necessary. Aboard the flight, we held hands and talked. It wasn't long before our plane touched down and we were greeted by Khedara and Lance. He seemed shorter in person but was still handsome with a contagious smile. After hugs and introductions, both he and Tricia stared at Khedara and me in awe. Though her hair was longer than mine, and she was slightly heavier, it was evident that we were identical twins.

We spent the first evening catching up and getting to know each others' mates over dinner and drinks. I couldn't wait to venture out onto the beaches the following day. Lance warned that it was possible to see all of Bermuda in a day, but I should pace myself. And that's what I tried to do as we started from the east end of the island and made our way west. Even though Khedara had a car, we got around on mopeds, which was really fun. With crystal blue water, magical waves, and beautiful pink sand, we were surrounded by postcard-like scenery. I enjoyed strolling along with Tricia in tow. We got romantic moments alone to ride horseback along the beach, while Khedara and Lance went off to kayak. Well, we were almost alone. Jessie had hitched a ride with us by taking a seat in my mind.

As Tricia's hands wandered to my body at night, my mind told me they were Jessie's. When I pulled her hair in ecstatic moments of pleasure, I felt locs, not the soft smoothness of Tricia's coiffure. With my eyes closed, I imagined Jessie's eyes glancing up at me as Tricia pleased me. Her skin was lighter, as if it were Jessie's. She *was* Jessie. My mouth was trained to only moan Tricia's name. She had me physically, but Jessie had me mentally. As I floated into a sexual abyss, I remembered the camera show that Jessie put on for me. It made every curve of her body fresh in my mind. I moaned as I began nearing an orgasm. Every feeling was intense and my body was extra sensitive to touches. Faster, deeper, and harder I traveled to new heights of pure bliss on a surge of emotions. I held onto Tricia tightly as the image and voice of Jessie brought me over the edge and into pleasure. I shuddered in an orgasmic release wondering what the hell had just happened.

I was unable to say a word after my climax. I swallowed hard and sank into numbness. I felt guilty. Very guilty. It would take me a while to get over the feeling. In the meantime, I became a better actress. Actually, after that night, the fire inside me seemed to calm down. I got enough of Jessie to sustain me and managed to continue the vacation without alarming Tricia.

The days went by blissfully slowly and Khedara and I continued to get to know the other's partner. We felt like family, enjoying picnics, bars, jet skiing, and even bird watching. Khedara did pull me aside a few times because she said she sensed something was up with me. I refused to reveal what ran rampant in my mind and promised her that I was fine. By the time the vacation wound down I actually felt great overall. Except for my mental rendezvous with Jessie, the trip was flawless. I took enough photos to fill at least three albums. And Lance had taped quite a bit with his camcorder. Khedara promised she'd send me a copy after they converted it to a DVD.

Back in New York, things continued to heat up with Jessie. It was hard to keep it all on the phone. I felt like I was going to explode if I didn't touch her soon. She fed my desire by teasing me with sexual innuendos, telling me about a Brazilian bikini wax she got and how all we needed was just one night. She and I both knew that there couldn't be 'just one night.' If we slept together we would do it repeatedly. I would devour her and surely overindulge.

My feelings for both women caused a great struggle within me. The extremes I experienced from the emotions, sensations, internal pressures, and constant pushing and pulling of my heart and mind as they fought each other were enough to asphyxiate me. Second after passing second I began to understand more and more the power of dependence. I needed Jessie. Every time I rode the subway I hoped that I'd catch a glimpse of her. I helplessly looked up and down the platform every time the train stopped at West 4th Street, which was a haven for gay people in New York. I knew it was farfetched, but still I hoped. I was dying without her but had to appear alive for Tricia. How long could I keep up this deception? Apparently, not long…

One night Tricia and I were out at a lounge with Warren and Josh. The evening had started off great. I even got on stage and did a poem for Tricia, but the entire setting and mood soon changed. If I didn't know better, I would have thought it was a set-up. "If Your Girl Only Knew" funneled through the speakers and my eyes widened when I saw Jessie and her friend Janae' walk in wearing sexy summer attire. Jessie was in all black, wearing a halter-top, Capri pants, and strappy slingback sandals. Her skin glimmered like gold. My heartbeat sped up and I felt a rush to my head. Tricia didn't notice Janae' at first and kept talking to Josh. With Tricia's attention on someone else, Jessie took the moment to wink at me. Janae' had a smirk on her face. *Fuck.*

I didn't know how things would go down. If Warren or Josh saw Janae', they would wave at her to come over to our table, and if she came up close with Jessie, Tricia would recognize her if not by the description I'd given her, then by the sweat that would probably boil on my forehead as I sat there shrinking from anxiety. I found myself silently praying that Jessie and Janae' wouldn't come our way.

As the bass from the music pumped through the speakers, I felt beads of sweat rolling down my back. I excused myself to go to the ladies room. Nerves and fear forced me to relieve myself. I heard someone enter as I was zipping my pants up, but I didn't have the nerve to call out a name to see if it were Jessie. What if it was Tricia and I said that? I kept my mouth shut, went to wash my hands, and tried to gather myself and not get too worked up over the situation. *Just be cool,* I told myself. I was scared. When I went back out toward our table, I saw Janae' talking to Tricia, Josh, and Warren, but Jessie wasn't with her. I stood so still in my confusion that it wasn't until someone bumped into me that I came back to reality. I took a deep breath and went back into the bathroom. I was afraid to go back to our table. Bracing myself against a sink with my head down, I tried to think.

"Sadira." The voice was soft, but unmistakable.

I looked up slowly and saw Jessie in the mirror. Blinking quickly as if it would make her vanish or take *me* away, I swallowed hard as a lump began to build in my throat. Jessie looked delicious, and had it been another night, I may have given in and slipped out of the lounge with her, but that night all I wanted to do was get away from her. I didn't want Tricia to see us anywhere near each other.

"Do you have a minute?" she spoke again.

"No…I have to go."

"Can I at least have a hug? It's been a long time."

My pulse quickened. *Damn she looks good.* Months of my wanting to touch her, lusting after her in my mind, and longing for her in my heart had passed and there she stood before me as if she were an angel. My hands trembled as I battled internal forces coaxing me to touch her.

"Just a few seconds," she said.

My eyes locked with hers and strength slipped away from me. I gave in and reached for her. It was a very quick awkward hug, not close enough, not tight enough, not worth the trouble I would get into if Tricia found out about it, and not…and just not enough! But I hadn't the time to melt into her the way I wanted to. I let go quickly and stepped out of the bathroom wondering how long I'd been away from Tricia.

When I got back to the table Tricia was livid. "Outside, now." She spoke between gritted teeth.

Without glancing at anyone, I followed Tricia outside.

"What's going on, Sadira?" She wasted no time questioning me.

"I don't know."

She clenched her fists as if she were restraining herself from hitting me. Again, she spoke slowly. "Sadira, what is going on?"

"Baby, I don't know. I didn't invite them here."

"Oh really?"

"What? Of course not."

She shook her head negatively.

"I'm not lying. Why would I ask them to come here? I don't want to run into Jessie with you?"

"So you wanted to run into her alone?"

"No! No, no, no, baby. Okay, wait." I reached for her. "Just wait a minute. Where are you getting the idea that I told them I'd be here?"

"Janae' said she *had a feeling* that she'd run into you here."

"WHAT?" Now things really weren't making any sense! I didn't know what the hell was going on! "Look, Tricia. I haven't talked to Janae' so I don't know where she got that from. Plus I didn't even know that she and Jessie had caught up with each other again."

"But have you spoken to Jessie?"

Oh, Jesus. I bit my bottom lip. "No."

"You're lying!"

Fumble. "Yes, I mean…" *Shit, shit, shit!*

Tricia's eyes narrowed on me in anger. It was as if the smell of blood were in the water and she was a preying shark. I felt my skin getting hot and knots forming in my stomach. Fear.

"Sadira!"

One word, my name, sounded extremely heavy when she said it. All of my lies and discreet conversations with Jessie were about to crash down on me if I didn't come up with something to say quickly.

"Baby, I'm telling you the honest truth. I don't know what's going on. I did not tell anyone we were going to be here tonight, and I have no idea where Janae' got her information from."

Tricia folded her arms across her chest and I could see controlled anger in her eyes. She exhaled deeply and rolled her eyes. "I'm not going to make a scene and let her think that she has control of the situation. You and I are going to go back inside and finish up here, but when we get home we're gonna talk." Tricia spoke with soft intensity. She was fuming.

"Okay." That was all I could say.

She pasted a fake smile on her face as soon as we got back inside

216

and I followed behind her, obediently. Silently, I repeated to myself *keep your eyes and mind on Tricia. Keep your eyes and mind on Tricia.*

I ordered another drink, but alcohol wasn't strong enough for me to block out the uneasiness I felt. Against my mantra my eyes stole glances to scan the room for Jessie. Tricia squeezed my hand under the table. Janae' looked over with a facial expression that was unreadable, and finally Warren said it was time to go.

Josh spoke next. "Yes, I think we should leave. Sadira, you look tired."

I got up with only an affirming nod.

By the time we got home Tricia had calmed down, but I wasn't nearly off the hook.

"You know it wouldn't have been so bad if you weren't looking around for Jessie all night."

"I wasn't—"

"Save it, Sadira. I saw you," she spoke firmly. "I felt you drawn away from me and into her. So please don't lie to me."

I sat quietly.

"Do you know how embarrassing that was for me? Do you?"

"I'm sorry, baby. I…" I didn't know what to say. I was sorry things went the way they did. I didn't plan it.

"I was so fucking embarrassed, Sadira!" She glared at me.

"Sorry!"

"Why did you have to do that? Damn it."

"I don't know. I apologize. I didn't mean to embarrass you. I didn't."

"But you meant to look for her. You were like a fucking hound just searching for her!"

Ouch. I had no response for her besides continuously asking for forgiveness.

She paced, ran her hands over her head, and looked at me with reprimanding eyes. "You know what? Let's just put this night behind us," Tricia finally said. "I don't want to dwell on it because it's just going to piss me off."

217

"Okay." That was a wonderful idea. I almost smiled.

We moved on from that night and tried to act as if it didn't happen. I was surprised she didn't press me more for information but was grateful that she didn't. In the back of my mind I wondered how often she reflected on that night. It wasn't like Tricia to just let things go, and I had to admit it scared me a little bit that things seemed to go on so easily.

Though Tricia didn't bring up Jessie, there were instances devoid of conversation when I was sure that Jessie still crossed her mind. I wasn't going to bring Jessie up though. Damn that. I didn't want to have to lie to Tricia, but I would…for her own good, and mine too. When I thought back on all the times I talked to Jessie and how I went so far as to use pre-paid cell phones, it dawned on me just how badly things could have gotten if Tricia had found out. She would have never believed that Jessie and I hadn't slept together again.

And as all the things I did in the dark began to come to light in my mind, I realized that I was still very careless by using instant messengers on the Internet so much. If Jessie wanted to be nasty, she could have very well saved copies of those conversations. I didn't think she would take it there though. ***Please*** *don't let her go there.* I liked to think I knew Jessie better than that, but then again she wasn't the same. Would she do something so spiteful to crush me for not giving her what she wanted? I didn't know, but I prayed she wouldn't.

I sat down and e-mailed Khedara to tell her everything. I didn't know what she could do for me, but I needed someone to talk to. After writing to her, I cleaned out my inbox and saw a note with an attachment from Jessie that was a week old. I thought about deleting it without opening it but went ahead and clicked on it so I could see what she'd sent. There were only four words in the e-mail, "I'm sorry for everything," but an image started to download. When it was finished the first thing that came to my mind was *tainted.* It looked like madness on a canvas. The auburn and brassy browns fused together and it was hard to tell where the painting started and stopped. It looked like us.

Without responding to it, I closed the message and signed off the Internet. I decided not to dig my hole any deeper than it already was. Whatever I needed and wanted to say to her would just have to be silenced. I was going to get myself together.

Things got somewhat back to normal with Tricia, but I ached when I was alone. Fleeting thoughts of Jessie traveled through my mind at the speed of light. Her face was in every drop of water that fell during my showers. I never asked her about the night she showed up at the lounge. I just let it be. And I never said anything about the separate world in my head. Instead, I suppressed my desire to speak to her and started looking for books and articles—anything that would help me get through my problems and perhaps reassure me that I wasn't alone. There had to be other people who had gone through what I was experiencing.

I knew my thoughts of Jessie didn't reduce my love for Tricia or discount it in any way. The sad fact was that I had lost control of myself. Yeah, I had lost control. Until Jessie, I never understood people who took their partners back or remained friends after they found out about infidelity, but I saw things in a different light when I found myself in that situation. I was *beyond* that situation. That wasn't just me wanting to take back a cheating ex. It was me going through withdrawal. It was me fighting a monster that I'd created. That was me being controlled by a burning desire. I dreaded a life without Jessie like I dreaded a root canal. And the more I tried to do the right thing and pull away from her, the more it ate away at me from within, which propelled me back toward her to avoid the pain.

When Khedara finally got back to me, she wasn't as hard on me as I thought she would be until I told her that I felt emotionally drained. I just wanted to stop. Literally, just stop. I didn't want to deal with my problems anymore.

"You should go see a therapist, Sadira." My sister spoke without a trace of humor in her voice.

"Hey, you know I've thought about it before but was ashamed to go. I'm not crazy…"

"Going to therapy doesn't mean you're crazy. It means you need help for something that is overpowering you and influencing your life." Her words didn't hurt or sting. She only said what I knew to be true.

She spoke again. "There's nothing to be ashamed of. I had a therapist for a while to help me get over Mom and Dad. Don't you remember?"

"Yeah." I remembered her seeing someone once a week while she was in college and I was in the Air Force.

"I can't help you get your life together, Sadira. But I'm serious when I say I think you should go. Tricia loves you. I saw it the way she looked at you and spoke about you."

"I love her too."

"I know. But you're cheating her. It's not fair. Either you get it together or leave her alone."

"Why are you taking her side?"

"I'm not. I'm on the side of women who deserve to have their lover's entire heart, not half of it."

"Yeah, yeah." She was going to start preaching at me soon if I didn't end or shift our conversation. "I'll look into therapy." I meant it. "Anyway, how's Lance and where's our DVD?"

"Do it, Sadira." She sounded maternal. "And Lance is a sweetheart as always. Girl, I'm daydreaming about having his babies! You're DVD will be coming soon."

I smiled. "I'm happy for you."

"Thanks, sis." We finished our conversation.

Chapter 25

The summer heat was unforgiving. Tricia and I were doing okay but not the way we used to be. I still bought her flowers and surprised her with gifts, but I didn't feel as connected as we used to be. We weren't moving in unhindered love the way we used to. I wanted things to work though. We'd put in too much effort for our relationship to fall apart and Tricia deserved to be happy. I didn't want anyone to bring her that happiness but me. She was *mine*.

I took my sister's advice and found a therapist. Once I stopped being afraid to open up, my sessions were great, but I didn't tell Tricia about seeing a therapist because I was embarrassed. It did feel good not to keep everything bottled up all the time. Every Thursday I could say whatever was on my mind and not feel judged. The therapist discouraged me from contacting Jessie again and I tried to follow his advice. I was weak one time and talked to her. The only part of my conversation with her that stood out was when she said, "I know what's in your heart." I didn't respond and she continued. "Not to mention I could see it in your eyes that you really want to be with me, not her. Sadira, I miss you, and I'm sorry everything is unfolding the way it is…" she sighed. "I'm going to step back and leave well enough alone."

I'd heard that before. Honestly, I had lost track of the number of times we said we were going to cut each other off. This time had to be the last time. "Jessie, look, if ever I am single again I will search high, low, far and wide for you. I loved you yesterday. I love you today. And I'll love you always…okay?"

There was a moment of silence before she responded. "All right. I can live with that."

That's when I hung up feeling like a major failure. I cried and then called my therapist to schedule an earlier session to talk through it. I told him that it was starting to be hard to even trust myself. I was having a difficult time distinguishing my thoughts from my feelings and wanted to give up. He calmed me down and told me that my situation wouldn't change over night. He encouraged me, told me I was stronger than I thought, and needed to put in more effort. This *was* something I could beat. And most importantly, I certainly wasn't the only person in the world who'd gone through an obsessive relationship. I listened, soaked up his words, and pushed myself to regain control of my mind and life. The last thing I needed to do was relapse. *It will take time, but you have to stay willing,* I heard his voice in my head long after I left his cozy office.

I was determined to get myself together. I started a new journal. Well, the journal was more of a log. I got the idea from one of the self-help books I was reading, and every time I thought of Jessie I wrote down what caused me to think of her and how it made me feel. After two days I realized I'd thought of her seventy-two times. *Call her, call her, CALL HER!* Oh, the sounds of yearning in my head! I'd felt everything from sadness to anger to joy to disappointment to rage while battling the forces in me that insisted I go backwards. Jessie was cocaine.

I picked up the phone to call her a number of times and hung up before I finished dialing. One evening I actually did let it ring until she picked up, but I did it from a pay phone in the subway so she wouldn't know it was me. I just wanted to hear her voice. My heartbeat sped up as the phone rang. Pounding. Speeding. Nerves running amuck. She picked up, said hello twice, waited a few seconds, and then disconnected. Something told me she knew it was me. I felt like a big idiot all over again. Pacing, I fought back tears and wiped my sweaty hands against my jeans. I had headaches. I was fighting.

Shit. *What's your problem?* Over and over again I asked myself that question. What was it that Jessie gave me that I felt I couldn't get anywhere else? Why did I have tunnel vision and act as though there was only one cure for me, and why the hell didn't I figure out what my problem was in the first place? What did she provide?

I began to explore those questions in my therapy sessions. And surprisingly it didn't take as long as I thought it would to crack the mystery. Jessie gave me what I was used to as a child, abandonment. But unlike everyone else, she came back. I was used to being left alone, forgotten and uncared for. After Khedara and I were split up as children, no one ever paid any attention to me…even in my adult relationships before Jessie, no one gave me the attention that I so badly wanted. Nobody loved me. Nobody cared. The Air Force was the closest thing to feeling loved that I ever got.

Jessie came back to me though. In all her beauty and goddess-like features, she told me *she* needed *me*. How exhilarating! Heaven was in her eyes.   She read everything I wrote, sometimes memorizing my words the way I'd memorized the exquisite details of her appearance. Her smile became my air. She had said I was important to her and that she didn't want to be without me. She was supposed to fill that deep hole I had, but she was too afraid. She was afraid I'd hurt her, so she left me abruptly before I had the chance to do so…only coming back when it was unbearable to be without me. A cycle. She fed me in small doses, giving me a sip of water when I was thirsty enough to drink an ocean.

The taste of how it felt to have someone care for me, especially romantically, was one I never wanted to live without again. It was too painful. The more she ran away and came back, the more I'd look forward to the sweetness of her returning. So I pushed harder, trying with everything I had to love her enough to show her that I meant no harm. I just wanted to give her the world if she'd let me. Meanwhile she sabotaged every chance we got at completing each other. A little bit at a time was good enough for her, but I wanted all of her. Maybe I smothered her. Maybe I was too much. I didn't know. I didn't mean to. Anyway, she would always eventually return. If I could count on nothing else, I could always count on Jessie to come back to me one day. And that comforted me. She was the one person who would *never* leave me for good. She loved me. How could I give that up?

"I worked so hard for her." I was talking to my therapist about Jessie on one of my down days. "Sometimes I feel like she should always be mine because I pushed and pushed and pushed until she would let her guard down. *I* tore down all the walls around her heart and I made her unafraid of love. No one else did, it was me."

He looked me directly in the eyes. "And what did she do to your heart?"

I stared at the floor. "She broke it. She crushed it and acted without regard for it. But that was a long time ago. Now she's different. She changed after we broke up and seems to want to fix what she's done in the past." I looked up at him. "You know, I hate that I'm so stuck on her. Sometimes I feel like an image of her face is painted on the walls of my heart. When she blinks, my heart beats, giving me life. It's like I live for her or because of her. I don't know. Listen to how crazy I sound!" I spoke in random and scattered thoughts. "Holy shit! And all this time I thought I was sane." I wanted to laugh at myself, but I was in pain. "Denial. Maybe I *am* damaged beyond repair." I remembered a while back thinking that I wasn't. I was wrong.

"You have to erase her from your heart, Sadira. You know what is real and what is fantasy."

"Not all of the time, I don't." I felt stupid and confused. "If I erase her, it'll leave my heart vulnerable to someone new who may end up leaving me. How do I know Tricia will stay?"

"You can't know, but you'll drive her away if you don't let go of Jessie. What is stronger, your desire to be free or your fear of the unknown?"

"My desire to be free...I think. I don't want to be left alone again. Jessie always comes back..." I fought tears. It was so hard for me.

We talked about Jessie more. I told him that I thought she was probably just as needy and bruised from a chaotic childhood. Her father left her family for days at a time sometimes returning to take out his anger

224

on her, her mother, and her sisters. Who knows what he was angry about, but his negative traits rubbed off on her. And somehow we found each other, perhaps latching on because of a common pain…I guess. I don't know, but I couldn't think of any other reason our relationship was so turbulent yet lasted so long.

When my session was over, thoughts of Jessie still passed through my mind. I'll never forget the day I met her on the train. Never. When I saw her, I saw life, but it was a fantasy. I gave that fantasy everything I could, but I couldn't breathe life into it. It took me a couple of weeks in therapy, but I finally figured out what had plagued me for years. Coming to understand everything was an exhausting and excruciating journey, but because I wanted to be free of Jessie, I made that new goal. I had to work just as hard at that as I did to get her in the first place. I had to undo the web in which I'd entangled myself and I had to do it quickly. I had to become strong. And I had to do it without alarming Tricia. That was selfish, but I didn't want to let her go. She was real.

I tried to stay focused on correcting my behavior and thoughts. At some point it wasn't even about Jessie anymore.   It was all a battle in my head, a battle that I began winning. I was able to follow my therapist's advice and my common sense. I still thought about Jessie, but I didn't contact her and eventually even my thoughts of her became non-existent. I kept reading self-help books to help me stay on track. My relationship with Tricia improved as a result. We drifted closer to each other once I stopped being distracted. Every time Jessie crossed my mind I kicked her out. I *finally* got rid of all correspondence that I'd saved over the years. That was major progress for me. I think I had almost every e-mail we'd exchanged since we'd known each other. I dumped them! I burned the journals that she'd given me. I had to let them burn! Watching them crumble into nothingness helped me in a way I cannot describe. And when necessary, I made myself remember the night Jessie's affair with another woman came to light. That was enough to piss me off and redirect my mind to Tricia.

In addition, I went through all of the photos that Tricia and I had taken over the course of the last year to remind me of what real happiness felt like. I listened to the songs that I had written for her, and I revisited all of the greeting cards and love notes that we'd exchanged. It helped. I noticed that she could still give me butterflies. I was beginning to fall in love again. True love. Jessie had finally been ejected from my life! God, it felt good to be free.

Day by day things got better until one morning while I was washing the dishes my cell phone rang and I told Tricia to answer it.

"Hello?" I heard her answer my phone. "This is who?" She paused to listen for a response. "Jessie?"

I could have collapsed when I heard Jessie's name. Tricia remained silent, listening to whatever was being said to her. Her facial expression was a mix of white-hot anger and disbelief.

"Excuse me?" she said, pausing to listen… "What proof?" Again, she became silent as Jessie delivered whatever information was going to be the demise of my relationship. Tricia soon hung up the phone, gazing at me in a way that put fear and sorrow in my heart.

"Baby, what—"

"Sadira I am SO through with you!" She spoke with disdain dripping from her words and headed toward the door, taking my cell phone with her.

"Wait, wait, wait, wait, wait! What's going on here?" By the time I put on decent clothes and slipped into my shoes I saw her getting in a cab. *Fuck!*

I went back inside. I paced, trying to remember Jessie's phone number. Because I used to have it saved in my cell phone, I never had to memorize it. I ran my hands over my head, wracking my brain trying to remember the digits that I so badly needed to clue me in. I got so pissed off I couldn't stand still. Sweat was forming on my forehead. I never thought Jessie would stoop that low. Never, but boy was I wrong! Seconds felt like hours as I tried to figure out what to do. I dialed my cell phone, but Tricia didn't answer. Back and forth I continued to pace trying again to remember Jessie's number until it finally came back to me.

I picked up the home phone and dialed Jessie repeatedly but got no answer. Anger began to twist inside me. Relentlessly, I kept trying to get a hold of her but was unsuccessful. My head was spinning as rage, anxiousness, and pain rose in me.

"God damn it. Fucking shit! Shit!!!" I yelled. I was losing my mind. I didn't know what happened or what *would* happen.

I then tried to reach Tricia again. I called several times in a row, but she kept sending the calls to voicemail. I even got on the computer to send her text messages via instant messenger. No response. I began to crumble. More than an hour had gone by since she'd left. And in a city as big as New York she could be *anywhere.*

I tried to call my sister but couldn't get her. I needed someone to talk to. When I called my therapist I got his answering machine. "Shit, shit, shit!" I couldn't dial Devonte'. I didn't want him to know what was going on. I debated calling Warren and Josh, but I didn't want to alert them that we were having trouble in paradise either. I was so stressed out I had to get my inhaler to help me breathe. I couldn't believe Jessie would do that to me. What a dirty bitch! Yeah, I messed up by talking to her in the first place, but what the fuck? I thought we had an unspoken agreement of some sort to keep that between the two of us. How could she expose me like that? Ohhh, Jessie! That was *low.* I could just scream. The clock was ticking and I was losing my mind without Tricia. My mind darkened with anger and hurt. "Jessie. Jessie. Jessie." I shook my head in disbelief. That was shady.

I tired to call Jessie again but got no answer. I logged online to see if she was there, but she wasn't. With time seeming to drag and fly at the same time, I sunk to the floor, curled into a tight position clutching the phone as tears filled my eyes. I'd gone back and forth between anger and sadness so many times that I had a migraine headache. And Jessie was still nowhere to be found. "Tricia, come back," I mouthed silently as if she could hear me.

Just when I thought I couldn't handle waiting anymore the phone rang.

I answered it on the first ring. "Hello?"

"Sa-di-raaa." The god-awful psychotically laced voice was unmistakable.

"Olivia..." My eyes widened.

"Yessssss, it's Olivia!" She laughed. "Mm hm. See, I told you that you'd regret the day you used me. Now Tricia will regret the day you used me too. She's on her way to my house right now...I'm going to carve your precious Tricia into little pieces. " She hung up.

Dropping the home phone, I grabbed Tricia's cell that she'd left behind and ran all the way to the subway station. My blood was boiling. That fucking maniac got Tricia involved! Every dark emotion ran rabidly inside of me. Pain, hurt, disappointment, regret, fear, remorse, and anger...everything. I felt myself plummeting over the edge of sanity. I was sickened by Olivia. Sickened!

Out of breath and drenched in sweat, I entered a hot and crowded subway. All I could think of was Tricia. I had to get to Tricia. My legs were shaking out of control. After the train crawled two stops, I realized it was a bad idea. It would take forever to get to the Bronx, and time was something I couldn't afford to waste.

Heart pounding and vision blurred, I exited the subway and hailed a cab. I fidgeted in the back seat, unable to stand the minutes wasted at red lights and in the horrific New York traffic. I started to wonder if maybe the train would have actually been faster. Stop and go, stop and go, the traffic was making me manic. Tears rushed from my eyes as I thought of Tricia. *Would Olivia really go that far?* I wondered. I tried to call Tricia again, but got no answer. I dialed and dialed and dialed and got no damn answer! Rubbing my hands against my pants to wipe the sweat off, I kept rocking back and forth in the back of the taxi. It was impossible for me to be still. Just then I thought of Jessie. Did Jessie even have anything to do with what was going on? At that point, I didn't think so. It was Olivia who called in the first place. She had to have known somehow that Jessie's name would set Tricia off. Shit. I tried Tricia again, but she didn't pick up the phone.

With no one else to call, I tried Jessie's number again. It went to voicemail. I was getting dizzy, and my mind was clouding with rage. If Olivia had done anything to Tricia, I would kill her.

I needed the cab driver to hurry it up! "Well, shit. Can you go any faster? This is a emergency!" I yelled. I didn't care if he had to make illegal turns or run red lights. I wanted him to MOVE. "I'll pay you extra to speed it up, man!"

"All right," he said and floored on it.

I dug my nails into the chair, holding back a scream. I wanted to sob. I wanted to holler. Tricia's cell phone soon rang. I answered without looking at the caller ID. "Hello?"

"Hello?" It was Jessie.

"It's me..."

"Sadira? You called me like twenty times! What number is this? What's going on? "

"Oh, Jessieeeeeeeeeeeeeeeeeee." I cried. Her voice broke me open.

"What? What? Baby, what is it?" She spoke hurriedly and with concern.

"Where have you been? Did you call me earlier? Where are you?"

"Slow down. I forgot my cell phone at home today. I just got here and saw all the missed calls from this number. What's going on?"

"So you didn't call me today, right?"

"No. Call you for what?"

Pain crashed down on me. "I can't even talk about it now. I'll tell you later."

"Wait, Sadira don't hang up!"

"What?"

"Tell me what's happening. I'm worried about you."

"I can't tell you right now. I don't have time." Almost an hour had gone by and we were nearing the area where I remembered Olivia lived.

"Where are you?"

"The Bronx." As I said it I remembered that Jessie lived in the Bronx, but at the moment I couldn't remember how close or far from

229

Olivia's apartment she was. It didn't matter. "Jess, it's a long story. I will tell you another time. I have to go." I hung up.

After paying the driver I got out and looked around for a moment to try to remember in which building Olivia lived. After a quick scan, I knew which one it was and went directly to it. I went to knock on her door. There was no answer. I tried to ring the bell, but it didn't work so I knocked again longer and harder, and then tried to turn the knob. I banged on the door and called her name. No answer. I even put my ear to the door but heard nothing. Frustrated, I tried the knob again, pulling and turning it with force. "Shit!" I pounded my fist on the door. A man walking by looked at me as if I were crazy, but I didn't care. I could hear her phone ringing on the other side of the door, but no movement. I clenched my fists and grinded my teeth to try not to explode in the apartment hallway. It didn't work.

"God damn it, Olivia, open this fucking door!" I continued to bang on the door. It was useless. I turned to leave and saw the man who had previously walked by me. My eyes locked with his, but I didn't say anything. I left and tried to reach Tricia again. That call didn't go straight to voicemail as they had previously been doing. She didn't answer, but it rang four or five times. *Maybe she just turned it back on.* I kept trying, but she never picked up.

With my stress level still at an all-time high, I called the police to report her missing. I told them what she looked like, the last time I saw her, and about Olivia's threatening message. They said they'd work on it. It didn't make me feel any better, but it was the only step I could think to take. I didn't know what else to do. *I'll **always** be here for you.* The resonance of Jessie's voice brought me back to the right side of sanity. I called her back. A ball of pain centered in my throat making it difficult for me to speak clearly when she answered, but I still managed to talk to her.

"Go home," she told me after I informed her of what was going on. "Go home now, and see if she's back there."

"Yeah, I'm trying to get a cab now."

There was a pause. "Where are you now?"

"Still in the Bronx."

"I mean where…what street?"

I looked up and told her the names of the streets at the intersection.

"I'm not far. Do you want me to drive you?"

"Can't do that. If Tricia *is* there and I show up with you, she'll kill me. No, no. Can't do it. Don't worry, I just got a cab to stop. Let me go."

"Okay."

We hung up.

When I arrived back at home Tricia still was not there. I called her incessantly to no avail. I tried got Olivia's number and dialed it too, but couldn't get her either. I flip-flopped between calling both of them until I got a cramp in my hand. I called Jessie back because she was the only person I could reach, and I needed someone. I went off on a tangent about how I was sorry I did all the flirting with her.

"Let's not go there. It's not me you should be apologizing to, and I think we both finally understand that we just don't belong together. Anyway, I know it's hard to do, but the best thing you probably can do is to stay calm and be alert. Did you tell anyone in Tricia's family what happened?"

"No, I—" Before I could answer I heard a car door slam shut out front. When I went to the window I saw Tricia. *Finally.* The long hours that had gone by since morning made it feel as though days had passed since I'd seen her last. It was late, and the sun had long since set. I hung up with Jessie and ran to the door.

Tricia wouldn't even look at me when she entered the apartment, but I grabbed her and hugged her. "Oh my God. That wasn't Jessie who called! Are you okay? Where have you been? Did you go see Olivia?"

She looked me directly in the eyes. "Have you cheated on me, Sadira?"

"No!"

"When was the last time you saw Jessie?"

"I haven't seen her since that night at the lounge, why?"

"So you haven't been talking to her at all?"

231

"N- no." *Oh my God I stuttered.* I should have just thrown in the towel right then.

"You're lying."

I was about to lie again, but I knew it would just make things worse. The disappointment in her eyes felt like a dagger stabbing me repeatedly. "I have spoken to her today, but I didn't cheat. I've never cheated. And I'm telling you the honest to God truth that I haven't seen her since that night at the lounge."

"Today?" She was a volcano ready to erupt.

I bit my bottom lip. "No, see I only called to ask if she had dialed my cell phone earlier!"

She looked at me in disgust. Her eyes were red.

"What happened today?" I asked again. I knew we had a lot to talk about but wanted to get back to Olivia.

"It was Olivia."

I sighed. "I know. Did you see her at all today?"

"What do you mean, you know?"

"She called the house and said she was going to…"

"What?"

"That she was going to kill you."

Tricia looked at me confused. "I did see her in Manhattan, but she didn't look like she could do me any harm."

"You didn't go to her apartment?" I was baffled. "Well then what happened?"

"No. I met her in the city. She took it upon herself to tell me that I'd *never* have all of you and that you were sleeping with Jessie behind my back. She went on about how she was looking out for my best interest, and that you were a snake because you broke her heart too. How does she even know about Jessie?"

"I don't know."

"Have you slept with Jessie?"

"No, baby no!" Shit. I was still trying to figure out Olivia's death threat. Forget about Jessie! "Where did you meet Olivia?"

Tricia wouldn't let up about Jessie. "But you've talked to

232

her…you've probably seen her when I specifically asked you not to. She had a picture of you and Jessie, Sadira. Stop lying to me!"

"Picture, what picture? I haven't been out with Jessie!"

"*This* one, Sadira." She shoved a picture at me. When I looked at it I realized it was from the night Jessie and Janae' showed up at the lounge…when Jessie and I were in the bathroom. *How in the hell did Olivia get this? What was she doing, hiding in a stall?*

My heart began to race to the beat of a thousand horses. In the brief seconds that I took Jessie into my arms, Olivia managed to take a picture. "Oh, this is nothing, baby. Really. It's nothing." I didn't know what to say and was tripping over my words. "I don't know how she got this picture, but I can assure you that I did *not* cheat on you. I swear on my life. You have to hear me out here, Tricia."

"Why? How do you explain this? You are *hugging* her!" She pushed me. "I don't trust you, Sadira! And what the fuck were you meeting Jessie for?" Tricia yelled. "Where was this? When? Oh my God!" She spoke in sharp abrupt statements filled with rage. And again, she shoved me.

"This was—"

A knock at the door interrupted us before I could respond to her. I was afraid to answer it. She glared at me with hate in her eyes before getting up to answer the door. I heard a deep voice speak as soon as she opened the door. The man identified himself as detective for the NYPD, and asked for me. I heard Tricia ask them why they wanted to speak to me.

"It's part of an investigation and we would like to ask Ms. Cooper some questions."

My eyes widened with fright, and I swallowed hard.

Tricia let them in. There were two of them, a woman who looked Puerto Rican and a black man. They introduced themselves to me, and the woman asked if she could have a seat.

"Sure," I said.

We sat down at the dining room table. The woman officer was closest to me while the man remained standing at a towering height.

"May I call you Sadira?" asked the female detective.

"Yeah, sure. What is this all about?"

"When was the last time you saw Olivia Bartlette, Sadira?"

"I haven't seen her in long time ago. I have a protective order against her. I don't know even know why you're here."

"Sadira, Olivia is dead. We found numerous photos of you in her apartment, and we have a witness who says that you were the last person at Olivia's apartment today."

I felt like I was drowning. "Are you kidding me? I didn't kill anyone!"

"And there were records that *she* pressed charges *you*." The man finally spoke. I didn't like him. He came off like an arrogant prick.

"Yeah, but she was unsuccessful. You should have seen that the charges were dropped and the judge granted *me* an order against *her*. Olivia was crazy, and I don't know how she died, but I had nothing to do with it."

"Were you at her apartment today?" He kept questioning me.

"Yes, I was. But I didn't go inside."

Tricia looked at me surprised and he took notice. He glanced at my wrists and then deep into my eyes.

"Look," I said to him, "I went there to look for my girlfriend, Tricia." I nodded in her direction.

The female officer leaned closer to me with the confused look of a concerned elder. "I don't understand. Why would Tricia be there? Sadira, can you tell us what happened today from the beginning to now?"

"Olivia called me and threatened Tricia's life. She said she was going to cut Tricia up into pieces. She said I was truly going to regret the day I hurt her...and Tricia would too. That's why I went up there." Recollection of the words sent a cold shiver down my spine. I looked at the guy. "Check your files, man. You'll see that *I* called the police hours ago to report Tricia missing!"

"What time did you go to Ms. Barlette's apartment?" the woman asked.

"Umm...I don't know. Hours ago I guess." I was scared. I was

234

upset. I didn't know what to do or say. I wasn't feeling like myself.

The male officer pulled out a notepad and started scribbling down notes. His eyes softened. "Is there anything else you can tell us about Olivia...maybe why she would send that kind of threat?"

I informed them of the brief relationship that Olivia and I'd had and how it ended up sour.

"How long were you at her apartment today?" asked the woman.

"Not long. I didn't go inside. The door was locked. I knocked, rang the doorbell, and tried the knob, but that was it. She probably killed herself. She was miserable. Miserable." *Or maybe someone else she was stalking killed her.*

The female detective turned her attention to Tricia. "Did you see Olivia today?"

"Yes..." Tricia's expression was unreadable. The detectives questioned her as they did me and made it clear that they would be in touch with us again.

"Fine. I have nothing to hide," I said and meant it.

Even though I knew I wasn't guilty. I was terrified. *Not again!*

After they left, Tricia and I sat on opposite ends of the couch. I wanted to talk. There was so much I had to say but didn't know where to start. I couldn't think of anything strong enough to really express how remorseful I was. And I still felt out of the loop as far as Olivia was concerned. The guilt that I was carrying was *old*.

Chapter 26

The death of Olivia had altered our emotions and attention that night. I looked at Tricia with pleading eyes. I had so much understanding to beg for I didn't know what to say first.

"Sadira, I know you are a lot of things, but a murderer is not one of them."

"I didn't even see her today."

"I believe you." Her voice sounded lifeless. She stared at the floor and then up at me with sorrowful eyes.

"She's dead?" I said softly more to myself than to Tricia. A part of me was still in shock. "What happened when you left her?"

"I don't know. I rode the subway up and down town before coming home."

The phone rang before I could speak again. Tricia answered it. "Hello?" She paused to listen to the caller and then responded. "Yes, she's here." Tricia handed me the phone.

"Hello?" I answered and sat down on the couch. Tricia took a seat next to me.

It was my therapist. He never called my home number but said he was concerned about me and I wasn't answering my cell phone. I told him that I was physically fine but going through a lot at the moment.

"I can't tell you everything right now, but I have to explain a lot to Tricia. Can I call you tomorrow?" I asked, and he said sure. We hung up.

"Who was that?" asked Tricia.

"My therapist."

"What?" She looked shocked.

"I've been seeing a psychotherapist for a while now, baby. I was ashamed to tell you."

She was taken aback by my revelation. I told her I thought it was necessary to help me move on and focus on my future rather than my past.

"Tell me something, Sadira. Explain. What were you doing with Jessie?"

"I wasn't with her. She happened to be in the bathroom when I was and asked for a hug. Nothing more happened between us. Nothing."

"And you *gave* her a hug." She rolled her eyes. "How can I believe you that nothing else happened?"

"I know what it may look like, and I know it's hard to understand, but I am telling you the truth. The reason I have a therapist is because of Jessie. I realized I had a problem a long time ago and he has been helping me deal with it."

"What kind of problem, Sadira?"

I kept rambling, not answering her question. "And I know it's asking a lot to beg for forgiveness, but Tricia I *need* you. I'm really sorry. Believe me when I say I regret that short moment. We can work this out. I know we can. We have to." I reached for her hand and tried to continue, but she pulled away from me and it stung. She pulled back as if I were trying to hurt her. There was a burning feeling in the pit of my stomach. "There's got to be a way that I can make things right."

"What kind of problem do you have?"

I swallowed. "It's a problem I think I had but have been on the right track. My attraction to Jessie wasn't a normal one. It was more of an obsessive one…before you came along I thought of her constantly to the point where I think I ingrained her in my mind and lived in a delusional fantasy that she was something she was not. I don't think I ever loved the real Jessie. I was in love with a magic person I created in my mind and clothed with Jessie."

She looked at me like I was nuts.

"It's like being addicted." That was the worst word I could have used, but I couldn't think of another. "People get attached to something because something about the substance or action gives them pleasure or

237

temporarily distorts reality or both. If they keep entertaining whatever it is that changes their reality in a compulsive way, they become addicted and it becomes a *need*. In my case it was to a human being." I was starting to sound like my therapist.

She rubbed her forehead. "I need a drink."

"Hear me out now."

Tricia bit her bottom lip, looked at me as if I were a stranger, and listened while I tried to explain myself. I didn't think it was wise to tell her the entire truth about my actions, but I owed it to her to be honest about my *feelings* and intentions. If I didn't purge myself, my thoughts would tear away at me. I had my therapist, but Tricia was the one who finally needed to know. I hated lying to her and sneaking around like a junkie. It was time to come clean.

Plunging into the meat of what I was feeling, I hoped, would show her I was truly sorry for involving her in such a mess and that I would do anything to repair our relationship. She asked me again if I had slept with Jessie and I told her no. She questioned me about how I felt about Jessie, and I told her that my eyes had been opened to the root of my problem and though I thought I had feelings, I knew they were wrong. I did not love Jessie and was training my brain to understand that. I loved Tricia. I did not tell her how much I entertained the thought of going back or hanging onto both of them, but I did tell her that I would not attempt to form any type of relationship with Jessie again. And I was serious.

As I sat there and vocalized what I was going through, I felt a sense of humility wash over me. I wanted her to stay, and I *would* do whatever it took to make things right, but I couldn't say that if I were in her shoes I would want to be bothered with someone who came with as much baggage as I did. All I could do was hope…and beg that the words of sincerity leaping from my heart and mouth would be good enough. I didn't find out anything that night though.

"I don't know about this," seemed to be the only words she could get out. Tricia looked worn out, and I felt it. "I can't even process everything from today," she said.

I remained silent.

238

"I mean if I was with someone and knew that she wasn't right for me I'd just move on. I wouldn't dwell on her. I don't understand any of what you're saying…well, I do, but I don't. I guess logically…Shit, Sadira, you're killing me here. What the fuck?"

A humiliated smile crept onto my face. It was contagious and made it's way to her, slightly lightening the mood. I spoke again. "I know. But my situation isn't your average situation. I am not the only one though. I've read books to help me understand. I've made progress. Believe me, Tricia, if this were something like drinking, I would have told you a long time ago, but because we're not talking about a substance it's really difficult to explain."

She sighed and glanced at the clock.

"I'm being honest. Hey, let's sleep on it. I mean…" I didn't want to sound as if I were pushing her. I wanted her to feel like she was making every decision and the ball was in her court. "Can we go to bed and talk more on it tomorrow."

She looked at me with disappointed eyes but responded, "Yes, I've had enough for one day."

Chapter 27

In the morning I went to take a shower and when I tried to go back in the bedroom I found the door locked.

"I need to be alone, Sadira."

"Okay."

I sat at the dining room table in shame and pain as tears fell from my eyes. Through my blurred vision I could see that a little puddle had formed in a glass that had caught my tears. Prayers began to mount in my mind as I wept. Tricia soon emerged from the bedroom.

"Check your e-mail," she said and walked past me.

"Right now?"

"I guess."

I took a deep breath. "Okay." I went into the bedroom to dress and then log onto the Internet to see what she'd sent me. I felt afraid and lightheaded as I hesitated in clicking on the message from her. *Open it.* I did.

Sadira,

I have to be very honest and let you know that I am seriously second-guessing our relationship. I appreciate your honesty last night, if that was really what it was, but the fact that you admitted to having an addiction to Jessie shows me that I cannot count on promises from you, nor can I count on us lasting. How can I believe that you will not fall back into whatever was driving you to be connected to her? How can I be sure? If Olivia hadn't told me about Jessie, would you have? I don't think so. I'm sure you don't even realize how you've managed to make me look like an idiot to Jessie. How could you do that to me?

I don't think that this is something that can be healed or fixed. I love you, but I don't trust you. You are no longer having a positive influence on me. You are causing me stress and depression, and I can't live like this. Sometimes people have to love enough to let go…and I think this may be one of those times. Everything we built up within the past year is shattered. I don't want to live with all this drama and chaos. Sadira, I don't want to talk to you at all in person until I have time to figure out what my next step is going to be.

Tricia

There could have been no greater punishment for me than to take in the enormous pain that was so evident in Tricia's words. My heart pounded with agony. I'd been hurt before, but nothing I'd ever felt could have been comparable to the hurt I felt for causing *her* anguish.

For hours I avoided Tricia so that she could have the silence and peace of mind she wished. In the late afternoon she was the first to break the quietness in the apartment.

"What did I do to deserve this? I don't even know what to do now." Tears slid down her cheeks. "We've already started merging our lives and it's all messed up."

"I'm sorry." I wanted to tell her to stop thinking it was her fault. It had nothing to do with her, but I knew that it would come out as a lame 'it's not you, it's me' speech, and I wanted to spare her the triteness of that.

She shook her head negatively and spoke barely above a whisper. "This isn't going to work out. I wasn't planning on a future without you, but I don't even feel like I know who you are now. You're a liar. You're addicted. You have people threatening to kill me because I'm connected to you. I can't do this."

Every sentence that fell from her lips was like a bullet to my heart. "Please…" I reached for her hand again and that time she let me have it. I exhaled with relief as I gently caressed her hand and spoke. "Baby, I don't have a plan B either. I really don't. When I look into my future, there isn't a scene without you in it. I'm so sorry I let you down."

"No. You don't understand. I won't let you trample my heart. I don't want to be sitting here a year from now looking like a fool again because I put faith in you."

I began to speak again but was cut off when the telephone rang. *Can things get any worse?* When I answered, it was one of the detectives. I sighed bitterly, not wanting to talk to him. I put him on speakerphone and Tricia and I listened to him say that I was no longer a suspect and Olivia's death was indeed a suicide. The detective didn't tell me any specifics. He only grazed over what had happened to her. Basically, the police found evidence in her apartment that exonerated me.

I wanted to know more, but that's all I was told. I could only dream up my own story of what had happened to Olivia, what she thought her suicide would do to me, if anything, and how she had known Janae'. I guessed she was there at the lounge that night everything went down with Tricia. Maybe I wasn't the only one she was following around. I had no idea, but it was over. *Man...* I thought.

I was surprised to even receive a call to let me know that I wasn't a suspect, but relieved I was nonetheless. There was a strange feeling in the pit of my stomach after I hung up the phone. Maybe I was numb; maybe I was in shock about the death. I don't know. I just didn't feel like myself, but I did realize that the call from the detective disrupted what was about to be a breakup speech from Tricia. I wanted to take advantage of it.

"Tricia, baby. Can we talk some more?"

"What, Sadira?"

"I'm just saying, let's not be in a haste to end things. You said you saw me in your future; if that is true, then we have to learn how to deal with the bumps that will come along. Every day isn't going to be a great day, but if we talk about things, then we can make most days good. We can't be in such a hurry to end things though."

She looked surprised at what I said. "I don't know if I can believe what you say anymore, Sadira. How do we make that work?"

"I'll do anything you want. I need you, Tricia. I really do. If you want me to go to work and come straight home, I will. If you want to monitor my phone records, you can." I felt guilty after saying that last statement remembering how I was so careful to see that she wouldn't find anything in my phone records. I didn't let her see my private regret, but that didn't mean I wasn't hurting even more on the inside for my dishonesty.

She folded her arms and made me wait for a response. Eventually words came from her soft lips. "Why, Sadira? Why? I've been hurt before, but not like this…and never did I think *you'd* hurt me. How could you do this to me? I have given you so much of me. Anything you wanted, everything you've asked for or desired, I gave to you!" She punched the couch. "Did you even think about me and my feelings? Damn it, Sadira!"

There was nothing I could say to convince her that I *did* consider her feelings. "I'm sorry." My voice cracked when I said the words. "I'm so sorry, baby."

"Sorry? You've undone so much. I can't even express my disappointment in you right now. You've been talking to Jessie after I…" she stopped, unable to revisit my reckless behavior.

Unable to think of anything to say, I sat still and absorbed the pain she was feeling as she verbally let it out. Tricia looked disheartened and got up to leave me sitting alone.

"Wait!" I reached out and grabbed her. I couldn't let her walk away from me. I had to make things right. She stopped and turned to me, this time her eyes were not filled with anger but with unhappiness. "I don't want anyone else loving you, baby." I proceeded to beg until I simply ran out of words.

I kept going on and on asking for her to believe in me and somewhere along the line something I said touched her and she began to cry. She sat back down and inched over closer to me, and I leaned back into the couch pulling her into my arms.

A warm tear from her face fell and touched my skin. "God." She spoke slowly. "I love you, Sadira. I do with all of my heart, but I don't give second chances."

Surges of pain shot through me as I listened to her speak. "You've got to give me one. You *have* to."

"I don't have to do anything!"

Put back in my place, I spoke again softly. "You're right, you don't. But I'm begging you for a second chance. I need to make you happy again. I can't even see my life without you." My groveling began again. On the floor and at her feet I pleaded.

I don't know how much time passed or how many words I said, but my begging was not in vain. Tricia said she was going to lie down.

"Can I come?"

She shrugged.

Neither of us went straight to sleep. We lay in the stillness of late afternoon as slits of dimming sunlight peaked through the blinds. She didn't come close to me in bed, but she was the first to break the silence. "Too much is happening in one weekend and I need to think," she said. "If I gave you another chance it would be the first time in my life I put that kind of faith in a person after she'd betrayed me."

"Okay."

"Let's just go to sleep." Tricia turned her back to me. I wanted to touch her but resisted. Instead, I lay on my back thinking about how everything was playing out.

We woke up hours later. Tricia slipped out of bed and into the bathroom, and didn't speak to me when she emerged, but I approached her for a hug. She didn't push me off, but she didn't hug me back either.

"I'm tired," was all she said before climbing back into bed. "Just leave me alone for a while."

The hours went by feeling like days. She went back to sleep, and I lay watching her, hoping that she would give me another chance.

We both called in sick when our alarm clock sounded and some time during that afternoon I made lunch and gave it to Tricia despite her wish for being left alone. She took it. "Thank you... Sadira?"

"Yes?" I answered her quickly and attentively.

"Can you bring me some aspirin, please?"

244

"Sure."

As the day faded into early evening we talked some more, and she settled on giving me not a second, but a last chance. *Thank, God.* I would give anything just to get things back to the way they had been. Yet, that night, there were big patches of silence when normally we'd be talking with each other or playing around. She looked at me differently. Something was missing. Trust. She no longer trusted me, and I had to somehow to change the way she felt.

When we got in bed, I beckoned her to me. I didn't want to go another night sleeping with, but not being able to touch her. That was torture. She came to me when I called, and I pulled her on top of me. I hugged her tightly and kissed her on the forehead. The room felt cold and solemn. Tricia began to cry. I'd wounded her through betrayal and broke my own heart in the process.

It killed me inside to hold her and feel her trembling as she sobbed. In my arms she wept, and in my heart I died. Her tears fell upon my cheek and made me feel like the scum of the earth. The sheets beneath me were bathed in the painful crystals that descended from our eyes. I felt useless, worthless, and deserving of nothing but heartache for bringing her so much misery. She had only been the perfect girlfriend to me.

She moved out of my arms and lay on her side to face me. "What if I did to you what you did to me? Could you handle it?"

I didn't say anything.

"How would you feel if you found out I was talking to another woman, flirting with her? What if I gave my body to someone else, Sadira?"

"I didn't cheat on you!" Just the *thought* of her last question was enough to keep me in check. I'd fantasized about being intimate with Jessie plenty of times, but even the suggestion of someone else enjoying Tricia hit me.

"You may as well have cheated. You stepped out on me in your heart."

"I'm sorry."

245

"Never mind. Never mind. We're putting it behind us. Just never mind."

That's what we tried to do, forget about the weekend and move on.

The next morning we went to work. I sent her two dozen red roses with a card that read *I'm sorry.* That seemed to lift her spirits. When she got home that night, I'd already prepared dinner so that she wouldn't have to do anything.

The next day, I sent her more roses, this time they were pink. The card read: *I'm **still** sorry.* She called me as soon as they were delivered. "You are crazy!" I could tell she was smiling.

"Crazy for you."

"Well, I can't talk long, but thank you for the flowers. Now don't send anymore because people are starting to get too nosey."

I laughed. "Okay."

That evening, though no where near normal, felt better than the previous two. She seemed a little bit like her old self rather than the lifeless shell that had been taking her place. She was even annoying me again by talking through the programming while we watched TV. I hadn't even realized I missed the little things I hated and smiled at the fact I was welcoming them back. That night we even made love. It was not heated make-up sex, but bittersweet exchanges...a reminder to me of whose body and heart I should forever cherish.

As days passed, my heart wouldn't let me forget about everything that had happened. Deep inside I was still hurting for everything I had done. The summer heat felt scorching against my skin as I made my way down streets. I was glad that I had another chance but felt horrible about abusing Tricia's heart. I never knew how heavy guilt really could be and how breaking the heart of someone I loved would crack mine simultaneously. I suffered streaks of depression throughout the days, but having my therapist to talk to really helped me feel better.

I left work alone and went straight home. When I got there one afternoon, I decided to take the instant messenger off my computer altogether. I deleted myself from message boards to which Jessie and I belonged, and while I was at it, I logged into my cell phone provider's

246

website and requested a new cell phone number. I did as much housecleaning as I could. I really wanted to do right by Tricia. After all, it was my last chance.

I finally called my sister to try to tell her about everything. Before I could finish telling Khedara everything I was in tears again.

"Oh, Jesus Christ, Sadira. I don't even know where to begin. I'm mad you waited this long to tell me what you were going through. I thought about you the other night but didn't get a chance to call. I should have checked on you."

"I'm sorry. Everything was happening so fast yet so slow."

"You've got a lot of making up to do. But you know I have to talk to you straight. And before you go rolling your eyes at what I have to say, I want you to think about how you would feel if Tricia did something to dishonor *you*. Would it hurt more than what your feeling now? I not trying to make you feel worse than you already do, but I just want you to think about your life without her before you do anything else."

Her statement hit me hard.

My sister continued. "I wish I were there to hug you right now."

"I sure do need one."

"You're lucky because I wouldn't take your sorry ass back. Hell no. Shit, I wouldn't trust you farther than I could see you, but Tricia must believe in you. Sadira, sis, you *can't* do this again."

"I know, and I won't. I don't ever want to see her in this kind of pain again. And I swear I will make it up to her and see to it she trusts me again."

"It's going to take a lot of time and patience on both your parts in order to get where you need to be. Don't rush it and don't pressure her."

"I won't. I'm doing everything she asks when she asks, and I was serious when I promised her I'd never contact Jessie again. My therapist is a big help."

"I'm glad you took that step. Do what you have to do."

My line beeped. "Hey hold on a second." When I saw that it was Tricia, I disconnected with Khedara.

"Hey, baby," I said.

"Hi." She spoke softly. "Let's um…let's go out tonight."

"What?"

"Let's go out," she sighed. "I was thinking about what you said the other night…how we shouldn't be in such a hurry to throw things away, and I figured since we are trying to piece things back together, we should start dating. It might help."

"Oh, that sounds great. We can go anywhere you want to go." I smiled.

"Surprise me. I'm going to be leaving work soon."

"Okay."

And with that I began to plan a special evening. I made reservations for a late dinner at a restaurant and bought movie tickets online for the last show. I wanted the extra time to put all of the photographs that I'd taken of us and begin creating a movie out of them. It was time for us to build a foundation of loyalty, love, trust, faith, and honesty for a new beginning.

Though I may have felt I needed Jessie in the past because I couldn't be happy without her, I knew that I would never be happy with her around.

Tricia and I continued to rebuild our relationship and move in love. There wasn't a day that went by that Jessie didn't cross my mind, but I didn't go back on my promise and never contacted her. Even when it ate away at me, I endured the pain. Sometimes I agonized in silence when I was fighting forces in me that wanted to talk to her. I went for walks, worked out in the gym, and read self-help books. I found things to fill in the times when I was alone and might be irresponsible. Perhaps if Jessie and I met up in another lifetime and could get things right, then we could just be, but until then I pushed her out of my mind and worked hard at regaining control of my life.

Some days, though, I thought I should break things off with Tricia and stop being selfish. On other occasions, things felt perfect between us. I wanted to do the right thing but honestly didn't know what that was. If I let Tricia go I'd regret it, and if I stayed with her, I would regret that too because I was cheating her mentally and emotionally.

As whirlwinds swirled inside of me, I finally knew I had to let her go. I knew she'd probably never forgive me for that night at the lounge and was suppressing resentment. *Do the right thing.* I kept telling myself over and over to do the right thing, but it was just too damned hard.

But one day I was distracted from Tricia by thoughts of Jessie. I'd seen her earlier in the day in passing but didn't speak to her. Still, the sight of her pushed a button in me. Tricia questioned me, and I just told her that I'd had a hard day at work. I went in the bathroom and took a long hard look at myself in the mirror.

It was time to do the right thing. When I stepped out of the bathroom, Tricia was standing in front of me. She spoke before I could.

"It's her again, isn't it?"

I looked down.

She sighed. "This isn't going to work."

"I know." A teardrop fell from my eye and hit the floor. Slowly, I looked up and into her pain-filled eyes. I took her hand. "I'm sorry, Tricia. I'm so sorry."

"I love you, I do…but, you are just incorrigible. I can't handle you."

I had run out of words. I was empty. And she deserved better than me. No more words were needed, as we both understood what had to happen.

I was exhausted from life. At that moment and in the days after I moved out, I contemplated ending my own life. The fear of dying had become less than the pain of living. I thought of Olivia. She was obsessed with me, and I was obsessed with Jessie. Wow. We were different trees from the same root. She just let mania get the best of her when I tried to work my problems out. *I tried so hard to fix myself.* A part of me sort of understood how she could take the easy way out. It wasn't like I hadn't thought of it before. I wanted to take the easy way out too. I walked around with a wound that was too big to be healed. I was weak. I was damaged and brought baggage that no one was strong enough to

249

carry…that no one should have to carry. I was tired. I just wanted to sleep…*I wanted to sleep…*

Alone in a dim hotel room, I sat on the edge of a bed sharpening a knife. My legs shook nervously as I rolled my sleeves up to expose my wrists. Perspiration formed on every part of my body. My lips trembled. Tears flowed from my eyes. I grazed the knife against my left wrist to test its sharpness. It cut me but wasn't sharp enough to do fatal damage. I only wanted to have to make one slash, so slowly, I continued to sharpen the knife. Earlier that day I'd had an overwhelming desire to talk to Jessie and I called her. I then got angry with myself for lacking strength of mind and hung up without speaking to her after she said hello twice. My anger boiled into silent self-hatred and the next thing I knew I was checking into a hotel with hazy, destructive thoughts. Holding the sharpened knife, I started to shake all over. I had to do it then or never. I wanted to vomit. Blood dripped onto my pant leg from the cut on my wrist. *Do it.*

I closed my eyes, took a deep breath, and brought the knife to my wrist. In the split second before I ran the blade across my skin, my cell phone rang and broke my resolve.

"Oh…" it came out in a high-pitched whimper and jagged exhale. My heartbeat was a sledgehammer. My wrist was hurting from the previous cut.

Jessie. Jessie. Jessie. The name flashed on the light blue caller ID screen of my cell phone. I stared at it but didn't pick it up. It stopped ringing and started a second later. Jessie.

My shirt was drenched in sweat. She'd broken my concentration and my will. I answered.

"Sadira?"

"Yes…" I didn't hear anything else she said. I felt dizzy and there was a few seconds of visual noise before I fell into deep darkness. My body gave out…complete paralysis, but my mind and spirit were fully aware. I could feel nothing, hear nothing, see nothing and smell nothing. *Did my phone really ring?* I was so unsure of where I was I didn't know if Jessie's phone call was reality or a hallucination. Floating in darkness, I hurriedly sent my love to my sister and to Tricia as if I could telepathically let them know something was happening to me. I said goodbye to Jessie. Though I couldn't move I realized sensations were coming back. There was a stretching, pulling feeling tugging at me; and then a very thin long light about as wide as pencil appeared diagonally in front of me.

Come on, Sadira, move. I tried to move a finger, a toe, anything to help me get out of wherever I was. But I felt that pulling feeling again. *Ahhhh!* I was being stretched from one realm into another. I wanted to scream, but couldn't. I was trapped. I wanted to cry. I wanted it to be over! Everything felt so drawn out I couldn't stand it. I trembled. *Tremble.* It made me realize I could move again. I tried with everything I could to bring myself back to what I knew was life, and finally the constant ringing of my phone did it. I opened my eyes, blinked, and looked around. A tear fell from my eye. *I'm in a hotel room.* I'm alive! I saw the blood drying on my hand and pants. I didn't know how much time had passed. It felt like hours there, but seemed like minutes when I looked at my ringing phone. I answered.

"Sadira, where are you?" It was Jessie again. She was frantic.

"In a hotel..." I spoke softly through a voiced wrapped in fear, shock, and pain. I told her exactly where I was. "Help me, Jessie...help me," I cried and spoke in slow soft whispers.

Jessie came. She held me. She cried. She said she knew it was me who had called her earlier and had a gut feeling that something was wrong. I was on her mind from the moment I disconnected and she later gave in to her feelings and redialed the number from which I had called. Bless her. I lay in her arms unresponsive, barely knowing if I were awake or asleep. She took me to a hospital. I don't remember what else happened that night, but something happened *after* that night.

Maybe it was being a breath or step away from death, I don't know. It could have been Jessie's holding my hand the entire time. It could have been whatever medication the doctors gave me. It could have been anything, but whatever it was, it changed the way I felt about life and myself. I found strength. At rock bottom, I decided to stand on the rock rather than crawl beneath it into non-existence.

The road to recovery was a long one. In addition to the psychotherapy that I'd already been going through, I was put on anti-depressants. I took a leave of absence from work and looked for another job. I wanted to change some things, a lot of things. Jessie contacted my sister and asked her to come to New York to help look after me. Khedara stayed for a week and came back every other weekend for the next two months. Jessie and I didn't attempt a relationship. She remained a friend to me. She said she'd always be there for me, and she was.

Piece by piece I constructed a new reality, rebuilding my mind and my beliefs, learning to love myself, the only love I realize I had ever really needed.

Tainted Destiny

End

Acknowledgements

There are many people who had a hand in helping me bring this project to completion. First and foremost I have to thank my partner, Monica Bey. I am forever in your debt for you unbiased support of my projects. I truly appreciate, love and respect you for your patience, understanding and encouragement. Thank you for putting up with my mood swings and my painful moments of trying to figure out if this story was worth publication. Also, I need to thank you for suggesting surprises for the ending for both *Intimate Chaos* and *Tainted Destiny*. Neither book would have been what it is if it were not for your input. I thank you. I love you. I need you.

J.J. Johnson, Yolanda Andrus, Richard A. Parks Jr., Jeremy Braggs, Ebony Farashuu, Gena Garrison and the rest of Soul City, I thank you for your continued support, suggestions, and pushing to make this book 'different.' I especially want to thank Kandyss Watson, Sandra K. Poole and Janita Diggins for reading the manuscript a number of times to help me get through rough spots. You are appreciated. Paris and Eshey Harris, thank you for your help when I first started writing this manuscript.

Byron James thank you so much for your guidance and PR coaching. I appreciate you.

Donna "Dee" Shands, Erin Sherrod and the LS family, I also want to thank you for your continued support and encouragement. As many, if not all of you know, the saga of Jessie and Sadira started on your message board three years ago.

Dr. Michelle Hutchinson, my editorial consultant, thank you. Renee' Johnson, my books wouldn't be as aesthetically pleasing as they are were if not for your beautiful cover designs and graphic artwork on my website. Thank you.

P. Stronger, I ought to thank you as much as I thanked Monica. This book wouldn't have been completed if I didn't have your guidance.

LaKeya Covington and Lynne Womble, thank you so much for being such dear friends of mine. Sgt. Cheryl McPherson, Michelle Clarke, Russell Hairston, Lavinia Lee Mears, and Tonja F. Jordan thanks a great deal for your assistance in law enforcement and legal research.

Last, but certainly not least, I want to thank all of my readers, both old and new. I truly appreciate your support and kind words, and hope that you've enjoyed this book. Please feel free to write me with your comments. I look forward to hearing from you.

Thank you all,

Cheril N. Clarke
Website: http://www.cherilnclarke.com
Blog: http://cherilnclarke.typepad.com
MySpace: http://www.myspace.com/cherilnclarke

E-mail: cherilnc@cherilnclarke.com

Snail Mail: 244 Fifth Ave., 2nd Fl., Suite J260, New York, NY 10001

Cheril N. Clarke

Biography

A native of Toronto, raised in Miami, and now living in Mount Laurel,
New Jersey, Cheril N. Clarke is the author of four novels, "Foundations: A
Novel of New Beginnings," "Different Trees From the Same Root,"
"Intimate Chaos," and "Tainted Destiny." She has been featured in *Curve*
Magazine, the nation's best selling lesbian magazine, as well as *Crain's
New York Business* newspaper. Clarke has also published poems, short
stories and reviews of hip-hop spoken word theater in various literary
magazines. She was a keynote speaker at an African Asian Latina
Lesbians United conference and has performed at events organized by
African American Lesbians United for Societal Change. In her spare time,
she enjoys indulging outdoor/nature photography.

Printed in the United States
77993LV00006B/178-201